Clifford Brown

Clifford Brown
The Life
and Art
of the Legendary
Jazz Trumpeter

Nick Catalano

OXFORD
UNIVERSITY PRESS

OXFORD
UNIVERSITY PRESS

Oxford   New York
Athens   Auckland   Bangkok   Bogotá   Buenos Aires   Calcutta
Cape Town   Chennai   Dar es Salaam   Delhi   Florence   Hong Kong   Istanbul
Karachi   Kuala Lumpur   Madrid   Melbourne   Mexico City   Mumbai
Nairobi   Paris   São Paulo   Shanghai   Singapore   Taipei   Tokyo   Toronto   Warsaw

and associated companies in
Berlin   Ibadan

Copyright © 2000 by Nick Catalano

First published by Oxford University Press, Inc., 2000
198 Madison Avenue, New York, New York 10016

First issued as an Oxford University Press paperback, 2001

Oxford is a registered trademark of Oxford University Press

Library of Congress Cataloging-in-Publication Data
Catalano, Nick.
Clifford Brown : the life and art of the legendary jazz trumpeter / Nick Catalano.
p. cm.
Includes bibliographical references and index.
ISBN: 978-0-19-514400-0

1. Brown, Clifford. 2. Jazz musicians—United States—Biography.
I. Title.
ML419.B75C37   2000
788.9'2165'092—dc21
[B] 99-27887

Book design by Adam B. Bohannon

Printed in the United States of America
on acid-free paper

For the East Siders
of Wilmington, Delaware

Contents

Acknowledgments

This book's existence is largely due to the generosity and time given by the musicians and performers who worked with or knew Clifford Brown. Also listed here are other figures who provided strategic information. They include: Annie Ross, David Amram, Don Glanden, Don Sickler, Dr. Billy Taylor, Harold Land, Herb Geller, Herbie Mann, Horace Silver, Jack Montrose, Jimmy Cavallo, Jimmy Heath, John Lewis, Junior Mance, Lionel Hampton, Louis-Victor Mialy, Max Roach, Milt Hinton, Roy Haynes, Teddy Edwards, Bobby Shew, Lou Donaldson, Tommy Walker, Clark Terry, Terry Gibbs, Claudio Roditi, Helen Merrill, and Dave Arbiter. A special thanks to Art Farmer, who, sadly, passed away as this book went to press. Art spent many hours with me discussing the wonders of Clifford Brown.

Among Clifford Brown's family and friends I am grateful to Clifford Brown, Jr., Cynthia Oates, Dave Clark, Margaret and Leon Brown, Geneva Griffin, Alice Robinson, Rella Bray, Bob Kelley, Kay Lacy, Boysie and Edna Lowery, Deanie Jenkins, Ida Mae Bey, Billy Norwood, Bop Wilson, Ralph Morris, and K. R. Swaggerty. These individuals provided a perspective and color that otherwise might have been missed.

In Wilmington, Delaware, I was given great help from Harmon

Carey, Valerie Trammel, and other city officials who continue to work indefatigably to showcase the music of their city's favorite son. Elizabeth Ahlfors and Dr. Joseph Antigalia were especially helpful in providing important information about Wilmington and its people.

I owe a great debt to my writing colleagues Eric Nisenson, David Hajdu, Arnold J. Smith, Stanley Crouch, and Gene Lees, who swapped stories, related anecdotes, and otherwise provided the encouragement that is always vital in this work. To producer Jack Kleinsinger goes a special thanks for his dedication to the musicians and his special interest in presenting Brownie's music to the public.

I want to acknowledge Joellyn Ausanka, Mary Ellen Curley, Penelope Anderson, Sarah Hemphill, and Susan Day of Oxford University Press for helping me get through the endless vicissitudes of book production, marketing, and publicity. To my editor, Sheldon Meyer, I owe much, especially for his prescience in recognizing the importance of Clifford Brown's music. I will be forever grateful to my assistants, Judy Allen and Joyce Farrell, for their patience and dedication.

Every biographer should have the assistance of an archivist who is generous to a fault in sharing his treasures. Norman Saks is such an individual. He asks nothing but to see his collections used to advance the cause of jazz, and I am eternally grateful for the material he provided.

I owe a great debt to my chief researcher for this book, Alan Hood, who conducted many interviews, spent weeks discussing the music, and supplied a steady stream of invaluable information. His scholarly work on Brownie's music and life will continue to be a vital principal source for jazz writers everywhere.

I would like to give special thanks to Clifford Brown's widow, LaRue Brown-Watson, who spent countless hours with me discussing her husband's life and music. For over forty years since Brownie's passing LaRue has dedicated her life to his legacy. Her work in jazz is legendary, and the support she gives to students and musicians everywhere is unmatched. We all owe her a great debt.

Introduction

In Warren Leight's critically acclaimed Broadway show *Side Man* (a roman à clef of the playwright's disturbing life with his parents) one of the lead characters, "Gene," is a trumpeter of a special sort. Although he is a virtuoso during one of the great periods of jazz, he is most remarkable in his knowledge of what made a truly great trumpet player. Here, Leight echoes a familiar theme: It is musicians who are often the best judges of musicians. In *Side Man* Gene worships the art of trumpeting like Christians worship Jesus, and his unequivocal hero is Clifford Brown. Gene adores Brown so much that he names his own son Clifford. In this, the play dramatizes the long held belief of the jazz virtuoso fraternity: As a trumpeter, Clifford Brown stands alone.

In addition to his artistic achievements, Brown exuded virtue and magnanimity. He wasn't just a "nice guy"; he was much more than that, and the pages of this book help to create the picture of an extraordinary person. As the veteran critic Nat Hentoff has declared: "Nobody I knew in the jazz world ever had a bad word to say about Brownie. He was too open, entirely without guile, without even a hint of malice toward anyone." Hentoff's remarks are indicative of the powerful effect Clifford Brown had on people who knew him. It was precisely this combination of his amazing talent and his virtuous life that set many musicians who encountered Brown on a different life path. Before he came along, droves of players used drugs in imitation of Charlie Parker. But because of Clifford Brown, many players cleaned up their act. He believed that in order to achieve success as a jazz artist, a performer had to live abstemiously with enormous focus and discipline. Because Brown was not a preacher it was only the respect that jazz musicians had for his enormous talent that led them to emulate his lifestyle.

As a youngster, Clifford Brown had created quite a sensation in his hometown of Wilmington, Delaware. One night when Dizzy Gillespie brought his band into town, Brown's friends urged the king of the bebop trumpet to let Brown sit in for a couple of tunes. Gillespie was awestruck. Immediately, he insisted that Brown, who at the time was attending a nearby college, launch himself into a performing career.

Clifford Brown had received considerable formal musical training and came from a family whose traditions included rigorous discipline and dedication. Soon after the Gillespie episode, he became a regular on Philadelphia bandstands playing alongside Charlie Parker, Miles Davis, and other bebop pioneers. Quickly, he encountered other young "second generation" boppers (e.g., Gigi Gryce) whose intention was to develop the new style and concurrently adopt aesthetic standards equal to that of serious classical musicians. A few of his black compeers would seek to establish themselves as rhythm 'n' blues stars, thereby gaining fortune as well as fame, but Clifford Brown would shun this life. His desire was to create the best music possible in the bebop genre, and after he realized that he could improvise with the best, he worked even harder, practicing inexhaustibly and living fastidiously. In addition, he was one of those rare musical artisans who could spend a few hours figuring out the essence of an instrument and then be able to develop immediate facility on that instrument; he could spend a few days in North Africa, assimilate the colors of the indigenous music, and create a composition incorporating those elements that would become a classic in jazz literature. At age twenty-three, alongside the quintessential bebop percussive virtuoso Max Roach, Clifford Brown created a musical explosion that continues to dazzle audiences to the present day.

What Brown and Roach achieved in their group of the early 1950s was unique. At a time when the art music of the great boppers was being diluted at "Jazz at the Philharmonic" blowing sessions designed to excite the appetites of screaming audiences, Clifford and Max turned elsewhere. Drawing upon training that had strong classical roots, Brown had found an unusual jazz colleague—a drummer who listened to Stravinsky. The two musicians spent long hours discussing new concepts of jazz performance that would incorporate many traditions inherent in classical forms. It soon became clear that only in the context of intellectually crafted compositions containing tapestries of exquisite improvisational design could the music achieve the artistic heights Brown and Roach desired. Solos, the raison d'être for any improvisational virtuoso, had to be economical, serving the needs of the compositional framework rather than the demands of egocentric players or hero-worshipping fans.

As an improviser, Clifford Brown created flowing lines of soaring melody and improvisation containing geometric symmetry and punctuated with an articulated attack and buttery tone that became the envy of trumpeters everywhere. With Max Roach, Harold Land, and later Sonny Rollins, the group played to audiences packed with musicians and other cognoscenti who were continually astounded at their performances.

Clifford Brown's artistry reaches its apotheosis in the area of improvisational design. Like Charlie Parker and Art Tatum, Clifford Brown commandeered the vast resources of his creativity to construct solos that contained revolutionary melodic language and new rhythmic subtlety. With the advent of academic interest in jazz in recent years, Brownie's achievement has been analyzed in dissertations and discussed in professional conferences. His focused approach to composition has influenced countless musicians, and, as bebop steadily gains a greater place in the aesthetic hierarchy of even the most establishmentarian critical circles, his art continues to emerge.

As is the case with all artists, environment played a quintessential role in the shaping of Clifford Brown's life. Too often, urban black neighborhoods have been stereotyped as centers of broken homes, drug dealers, and social unrest. The situation could not have been more different in the Wilmington east side where Clifford Brown grew up. Because of several factors, including the quirky post–Civil War history of Delaware's black population, the east side evolved into an intriguingly stable area during the time Brown lived there. Families were close-knit, social life was highly ordered, and the cultural atmosphere was rich. Above all, the segregated public schools of the neighborhood provided curricula that rivaled the best that the white schools could offer. Brown, his siblings and friends, received heavy doses of science, mathematics, and language courses that enabled them to enter colleges and universities in unusually heavy numbers. As a result, large groups of east siders wound up in important professional careers, which resonate to the present day. Ironically, the practice of segregation in Wilmington infused a strength and cohesiveness to the community that later integration legislation would dissipate.

Geographically situated very close to Philadelphia (about twenty-seven miles), Wilmington took advantage of that city's rich cultural legacy, particularly focusing upon the enormous jazz activity that developed there after World War II. In this context, Clifford Brown's life brought him into seminal musical contact with several other artists whose enormous contribution to post–World War II jazz remains largely unexamined. During a very short period in his life Brown worked very closely with Tadd Dameron, Fats Navarro, Gigi Gryce, Horace Silver, Lou Donaldson, Max Roach, Sonny Rollins, Art Farmer, and other important figures who have never been subjects of sustained biographical study. Thus, in this biography of Clifford Brown, frequent references to these artists appear, enabling readers to reexamine this pivotal period in jazz history.

This book attempts to trace the stages of Brown's life and simultaneously illustrate his musical accomplishments in language intended for the general reader. Throughout, the approach has been to present the man and his music and avoid protracted judgments and distracting commentary. Included in the account are specific examinations of all of Brown's published recording sessions (and a few important unpublished ones). As greater critical attention is focused on Clifford Brown's music, which is inevitable, others will follow who will provide specific instructional insights and finely tuned critical guidance. However, even though the analysis of Clifford Brown's artistry contained herein exists in base outline, certain developments emerge. That his improvisational vision and execution achieved a new aesthetic plateau in jazz is inescapable; that he and Max Roach advanced the bebop form in their performances is indisputable; that Brownie's achievement as a composer deserves greater attention is clearly apparent.

In conclusion, I have followed John Keats's dictum of negative capability and tried to spare the public my own whims and opinions. In this manner, I hope that readers will discover on their own the compelling character of this remarkable American artist and that new audiences will be drawn to his musical achievements.

Clifford Brown

One
The Brown Family
of Wilmington

"If you don't practice, I'll whip you," said Joe Brown, addressing his family at one of the frequent songfests at their house on Poplar Street. Although he was a loving father who deeply cared for his family, Joe Brown was serious about the importance of music.

The family lived in a row house built before the turn of the century, in a modest Wilmington neighborhood that remains charming to the present day. The father of eight children, Joe Brown was chastising his sons; there were five, four of whom he was trying to organize into a vocal quartet (the oldest, Harold, had moved out by this time). His older daughters had already begun to distinguish themselves: Marie, the eldest, early on became a soloist at Mt. Carmel Church; and Geneva was an outstanding singer who would one day earn her B.A. in music at Howard University and have an important career in opera.

But the boys were another story. Leon and Eugene reluctantly obeyed their father, while Elsworth purposely sang off-key, pretending he couldn't carry a tune. "We'd be laughin' at Elsworth," recalled Leon, "and my father would stand there with that strap in one hand. Maybe that turned me off from music."[1]

Joe Brown's frustrations continued. As long as anyone could re-

3

member, he had surrounded himself with musical instruments—violins, horns, percussion—and had kept collecting, playing, and repairing them. He proudly told his children about his brother, Uncle Arthur, who was leading a band in New York. Estella, his wife, had a sister who was a successful concert singer. His neighbors and friends played instruments and sang. But, alas, his sons' vocal quartet struggled without results.

Finally, one day when his youngest boy, Clifford, had turned twelve, the lad asked his father if he could play the shiny silver trumpet that Joe kept carefully stored in a closet. "He took to it like a fish to water," said Leon. "My father played trumpet and violin and piano for his own amusement," recalled Clifford Brown years later, "and from the earliest time I can remember it was the trumpet that fascinated me."

Even today, Wilmington, Delaware, appears to be an odd little city. Surrounded by much larger cities, Wilmington has long been an international corporate stronghold. Low taxes have attracted large companies, many of whom register as Delaware corporations. The city is quite small, its population about 43,000, and the corporate towers dominate the downtown area, with black working class neighborhoods surrounding them. It is a short walk from Rodney Square in the center of town along Delaware Avenue or Ninth Street to the Christina River at the edge of the city. The row houses have been constructed in a Federal style that gives an antebellum look to the area.

The ancestors of the people living in these neighborhoods had, of course, been slaves, but for a state that had practiced slavery since its founding, Delaware had a singular history. In Wilmington, "slavery was practically unknown in the city even before the Civil War."[2] In fact, before the war began in 1861, only 1,798 slaves remained in the entire state, while freed Negroes numbered 19,829.[3] Most historians feel that manumission (liberation from slavery) continued steadily in the state largely because of economic reasons. Since the climate did not permit a long growing season, slavery simply did not pay. Had there not been a war, it is certain that the role of blacks would have run a far different course in this period. During the Civil War, however, "slavery became a symbol of opposition to the northern government, a gesture of defiance."[4] Although Negroes had the right to vote after the war, they faced great difficulties in exercising this right, with the state Democratic Party taking a tough anti-Negro stand. In his inaugural address, Delaware Governor Gove Saulsbury declared: "The true position of the Negro was as a subordinate race excluded from all political and social privileges."[5] Anthony Higgins (later a United States senator) stated that "the enfranchisement of the Negro would guarantee a majority for the Republican party."

In the 1870 election, although the Republicans counted on support from 4,500 newly enfranchised Negroes, they lost convincingly to a Democratic Party that had campaigned on a vigorous anti-Negro platform. It was a violent time during which Democrats accused Republicans of importing Negroes from other states to vote, and Republicans accused Democrats of trying to keep Negroes from the polls. At one polling place in Wilmington shots were fired, and several people were reported injured.[6] Anthony Higgins telegraphed President Grant to request military intervention because Negroes had been driven from the polls by "clubs, bludgeons and revolvers."[7]

The *Delaware Gazette*, a Democratic newspaper, declared that "Negroism is dead and buried forever."[8] But in 1888, when the Republicans won the legislature with the aid of the Negro vote, the former slaves' status noticeably improved. "Formerly spurned by officeholders, (the Negro) was cozened, entreated, or even paid to vote."[9] While this development exacerbated a growing racism among the white population, the Republican administration began to help Negroes, mainly through providing for their education. A multimillion dollar gift from Pierre S. duPont made it possible to construct schools for Negroes in every district, and a new school code, adapted in 1921, forced standards, teachers' salaries, and length of sessions to be equalized in colored and white schools. By this time Wilmington's Howard High School, under the guidance of a legendary black principal, Edwina Kruse, had become "one of the best, possibly the best, in the entire school system."[10] This would be the school in which Joe and Estella Brown's eight children would be educated.

Joseph Leon Brown was born probably in 1891 in Seaford, Delaware, in the southern part of the state. "The best guess is sometime in November," says his older surviving daughter, Geneva Griffin. He was raised by a foster mother who was "very mean." One of the earliest musical recollections alludes to Joe's ability to "buck dance," an activity he could have acquired from traveling minstrel shows.

Estella Hackett was born in Marydel, Maryland, and moved to Wilmington to stay with her Aunt Fina and finish high school at Howard. Her sister Rella had musical talent and became a concert singer. Intellectually gifted—"I can spell any word in the dictionary," Estella would say—she was one of eleven graduates from Howard in 1912. The yearbook says she helped write the school's alma mater, but Geneva feels that her mother only wrote the lyrics.

In 1913, Joe Brown was working as a laborer and living at 1013 B Street. City records show that Estella was boarding at 1009 B Street, probably while attending normal school studying to be a teacher. She was going with Enos Dickson when she met Joe Brown. Joe wore "country boy" outfits and "thought he was hot stuff," recalled the urban-bred Estella, but, evidently, he finally charmed her, and soon they were married. (The rejected Dickson was so frustrated that he continually harassed the couple.) The couple moved in with Joe's Aunt Sarah, and on January 9, 1914, their first child, Harold Boyd Brown, was born. Joe and Estella soon moved out of Aunt Sarah's house and would live in a number of houses in the next few years as their family grew.

Although poor by any economic standard, the Wilmington Negro neighborhoods were far from being socially, educationally, or culturally impoverished. A contemporary of the Brown children, J. Saunders Redding, whose family lived close by, was one of the many students who benefited from the rigorous education at Howard High School. Born in 1906, Redding, one of the first three Negroes admitted to Brown University, later wrote a compelling narrative describing life in Wilmington. "In the early years, when we were a young family, there was always talk at our house; a great deal of it meal talk, a kind of boundless and robust overflow of family feeling. Our shouts roared through the house with the exuberant gush of flood waters through an open sluice, for talk, generated by any trifle, was the power that turned the wheels of our inner family life. It was the strength and that very quality of our living that made impregnable, it seemed, even to time itself, the walls of our home. But it was in the beginning of the second decade of the century, when the family was an institution still as inviolate as the swing of the earth."[11]

This strong family connection that Redding found so important persists on the Wilmington east side to the present day. When I went to visit Clifford Brown's neighbors and friends, I encountered a warmth and cordiality that was very stirring. These things are available in large urban centers, but in Wilmington, the east siders meet and greet with a genteel enthusiasm that can only be a relic of southern antebellum aristocracy. To have dinner at one of the row houses in the east side on a warm summer evening is to go back in time. The tempo of the evening is slow paced, but the lively conversation, punctuated with animated but delicate humor, makes one feel that dinner is over all too quickly. The subjects of conversation echo the sophistication of an urban coffee house: literature, art, government, and, of course, music. Each conversation is orchestrated by unusual counterpoint between avid listening and purposive talk. It is the art of conversation referred to by Hazlitt, Carlyle, and other nineteenth-century stylists that has been obfuscated in most present-day American families by television, constantly ringing telephones, and fast food dinners. And yet today in Wilmington's east side one can still feel the shadows of the old southern ways.

All of the Brown children currently living—Geneva, Rella, and Leon—wear bemused expressions when the "talk" element of their family is recalled. "Talk," Geneva recalls, "my father was such a droner that it was dangerous to ask, 'how are you, Joe?' Momma was a talker too." Conversation would range over a wide variety of subjects, but often it revolved around education. Many times "we called the library to check things out." In the Redding family, "we children were all trained at home in the declining art of oratory and were regular contestants for prizes at school."[12] In the Brown family, the emphasis on speaking correctly would seem unusual in today's society. "Where's the jelly at?" a youngster would ask. "Right in back of the preposition," was the retort.

The Brown family grew steadily. Marie Vendetta Brown was born in July 1916. "She was the first to ever graduate from high school at fifteen years of age," recalled Leon Brown. "She graduated with honors. Magna cum laude or something." Three sons followed: Leon Robert on September 22, 1918; Joseph Ellsworth on April 7, 1920; and Eugene Anthony on June 30, 1923. During these years the Browns had moved from B Street to Townsend Street and then to Buttonwood, outside Wilmington. By the time Geneva was born on December 12, 1925, they had moved back into the city and resided at the row house on Poplar Street.

Joe Brown worked at a number of jobs to support his family. He became a fireman and continued to hire out as a laborer. He would work as a porter, a janitor at Fraim's Dairy, a molder helper, stevedore, housing authority guard, and even deputy sheriff. In order to help out, Estella would eventually run an employment agency in her home.

Despite the poverty, the life of the Negro families on Poplar Street and the surrounding areas of Wilmington's east side had unique advantages. In the years between the two world wars the children had positive memories of their daily lives and social milieus. Ralph Morris, who lived up the street from the Browns at 1023, recalled that "at that time it was a close-built block. And everyone knew everyone very well. . . . We were all in a sort of 'extended' family kind of situation."[13] Kay Lacy, a close friend of the Brown family, summed it up this way: "You were brought up with dignity—to be proud of who you were, to be able to walk and stand with any man. That's the kind of confidence that was instilled in you. It just carried through. Most of the kids that were brought up at that time were . . . outgoing, self-assured people. And it wasn't until later when we were older, teenagers, that we realized the injustice of society. It did not bother me that we could not go to certain places, because we had our own. . . . Another lesson that my grandmother taught me— never want anything that anyone else had. . . . In order for them to protect us, they were teaching this whole pride in self, or pride in race concept. We went to church, we went to school, we went on picnics. We stayed away from places that did not want us. It never occurred to me, when I was growing up, to want to go. I don't remember race being an issue in the home. I don't remember that kind of talk."[14]

Many people lived in the same house—"the more people, the more adults you have, the more money was brought into the house . . . the whole 'extended family' thing." Role models were the key: "The school teacher and the minister were the epitome of society, even more so than a doctor. These people were like gods. And you had to be good so these people would notice you."

Dave Clark, who became Clifford Brown's close friend, ascribed some of this cohesiveness and strength to the long periods of slavery the Negroes endured. "After all of that," said Davey, "there was no way that my father could get broken by any injustice that may have been left over in the twentieth century."

Many of the Delaware east siders struggled fiercely to overcome the legacy of unjust laws governing education and social and economic status, but the toughness woven into their ethos because of slavery gave them enormous strength. Often this strength manifested itself in social behavior. The quiet affability and humility that many east siders constantly exhibited had its roots in this tradition. Albert Murray, the noted contemporary writer, believes deeply in this idea. In his recent book, *Black Genius*, Dick Russell paraphrases Murray's philosophy: "Murray viewed the degradation of slavery and subsequent oppression of African-Americans as actually having forged something heroic and life enhancing."[15]

Modern stereotypes of broken Negro families, with absent fathers, were unknown to Rella Brown, the youngest daughter, born in 1928, who had to wait until she went to college at New Jersey's Glassboro State to encounter this phenomenon. "You took the best your community had to offer," Kay Lacy said, "and you capitalized on that. . . . In the end even the poorest families had things that they could be proud of. . . . Everyone graduated from high school—that was drilled into your head."[16]

Into this stable Poplar Street environment arrived Clifford Benjamin Brown on October 30, 1930. "I was sittin' on the steps, I'll never forget that," said brother Leon, who was twelve at the time.

"It was the day before Halloween, and I thought he was gonna come out lookin' like a goblin or somethin'." Rella uses the euphemism "mischief night" (the night before Halloween) to describe the event.

In addition to a steady stream of boarders, the Brown family now included eight children in a house containing only three bedrooms. Joe and Estella always kept the youngest child in with them, and the new baby was no exception. Sister Rella recalls: "Clifford was the youngest and I was next to the youngest, so Clifford and I were very close. We played together, we learned to swim together, we bowled together, and we learned how to get water out of our ears together." Quick intelligence, long a trait of the Brown children, appeared early in the little boy. "Clifford started reading before he even entered school," said Rella. "We used to get these little nursery rhyme booklets from the Metropolitan Insurance Company, and Clifford just picked it up. He heard somebody read a poem one time and he learned how to read from there. He did everything fast." The picture of the youngster picking up learning habits very quickly is significant. Continued Rella, "He rode a bicycle when he was two. Because his legs were too short, he had to ride a girl's bike so he could get in between that space, because he couldn't sit on the seat and reach the pedal."

In order to provide amusement for his children, "Daddy would go to a secondhand store," recalls Geneva, "buy used toys a lot and fix 'em up and paint 'em. And we didn't know the difference, we didn't care."[17] But young Clifford received a new silver airplane wagon. "You know, kids have carts with pedals and you push your feet. [Daddy] bought that wagon brand new so that was something." It is evident that the Browns' youngest child quickly became a favorite with his parents. The silver wagon was an "indulgence" for the family, "as poor as we were," but Clifford had become a fresh source of joy for the family, so Joe and Estella had squeezed out a few extra dollars to pay for the wagon. "Kinda quiet and very sensitive," says Geneva of her earliest recollection of her brother. One time Clifford was playing and had lost a yo-yo, and he was walking around crying. Geneva said, "What's the matter, Cliff?," and he said "Well, I had my yo-yo and can't find it. Lord [he prayed], please help me to find my yo-yo." Geneva laughed because he was so earnest and was prepared to do anything to find his toy.

The boys were crowded into one room, "two, three, four people almost in one bed" in the back bedroom. The girls all "slept in the middle room, and my mother and father had the front room." Leon and Clifford slept in the same bed for many years. "I was twenty-somethin' years old when me and Clifford was sleepin' in the same bed," chuckles Leon, recalling the predictably amusing antics that occurred with the boys crammed together in one room. Geneva said, "You had your ups and downs and your little peculiarities and things. My sister Rella didn't want anybody to get too close to her food. In order to tease her, Ellsworth would always get real close and breathe heavily on her food. Disgusted, she would say, 'Well, you can have it, I don't want it.' From infancy Rella was a spitfire. Ellsworth was ornery—he liked to fight. I was kind of a sickly child. Clifford was more quiet; he was not the violent type at all. He was an easygoing kind of guy. That was just his basic personality."

Rella remarked: "We were raised by the golden rule. We were always taught, 'Do unto others as you would have them do unto you.' My mother had a quotation either from the Bible or an old adage for almost every situation . . . one of them was 'Grin and bear it,' one was 'A rolling stone gathers no moss,' another was 'Work while the sun is shining.' Her most famous one was 'Do unto others.' Clifford lived by the golden rule, and that's why he was such a good-hearted person. He would never do anything to anyone that he would not want someone to do to him. He was a beautiful person from that."

This theme echoes and re-echoes from many people associated with the mature Clifford Brown. When LaRue Brown, the musician's future wife, was about to meet him she was told "what a beautiful person he was. So of course I was expecting this tall, gorgeous thing . . . I found out it wasn't the physical beauty that they were talking about, it was inner beauty. Believe me, he was the most beautiful human being that I have ever known in my life."

At Thanksgiving time through the years, the Brown family celebrated in comfortable fashion despite having to pinch pennies. Leon recalls: "The bigger the turkey, the less it cost per pound. And my brother Eugene was at the table eatin', and all of a sudden he started cryin'. So our father said, 'What are you cryin' for?' 'I'm cryin',' Eugene eventually blurted out, ' 'cause I can't eat no more.' So we could eat all we wanted," chuckles Leon, relating the good holiday times. The eating was hearty, but there was no alcohol. Neither Joe nor his wife was a drinker, and the children followed suit. In his working years Clifford Brown was conspicuous as a teetotaler. Many musical cohorts speak impressively of his steadfast clean living. In a jazz world flooded with figures addicted to alcohol and drugs, Brown eschewed these habits with a firmness traceable to his early family upbringing.

When Clifford was quite young, Joe Brown was racing a large used Cadillac he had purchased in Marydel, Estella's hometown. With the young Clifford, his wife, and other passengers in the car, Joe was forced to turn abruptly to avoid a collision. "The car turned over three times," recalled Leon, but somehow Clifford escaped injury. Estella suffered a sprained arm, but everyone was very lucky.

The trip to Maryland was part of a tradition dating back to the days of slavery. Margaret Brown, Leon's wife, recalls that a large group of buses and cars would gather on French Street in Wilmington. There would be singing, followed by family cookouts, and the festivities would wind up in Marydel. It was an exciting event that the young children looked forward to all year.

The families on Poplar Street received great benefit from the neighborhood schools. Public School 29, which young Clifford attended, located at 12th and Poplar, down the street from the Brown residence, possessed fine teachers and a challenging curriculum. Because of such schools on the east side, many of these children went on to successful careers. Next door to the Browns at 1011 lived the Whittens. A daughter, Ann, would one day major in music at Howard University with Geneva Brown. Ann's brother, Charles, a physician (Geneva is proud to say), is a contemporary expert on sickle cell anemia.

Gwendolyn Redding, sister to the aforementioned Saunders, became Howard High's most feared English teacher. Cynthia Oates, one of the neighborhood's many college graduates, recalls "going to summer school to avoid Miss Redding's class. She failed one kid twice."[18] Generally, the students responded well to their mentors. "I can't remember having one bad teacher," said Cynthia.

From early on, Joe Brown taught his sons how to box. Rella remembers how "our father trained boxers. Leon and Harold were matched together to practice, and Ellsworth and Eugene were also matched. Clifford didn't have a match; the next one to him was a girl. We young ladies didn't box. So he didn't have a partner for boxing." As a result, Leon says, "that's the only thing he didn't do." But Clifford didn't lose out, because his brothers protected him. Toward the end of the grammar school days, this "gave him the chance to study music without having to worry 'bout going down to school and somebody jumpin' on him, because all of his brothers could fight."

With unwavering determination, Joe Brown strove to have his children follow his interest in music. He went to great lengths to encourage them in formal musical training. Geneva recalls: "My daddy was a person who loved music. I guess he must have had some musical talent, but it never had a chance to be developed. . . . He had all sorts of musical instruments in the house. We always had a piano. He had a guitar, he had a violin, he had a trumpet and a cornet. I can't remember if he had a saxophone or not." When asked if Joe could "play" any of these horns, Geneva responded: "He could make music on 'em. He was funny 'cause he got a little tune that he's bangin' on the piano, got a little tune that he'd play on the trumpet. I remember how it went. He could play his little melodies that he picked out himself. And he kept hoping that one of his children would be an instrumentalist."

Since his brother Arthur had led a jazz band, Joe was naturally interested in the big band dance music that was sweeping the country in those years. This band music was constantly playing at home, according to Geneva, and the Browns enjoyed dancing to it. Geneva remembers listening to Lionel Hampton's music together with Clifford when he was "about nine or ten." Hampton would later play an important role in Clifford's musical career.

Joe had far more than a casual interest in his family's music training; he can be remembered threatening to whip them if they failed
to practice. Leon tried the slide trombone for a little while. "I wasn't
too interested," he said. "And then there is Eugene, who played
trumpet better than Clifford when he grabbed it." According to
Leon, it was Eugene's "messin' with the trumpet" that caused his
younger brother "to decide to mess with it too." "As time went on,
he went down to school; they had a band and they gave him a
trumpet. . . . It was a little better than the one we had. That's what
he'd play. That's how he picked up the trumpet." So the vocal quartet is practicing, Joe Brown is collecting and toying with all of his
instruments, his daughters are singing (Marie and Geneva already at
a high level), at least three of his sons are "playing" brass instruments, and all of the children are at some stage on the piano. More
than just your usual family music-making.

Meanwhile, Joe continued to play the piano. "He played the same
tune for twenty years—I can hear it right now," says Leon. Joe did
not take too kindly to any negative comments about his playing. He
just played on, undaunted, evidently buoyed by his own musical
feeling.

Leon indicates that Clifford was nine or ten when he started "messin' " with the trumpet. Clifford Brown's own aforementioned recollection corroborates this: "My father played trumpet and violin and
piano for his own amusement," he said, "and from the earliest times
I can remember it was the trumpet that fascinated me. When I was
too little to reach it, I'd climb up to where it was (in a closet), and I
kept on knocking it down."[19]

It has been reported that Joe Brown initially discouraged Clifford
from access to the "shiny silver trumpet" because it was not a toy,
allowing him only to play a bugle that lay among his vast collection.
But after Clifford's "messing around with the trumpet," he began
playing a horn at school. Soon he began actively to take up the
instrument. By age twelve, Clifford showed such interest that Joe
decided to provide him with private lessons.

Clifford Brown's own recollection is crucial. "So when I was thirteen, my father finally bought me one—and only because of that

fascination with the horn itself. Otherwise I had no noticeable interest in music as such at that time. That developed later."[20]

Thus, despite the intense musical atmosphere that we have seen in the Brown home, Clifford, perhaps at one with Leon in forming an early musical antipathy to music, had no noticeable interest. His desire was more to possess the shiny silver trumpet than to play it. Jazz saxophonist James Moody, two years older than Clifford, had a similar experience growing up in Newark, New Jersey. "When I was about sixteen," he recalled, "I used to walk to Kirschner's music store that had a front window filled with all kinds of saxophones. I used to press my face against the window and dream that one day I would get one of those beautiful horns. Finally, my uncle got me one, but it wasn't beautiful like the horns in that window."[21]

"Little Comache," a nickname that young Clifford acquired (Leon was "Big Comache," a name that referred to his fighting prowess), was seen regularly during this time walking back and forth from school carrying a trumpet.

Two
Boysie Lowery
and Howard High

In addition to its being a neighborhood that would produce future doctors, lawyers, and academics, the Wilmington east side also spawned more than its share of artists and musicians. One of the main forces in the east side's musical life was a band leader who fast became a legend. His name was Robert Lowery.

Known as "Boysie," Lowery had settled in Wilmington in the early 1940s. Born in Kingston, North Carolina, on August 9, 1914, Lowery came from a family that was highly musical. His father, a blacksmith, "had a thirty-two-piece band."[1] His older brother led "a sixteen-piece dance band dubbed the 'Kingston Night Hawks,' " featuring Tap Smith, an outstanding alto player. A musical natural, Lowery learned to play the trumpet in six months. He later played other instruments with facility, and by the time I visited him in June 1995 he was focusing on soprano saxophone, since he had breathing problems. "I went with Keter Betts to join Kelly's Jazz Hounds," and so traveled a lot, recalled Lowery. He described a gig in Pinehurst, North Carolina, to play in a "gangster club." He joined "Dr. Robertson's Medicine Show," a minstrel show that included comics and chorus girls. When he headed north he was a member of The Three Keys, making an appearance in Chester, Pennsylvania. Eventually

16

Boysie's brother, Willie, started The Aces of Rhythm. There is a photo of this group in Lowery's basement at 609 North Broom Street. This band would become his mainstay, and it included Mr. Horse Collar, Billy Jackson, Bud Lowery, Jimmy Turner, Robert Townsend, and Daisy Winchester.

As Boysie Lowery played in the Carolinas, he kept coming across references to a young trumpeter by the name of John Birks Gillespie, who hailed from Cheraw, South Carolina. On one occasion Kelly's Jazz Hounds played a gig at the Laurenburg Institute in Gausenburg, North Carolina, where young Gillespie was a student. Later Boysie's brother, also impressed with Gillespie's growing reputation, auditioned him for the Kingston Nighthawks. A cutting contest ensued between Gillespie and Lowery, and so began a long friendship between the two young trumpeters. It developed that Gillespie didn't like the job with the Nighthawks. His family had moved north, so he decided to follow them to Philadelphia, where he began playing with Frankie Fairfax and his band.

Because the Philadelphia jazz scene was so active at that time, many southern musicians were drawn there, so it followed that Boysie Lowery and the Aces of Rhythm began to find work in Philadelphia and in Atlantic City. Eventually Lowery settled in Wilmington, which was only twenty-seven miles from Philadelphia and offered a more peaceful setting. Here he could play, book gigs for the Aces, and at the same time develop his other passion—teaching. By the time Boysie Lowery settled there he had extensively explored many of the changes in jazz that had occurred since the music's inception. Together with his knowledge of minstrel literature, he grew up listening to and playing a variety of blues styles (the various groups in the Carolinas would be his inspiration) and wound up making a living from the new dance rhythms of 1930s swing. Perhaps more significantly for our story, his relationship during the Philadelphia period with Dizzy Gillespie and other pioneers enabled him to participate in the bebop revolution of the early 1940s.

Clifford Brown was a junior high school student when he was brought to Boysie Lowery. He had advanced considerably beyond his initial fascination with the shiny trumpet and had developed a serious musical interest "through experience with the junior high school band."

"I didn't start him in a book," Boysie Lowery recalled years later. "I taught him how to hear. The most important thing is to be able to hear. I know a lot of guys that have been to college, but they don't have what it takes to improvise. They can't hear. You've got to be able to hear things before you can do them."[2] Lowery's system has now become legendary. He calls it "the classes." Briefly, it teaches the student how to hear chord changes and then to improvise on the basis of what is heard. "The classes gave you the freedom to execute and develop a style," he said. "It gives you a chance to know what you want to do." Improvisation? Chord changes? Certainly not the stereotyped exercise books and uninspiring classical practice pieces that comprise the bill of fare for most young music students. Lowery's approach cut to the chase. It gave great motivation to youngsters who wanted to play jazz, which was where Clifford Brown's aspirations lay. "He really knew what he wanted to do as far as music was concerned,"[3] Boysie Lowery later told jazz scholar Phil Schaap. "All he needed was the right person, and I think I was the one at the time."

Clifford Brown was not the only young talent that Boysie Lowery would help. His jazz theories played a big role in the development of Ernie Watts, who recalls that he "led me through the cycle of fifths and gave me a solid foundation in the jazz harmonies of bebop."

Clifford used the term "jazz" in conjunction with his earliest recollection of interest in music. Soon after he began studying with Lowery, he joined "a jazz group that Robert Lowery organized to stimulate interest in jazz among the younger musicians in town." The group was dubbed The Little Dukes.

By this time there are three forces at work shaping the goals of a young Clifford Brown: the junior high band, lessons with Boysie Lowery, and playing with The Little Dukes—a busy schedule.

When I visited Lowery I asked what kind of structure his teaching sessions had. "He [Clifford] came by the house, and we had jam sessions," he said slowly. He was certainly glad to talk about Clifford

Brown. "Jam sessions and teaching. He would come by anytime, I guess," Lowery continued with a warm smile. "What were you charging for the lessons in those days?" I asked him. He shot me a quick glance. "Nothing," he said. "If somebody said 'today I can pay a dollar for a lesson and so on,' that was fine." His voice was full of pride as he spoke. The whole ethos of the east side seemed to be summed up in his last comment.

I asked Boysie Lowery to evaluate Clifford Brown as a student. He quickly responded that Clifford was not the most talented in his group. "Charlie Robertson—I thought he would be better," he said. "Well, what do you think eventually made Clifford so proficient?" I inquired. Boysie looked at me hard again. "Because he was determined to succeed," he said, slapping his hand down hard on the sofa arm to emphasize the word "determined."

Boysie Lowery soon selected Clifford Brown as the leader of The Little Dukes, and the group began to work some of the jobs that the Aces of Rhythm could not make. Progressing rapidly, the youngster soon became good enough to play with the Aces, even though he was not old enough to play in the Wilmington clubs. Lowery tried to get permission for him to play, but Clifford's young age proved a barrier.

"He showed his ability pretty early," Lowery recalled. "I remember one night in a club in Salisbury, Maryland, he played 'Star Dust,' and the way he played it, the way he improvised it, everyone in that club started paying attention to what he was doing. That ad lib made everyone notice it."

As is the case with many young musicians with talent, Clifford Brown now looked for new challenges. Soon he began to pick up other instruments and, under Lowery's tutelage, started playing the vibraphone, string bass, and piano. He would eventually develop enough mastery of the piano to play jobs, and his proficiency at the keyboard continued to progress.

By age fifteen, Clifford Brown attended the high school division of Howard High, which was a junior-senior high institution. The many advantages that this school had to offer would certainly not be lost on the determined youngster.

During Clifford's early teens his siblings had also begun to achieve goals that would distinguish the Brown family. As noted before, sister Marie, born in 1916, had graduated from Howard High at age fifteen and had showed vocal ability. She was certainly precocious and would lead the way for her sisters, Geneva and Rella. The girls developed an academic track record that was the pride of the family but a source of some frustration for the boys. Because the girls were "so brainy," Leon recalls that "the teachers were givin' me B's 'cause my name was Brown." The boys "were no dummies" (the college prep curriculum had them studying Latin, French, and physics at the same time), but Marie was truly outstanding. Later she applied to nursing school, "but got rejected when she had to send a picture," recalls Rella. It was one of the few early painful recollections of racial prejudice.

Among the five sons, it was Eugene who would set standards for academic achievement. "Genie" was "president of the student council," recalls Geneva, and also played football. Upon graduation from Howard High he entered Lincoln University, took his baccalaureate degree, and then finished a Master's degree "in record time" at Columbia. Eugene would go on to a distinguished career as an educator specializing in guidance. His work in New York at the Wiltwick School for Boys (boxer Floyd Patterson was one of its alumni) was significant. "Helping young people" became a source of much pride in the Brown family.

The Brown children received wise and loving support from Joe and Estella. Although the atmosphere at home was characterized by the "yes sir/no sir" form of address Joe required, there was no sense of the repression that occurred in many other cultures of the period. Religion, for example, did not induce fear. Although both Methodists, Joe and Estella attended different churches. Joe went to Zion at 9th and Walnut, where the children would go. Marie sang in the choir there, and although Joe was not a weekly attendee, he found the church and the people very suitable for his eclectic religious needs.

Estella attended Mt. Carmel (the two churches later merged) because she "felt she could be more helpful there." She became a deaconess, served as treasurer, and never missed a service. The strong, although different religious connections in the family underscored a highly moral value system ("If you lie, you steal") that was clear but never rigidly orthodox.

Family get-togethers always focused on music. When Uncle Arthur and Aunt Corrine (his piano player) visited from New York, the talk centered on the music business and the increasing success of many of the black swing dance bands. Geneva recalls many occasions where she and her older brothers were "quite the jitterbugs." Geneva and Marie danced, "and my mother and father would sit there watching and enjoying it."

Geneva recalls that the Brown youngsters would often go to the Howard High senior prom (even though they were underclassmen) in order to see and hear the black dance bands. The Sweethearts of Rhythm, an all-girl band, was Geneva's favorite. Although her recollection is a bit hazy, she says that "Tuxedo Junction," a signature tune of the Erskine Hawkins band, was very popular. This memory tallies with the date that this famous tune was written (1939) by Hawkins and Julian Dash.[4] It was, of course, later appropriated by Glenn Miller with great success. These teenagers were also well aware of such famous black bands as those of Jimmie Lunceford and Fletcher Henderson. This dance music provided an important backdrop for Clifford Brown while he was working with Boysie Lowery and learning to improvise.

East side neighborhood social life focused on the Walnut Street "Y," Brinkley's Pool Hall, and the Odd Fellows Temple. The Y was an important social and education center for families like the Browns. Chess attracted the Brown boys, and Ellsworth actually became a teacher of the game at the Y. Clifford Brown's mastery of chess is well known, and Geneva's recollection is that Ellsworth taught him how to play. The Y also became a natural meeting place and rehearsal space for the neighborhood musicians. Clifford's other boyhood pals, Bobby Ennis and Billy Norwood, recall Room 214 at the Y as being the scene of important jam sessions during Clifford's teenage years.

Pool halls conjure up a negative image. But by all indications,

Brinkley's was a place that Clifford Brown and his friends frequented with parental approval. The extended family structure of the neighborhood assured the locals that the kids were not going to get into trouble here. The Brown boys were regulars, and Leon recalls that Clifford quickly learned to shoot well and could always hold his own with a cue stick. "We taught him how to play pool," said Leon proudly.

Because of the Walnut Street Y, the Odd Fellows Temple, Brinkley's Pool Hall, the ball fields and picnics at Kirkwood Park, and the Armory for dances, the east siders had a much richer social and cultural life than many inner city youths have today.

Back at Howard High, Clifford Brown's musical horizons were expanding considerably. He now played in the senior high school marching band at Howard, and during this time the school hired two new teachers, Harry Andrews and Sam Wooding.

"I can't remember having a bad teacher at Howard High," recalled Cynthia Oates, a 1953 graduate who remembers Harry Andrews as the epitome of this teaching tradition. A tough taskmaster, Andrews required each individual student to sing specific passages, "and you better know it," said Cynthia with fond memory. Unassuming and modest, Andrews preferred not to have his photo in the school yearbooks.

A World War II veteran who had directed an army band, Andrews arrived at Howard High in 1946, when Clifford Brown was a junior. He had a Bachelor's degree from West Chester (Pennsylvania) University (1934) and a Master's from Columbia University, and he did graduate work at the University of Michigan. While at Howard High, Andrews became heavily involved in community music groups, earned outstanding teaching awards, and conducted numerous music camps. He was famous for developing young talent; in addition to Clifford Brown, he taught jazz luminary Ernie Watts. Watts was a student at Wilmington High in the early 1960s, and by that time Andrews was teaching there. Watts's early studies were heavily classically oriented, and Andrews was his music theory teacher. "The first time I ever heard a symphony orchestra was when Mr. Andrews took us to Philadelphia" recalled Watts. "I was sixteen or seventeen, and I saw [Eugene] Ormandy conduct; and it was Harry Andrews who taught me the sonata-allegro classical forms."[5] This classical legacy continues with Ernie Watts to the present day, for he plays classical music dates quite frequently in addition to his jazz work.

Late in his career Harry Andrews returned to West Chester's music department to teach, and at this time, he told writer Hollie West about his relationship with the teenaged Clifford Brown: "Clifford had some experience in a local Elks band when he came to our school. I started him on the Prescott system, which is based on Arban's method.[6] We used the Arban book to teach the Prescott system. One of the exercises, for example, was to play 16 or 32 bars in one breath. We put a maximum of eight weeks to work on an exercise. I also introduced him to the non-pressure system.[7] He had been using a lot of pressure on putting his lips to the mouthpiece. I also remember that he had an excellent embouchure. He put two-thirds of his lower lip in the mouthpiece." (Eventually, Clifford modified his technique of opening the aperture on strategic notes, enabling him to achieve a deeper, richer tone. After maneuvering the opening thus, he would then close it down in order to play other notes more easily. The result was an evenness of tone that became his trademark.)

"He perfected making octave jumps very early. Sometimes on certain marches in parades, he'd play an octave above the rest of the trumpets. And he developed a very beautiful range. When he came to us, he was a very good intermediate trumpet player. But he played the 'Carnival of Venice' as his graduation solo, and I mean he really played it. He had great drive. Many times I'd be cleaning up my desk after school, and he'd stick his head in and ask if I had time for another lesson. And we'd go to it. But he was ahead of me. He knew polytonality. He played all those little grace notes. From the beginning in high school, he was very Gillespie-oriented. He took our small theory class and started developing some jazz arrangements for the band."[8]

Andrews and Clifford Brown appeared to have that rare relationship between a brilliant pedagogue and a dedicated student. Each had focus and drive, with no egos intervening, and this produced extraordinary musical growth in Clifford. "When he concentrated on the piano he played very well for a guy who was just starting," recalled Andrews. "I don't mean he was an Erroll Garner. One day I went by a little club where he was playing piano at a jam session. Some of his friends were playing, and he didn't want to play while I was there. He said, 'Mr. Andrews, I get so nervous when you listen to me.' " The teacher acknowledged the superiority of the student ("He was ahead of me"), and the student recognized the great contribution the teacher had made to him.

Clifford Brown continued to be well aware of Harry Andrews. Years after graduation, even after Brown had become famous, he would drop into Harry Andrews's office when in Wilmington and talk about music with his old mentor.

Since Boysie Lowery relied on his students' listening to music while they improvised, he was also up on the latest in recording technology. Thus he constantly encouraged his students to record their practice sessions to develop their skills. In the 1940s, wire spool recorders and disc cutters were developed and targeted for a mass market audience. Clifford Brown became one of the first jazz men to use these devices, and he would continue to do so throughout his career. Many of these sessions, especially those on piano, provide great insight into Clifford's musical development.

The practice sessions themselves have become the stuff of legend. With his quiet manner and calm determination Clifford followed the regimen established by his teachers. He would practice for hours at a time. Leon Brown recalls one Sunday when Clifford practiced in a closet so he wouldn't disturb the Sabbath.

Initially, Clifford's playing failed to impress the manager of the Aces of Rhythm, Ben Cashman, who himself played the trumpet. He recalled the young Clifford Brown's hanging around the band shortly after he had begun to study with Boysie Lowery. "I never thought he would amount to anything, to tell you the truth," said Cashman. "He had such poor tone, and he was so sloppy."[9] After managing the Aces for about seven months, Cashman departed for

Florida. Upon his return to Wilmington a couple of years later, Boysie Lowery urged him to come and listen to Clifford. "Brownie's really blowin'," said Lowery, so Cashman went down "to a little club, I think it was called the Baby Grand," and was instantly enthralled. "I never heard anything like it in my life," he said. "It was just like you hear Clifford now on record. How could a guy get that kind of technique in that short a time? I'll never forget it!"

"Brownie" had actually been Clifford's father's nickname, but Clifford too began to be called Brownie during these teenage years. The nickname stuck with him all his life, and musicians and writers have referred to him by it ever since.

Trumpeter Marcus Belgrave, who studied with Lowery later, often heard Brownie practice. "When he played, everything was scientifically laid out," stated Belgrave. "He was into writing ideas down; he would always tell me to write things down. He'd play everything through the keys."[10] Even though Clifford Brown was beginning to play jazz gigs, he would still appear at the marching band practices. "I asked him why he bothered to show up to play these circus-type tunes," said Belgrave, and Brownie responded, "I like all kinds of music." And he continued to be interested in a wide range of music throughout his life.

At Howard there were four main musical aggregations: marching band, concert band, choir, and orchestra. According to Kenyon Camper, a member of the band, the orchestra was the only coed organization.[11] Band practice began before classes at 8:10 A.M., and the repertoire included plenty of Sousa marches, a piece called "Field Tactics," and the band's theme song, "Rhapsody in Blue." Andrews was an admirer of Fred Waring, and the band played Waring's arrangement of "Battle Hymn of the Republic." There were usually forty-eight musicians playing, and the band marched on the field before the football games, played there at half time, and performed in the stands during the game, like so many other marching bands. They also played for parades in Wilmington. The sight of the Howard band "marching up the street and turning by the post office" was a great source of pride for the east side community.

In addition to Clifford Brown, "we had a lot of talented musicians, even trumpet players . . . a guy named Ben Jackson, and Alan Williams (who became a physician) was called Diz." The band wore navy blue and white uniforms, but they only arrived during Brownie's senior year, 1947–48. A picture in the '48 yearbook shows him in this new uniform.

Because Andrews arrived at Howard when Clifford Brown was a junior, his influence on Brownie was crammed into two years. It is clear that Andrews's disciplined approach rubbed off on the youngster. "He took the roll, and, if you were late, it affected your grade." Even the Howard principal, George A. Johnson, was a disciplinarian who "would paddle you if you got out of hand." Years later, Sam Dockery, an early cohort of Clifford's, always admired the fact that he arrived on time for every job.

Kenyon Camper, president of the student government his senior year, was a dedicated Howard student. He recalled that the segregation of those days, ironically, had positive features. Although almost all facilities were segregated, the east side community still had a very strong sense of pride.

No one had much money. "We were so poor we could only say 'po,' not 'poor,' " says Kenyon Camper, but he laughs as he says it. He has very positive memories of the scene at the Y, with its swimming pool, gymnastics, bowling alley, dancing, and a sort of teenage nightclub dubbed El Trocadero. Because of the dedicated faculty, the schools had excellent standards; because the population was small, the students had unusual opportunities for intellectual, spiritual, and cultural growth. In contrast to the hi-tech, sports-oriented schools in present-day suburban communities, Wilmington's east side schools of the war years were model academic institutions.

The image of a teenage Clifford Brown running from trumpet lesson to band practice, to school, to the Y, to his long practice sessions, to gigs with The Little Dukes and the Aces of Rhythm provides a graphic picture of a busy youngster whose world is largely dominated by his horn and his music. His teachers had taught him lessons that would stand the determined youngster in good stead. His parents always supported him strongly. His siblings loved "Little

Comache" and protected him. His neighborhood created an environment that would spawn many successful careers. With this background and his own dedication and talent, it is little wonder that Clifford Brown would become another important story in the remarkable tradition of the east side.

Three
On to
Philadelphia

By the time Clifford Brown was an upperclassman at Howard, his musical pace had become frenetic. When not at school or with all of the bands and groups, he led jam sessions at 1013 Poplar Street. His reputation was developing, and musicians would arrive for the jam sessions at the Brown house from as far away as Philadelphia. His parents took notice, of course, but never objected to the hordes of players that would invade their house. "Estella never said a word," recalled Deanie Jenkins. "All she did was be out in the kitchen cookin' . . . the first two rooms of the house were all ours."[1] Soon the crowds began to overflow. "What would happen," said Jenkins, "there were so many guys, that's why we had to go to the Y."

At school, Clifford Brown began to arrange music for different jazz groups. Neighbor Bobby Burton, also a student of Boysie Lowery's, was part of the trio that Brownie led with Donald Criss (Rashied Ali). "I wasn't good enough to be in it," said Deanie Jenkins.

The group caused a big ruckus among the student body on one occasion when they played a tune that Brownie wrote, "Blue Feathers." "They [the teachers] made everybody leave the auditorium and go back to class," said Jenkins, chuckling as he recalled the incident.

"When they heard 'Blue Feathers' they [the students] were so over-whelmed they got unruly."

Back at the Brown house jam sessions, the level of musicianship constantly improved. "The guys that came to jam sessions were just a step below Jimmy and Percy Heath," recalled Charles "Bop" Wilson, one of the young Brown's protégés. "They were top guys."

Deanie Jenkins had originally encountered Clifford Brown at one session at the Walnut Street Y. "I sneaked up to the Y," he said, "and Clifford showed me the chord changes to 'I Got Rhythm.'" Brownie constantly taught and encouraged his friends and classmates, but his playing often intimidated them. "He scared me so much I switched to trombone for a while," said Bop Wilson. He laughed: "Then I started copying Miles [Davis] . . . Miles is easy . . . simple stuff. . . . But I was always around Brownie's licks . . . I would be on a gig and Clifford would show up and I'd go to pieces, man."[3]

As winter turned to spring in 1948, the tempo of the senior class activities picked up at Howard High. Although by this time Clifford Brown's reputation as the school's leading trumpeter was secure, he had also developed a strong aptitude for mathematics. The college preparatory curriculum at Howard included math sequences through trigonometry; science courses that emphasized biology, physics, and chemistry (the latter courses were strong enough to propel several graduates into pre-med majors in college); and language studies in French and Latin. Although Brownie was doing well in math, he was not a leading scholar in the class of '48. He had some difficulty in English, and Leon recounts that Clifford had to talk the teacher out of giving him a D. He got along but could not match the academic success of his sisters. But neither could the other Brown boys.

Despite the quality of its teachers and the discipline of the curriculum, Howard High did experience the fact of segregation, since the textbooks, as Kenyon Camper says, were dog-eared "hand-me-down books from the white schools."

That spring, the music department presented arias from "Il Trovatore," and the sixty-eight-piece choir, as they had done before, scored a second place finish in statewide competition. The jazz groups jammed, the concert band paraded, and the orchestra gave concerts. As graduation neared, expectations were heightened in the Brown household—Clifford was to play "Carnival of Venice" as his featured selection. When he gave his performance, he brought down the house, and the occasion became a major story told over and over by '48 alumni. "He really played it," said Harry Andrews. "Nobody ever did that," said Bop Wilson, "and nobody has done it since."

By this time, Clifford Brown had become a hero to his young musical cohorts. Ralph Morris claimed that Brownie did it all alone. "Clifford taught himself. He really did. He did things with books. . . . If he had never met Boysie or Andrews, he would have been just as great."[2] Deanie Jenkins and Bop Wilson agreed.

During the summer after graduation, Brownie continued his gigging around the Wilmington area and began to make more frequent visits to Philadelphia, a city that would remain pivotal for him for the rest of his life.

In the fall of 1948, Clifford Brown matriculated at Delaware State College, an all-black school in Dover. It has been incorrectly reported that he had a music scholarship, but that fall the school had temporarily suspended its music program, so he enrolled in a course of studies that listed mathematics as his intended major. Clifford's sister Geneva had obtained an Elks Scholarship to Howard University, and this may also have been the source of his grant too.

Tuition at the school, including room and board, was "about $1000 per year," according to Irving Williams, who graduated from Howard in 1947 and entered Delaware State with Margaret Brown, Brownie's future sister-in-law. In 1948 Delaware State College was an institution caught in the time warp between old time segregation and the new civil rights struggles. For decades the school had served as both the only college for blacks in the state[4] and the only black high school outside of Wilmington. Because it had serious funding problems, the school had an inadequate library, no laboratory equipment, and questionable academic standards. By 1948 it had lost its accreditation. In January of that year the Board of Trustees voted to admit blacks to the University of Delaware (Newark) graduate schools and engineering school, which made the university the first institution of higher learning ordered to desegregate.

Irving Williams speaks favorably of Delaware State. The activities included "music clubs and sports and things like that." There were three or four fraternities and a fairly typical formal dress code.

Delaware State had about five hundred students, with two male dorms, Cannon and Jason halls, each one housing about fifty young men. The first recollection Williams had of Brownie was his "leaving the dorm on Friday with his horn in his hand. We knew that he did go to Philadelphia and New Jersey and played at different night spots on the weekends." When pressed, Williams says "every weekend." Brown probably played of campus at various functions during the school week, and his reputation as an important musician from Howard High was certainly carried onto the campus at Dover. But there is little evidence that he developed musically at Delaware State in any significant way. What was more important for him were the musical activities on those weekend trips to Philadelphia.

The city was a jazz mecca during this period. It was, like Delaware, home to large pre–Civil War neighborhoods of freed Negroes. Divided into north and south by Broad Street and into east and west by Market Street, Philadelphia was teeming with jazz venues when Clifford Brown first arrived.

In the black sections along South Street, during the early swing era, there were many theaters—the Pearl, the Lincoln, and the Dunbar—as well as nightclubs and bars. Most were located between 10th and 17th streets. Many revues and touring companies appeared here. During the war and immediately thereafter, the scene changed to small jazz clubs, just as it had in New York. Such clubs as Pep's Musical Bar at Broad and South streets and the Blue Note at 15th Street and Ridge Avenue were thriving, and many local musicians who played there would soon became nationally known. When the bebop revolution occurred in the early 1940s, Philadelphia was second only to New York as a center for the new jazz. The list of local musicians who became stars is a long one: the Heath Brothers, Benny Golson, Philly Joe Jones, Lee Morgan, and Red Rodney are only a few of the best known.

Rodney recounts a story about the young Clifford Brown, perhaps when he was visiting the city on one of his weekend jaunts from college. There was a ring on the doorbell at the Rodneys' house one afternoon, and Red opened the door to find Brown. After announcing himself, he told Rodney: "I'm a trumpet player. I'd sure like to speak to you and study. I'd like to take lessons from the man who plays with Bird."[5] Rodney was not giving lessons, but he was struck by the youngster's determination and so invited him into his house. Rodney asked him to play. "I could see from his questions, he was no ordinary kid," said Rodney, who quickly became astounded. "He knocked me out even then. He was tremendous. He already had that gorgeous sound and was just getting his ideas together. I told him, 'There's nothing I can show you, you just have to keep playing like you are.' "

It is difficult to pinpoint the date of this incident. Ellis Tollin, who operated Music City, a store/concert venue that sponsored jam sessions, recalled an evening featuring Bill Harris, Charlie Ventura, and "a little kid about fifteen or sixteen years old named Clifford Brown." So it is possible that Brownie may have played in Philadelphia as early as 1945. Red Rodney later stated, "I knew Clifford when he was just a young boy who used to come around and listen to all of us. He was very nice. He was a modest, humble person and very gentlemanly, even as a youth. I saw great promise in him when he was fifteen or sixteen years old. Even then he sounded very much like Fats."[6]

It seems unlikely that Brown had heard Fats Navarro as early as 1945, but, when he did hear him, he was immediately struck by his style. Most observers feel that the first Brown-Navarro meeting took place later. Nevertheless, it is abundantly clear that the Philadelphia music scene played an important part in Clifford Brown's musical growth during high school and college years. Equally significant, it introduced the youngster to a musical revolution in the making—bebop.

Benny Golson recalled that he first met Brown in Philadelphia "when I was nineteen and Brownie was about sixteen." (Golson was actually only about one and a half years older than Brownie.) This would place the meeting somewhere about 1946. "He sounded good even then," added Golson.

Of all the musicians whom Brownie encountered on his trips to Philadelphia, Fats Navarro was the one who would matter most to the young trumpeter. Born of Cuban, Chinese, and black parentage in Key West, Florida, on September 24, 1923, Theodore "Fats" Navarro played piano and tenor saxophone as a youth. By age seventeen, however, he was playing trumpet and performing with dance bands. He played with Snookum Russell and toured in 1943 with Andy Kirk's jazz orchestra, which then included trumpeter Howard McGhee. He did a stint with Lionel Hampton, but his most important modern jazz band gig came in January 1945, when he replaced Dizzy Gillespie in Billy Eckstine's band. This short-lived aggregation had more young bebop innovators in it than any other band. As the principal trumpet soloist, Navarro broke new ground in the bop idiom.

After he left Eckstine in 1946, Navarro played in small groups, which had become the major vehicle for the new music. Between 1946 and his death in 1950, he performed on about 150 small group recordings. He played with Kenny Clarke, Coleman Hawkins, Bud Powell, Charlie Parker, and many others. It is in his recordings with Tadd Dameron, an innovative bebop composer, that Navarro's talent is particularly evident. Here the rapid eighth-note delivery, the broken rhythms, and new chord phrasing, which Navarro had adopted from the Charlie Parker–Dizzy Gillespie canon, evolved into a truly individualistic style. Dizzy Gillespie had set the standard for bebop trumpeters a few years before with his rapid-fire technique and high register solos. Navarro quickly focused on tone and developed soft subtlety in the middle registers of the horn. His solos were structured with classical balance and a good deal of logic.

Whitney Balliett has described Navarro's approach aptly: "Set against the background of his often disheveled peers, a Navarro solo was like an immaculate fairway flanked by ankle-deep rough. His solos compare extremely well with Dizzy Gillespie's most famous effusions of the time, but they got less attention from the public because they lacked the italics and bold face that Gillespie always set himself up in. Gillespie liked to clown and blare and do the fandango up and down his registers. He liked to mow the grass flat and divide the waters. But the truth is that Navarro was the better trumpet player. He concentrated on his tone, which was generous and even; on his chops, which were almost perfect (he rarely split or dropped notes, the way most bebop trumpeters did, Gillespie included); and on his classic sense of order, which gave his solos a Churchillian ring and flow. He stayed largely in the middle register, but his occasional ascensions were consummate. The notes, though high, were big and smooth, and there was none of Gillespie's occasional pinched quality. Sometimes Navarro's phrases lasted ten or twelve bars. They crossed meadows and stiles and copses before finally landing. But every so often he would insert a clump of whole notes that would have the effect of briefly throwing his solo into slow motion. He would punctuate these serene juxtapositions with silence, and shift back into his handsome parade of eighth notes. At first, Navarro's solos seemed as cluttered as most bebop players', but there was no hot air in them; his loquacity had content and purpose and grace."[7]

In his "Fats Navarro" entry in the *New Grove Dictionary of Jazz*, Thomas Owens has transcribed a Navarro solo performed on Bud Powell's "Wail" clearly showing Parker's influence upon him. Owens notes the "nearly continuous flow of eighth notes with an unpredictable sparkling of accents between the beats" that Parker brought to jazz. But Owens also mentions a motif in the solo that "connects by chromatic descent the 13th and raised 11th of each chord,"[8] which is a singular Navarro habit.

Although Dizzy Gillespie was by far the most widely admired trumpeter of the new bebop, it is significant that Clifford Brown chose, perhaps as early as age fifteen, to follow the path of Navarro. During his Philadelphia excursions it is evident that he saw Navarro frequently perform. He sought to develop the "fat sound" that has long since become identified as the essential Clifford Brown style. Following the lead of Navarro, Brown eschewed the high register solos that made bebop such a crowd-pleaser. He preferred the middle of the horn, and it is there that he developed his long improvisational lines.

Clifford Brown was well aware of Gillespie's innovations, but he refused to become a Gillespie clone. Even at this early age he recognized that he could achieve more if he utilized ideas that Navarro had developed. In time, his tone would become sweeter than Navarro's, his improvisations more complex, and, above all, his articulation and clarity more pronounced.

Benny Golson describes what was probably the first meeting between Clifford Brown and Fats Navarro. One of the Philadelphia clubs "had local talent there, Clifford Brown, an alto player and a rhythm section—and Fats was a little late getting in. Clifford was playing as he entered, and Fats sort of realized halfway between the door and the stage what was going on—you could see him slow his pace just a little and sort of look up to see where all this playing was coming from. He proceeded to take his trumpet out; he got up there, and they called another tune off and began to play. Being the star, as it were, at the time, Fats played the first solo, and then Clifford began to play. Fats held his horn in his arms the way trumpet players do, and sort of stepped back—not in awe, but sort of like in respect. And I'll tell you, Clifford was really holding his own. In fact, as kind and meek as he was, when he picked his horn up and the tempo really went up, he became almost like a vicious person, you know—darting and dodging and badgering and manhandling—yet it was all very beautiful, very controlled and colored with emotion."[9]

It is probable that this first meeting occurred on one of the Philadelphia trips taken when Brownie was still in high school. Golson recollected that "Fats tucked his trumpet under his arm, stood beside Brownie and applauded." This coincides with the 1946 date that is Golson's first recollection of seeing him. Navarro was sincerely appreciative of Brown's talent and, it appears, advised him on many occasions, most of them in Philadelphia.

Years later, in 1954, when Clifford Brown became a jazz star and *Down Beat* critics' poll winner, he was asked by Leonard Feather to fill out a questionnaire. Feather was preparing entries for his forthcoming *Encyclopedia of Jazz*. His form included the question, "Who are your favorite musicians on your instrument?" Brownie wrote down only one name: "the late Fats Navarro."[10]

Benny Golson was another Philadelphia jazzman who played an important part in Clifford Brown's life. Born on January 26, 1929, Golson studied piano, organ, tenor saxophone, and clarinet as a youth and later attended Howard University (1947–50). In 1951, in Bull Moose Jackson's band, he met Tadd Dameron. By this time Dameron had begun to write in the new bebop idiom, after having written for swing bands in the 1930s and 1940s. Dameron's innovative writing strongly influenced Golson, motivating him to devote more time to composition. In 1953, Golson played in Dameron's band alongside Clifford Brown. Once again Philadelphia and neighboring Atlantic City was the scene of these musical associations.[11]

The Heath Brothers, also from Philadelphia, are one of the most famous families in jazz. Bass player Percy, the eldest, gigged around the city and studied at the Granoff School of Music. A few years later he played with Fats Navarro in Howard McGhee's band, and he would eventually play on one of Clifford Brown's first recordings. Later, he became a mainstay of the Modern Jazz Quartet. Jimmy Heath, the middle brother, a sax player, also played in McGhee's and then Gillespie's band. While moving back and forth between New York and Philadelphia in the middle 1940s, he kept a rehearsal band going at an odd studio/store called Music City.

Music City's operator, Ellis Tollin, intended to present jazzmen who were being featured at the main Philadelphia jazz clubs. Many Philadelphia youngsters had no place to see their heroes live. In a makeshift concert hall located on the second floor of the building at 1711 Chestnut Street, Tollin produced jam sessions, usually on Tuesday nights. By paying token admission, the young jazz fans, many of themselves players, could experience the music firsthand and, if they had enough talent, get up on the bandstand and join in. Two of the more prominent names in the youth groups were Clifford Brown and, later, Lee Morgan.

Of course, Charlie Parker, the foremost player in the bebop revolution, made a great impact on the young players when he appeared at the clubs in Philadelphia. Bird's comings and goings touched the lives of many budding jazz musicians who saw him in the city, some of whom were fortunate enough to share a bandstand with him. It did not take long for Boysie Lowery's jazz students in Wilmington to adopt Charlie Parker and Dizzy Gillespie as their improvisational idols. Clifford Brown, as early as age twelve, had encountered the Parker-Gillespie revolution through Boysie Lowery's early connection with Dizzy Gillespie. By the time he had graduated from Howard and begun college, he had become a Parker-Gillespie disciple. Boysie Lowery recalled that a good deal of their sound had crept into Clifford's playing. On occasion, he had to rein in his student and keep him focused on developing his own style. Brownie responded positively to Boysie's advice.

When I visited Boysie Lowery's Broome Street home in Wilmington, he showed me his photos and souvenirs. He came across a record of a tape that he had made with Brownie when Clifford was still in early development. The recording is a practice session that finds them both playing the legendary Parker tune "Ornithology." Lowery is playing alto, and the two go through a charming harmonized duet. Although filled with scratches and static, the record shows Brown playing a plethora of neatly phrased triplet figures à la Parker that he would incorporate into his improvisational style. We also hear the sweet, soft tone from the trumpet's lower register that would become his trademark. Lowery and Brown play the tune at a medium tempo, which allows them to improvise comfortably. Brownie's phrasing of the sixteenth-note passages in the melody is more even and more articulate than his teacher's, and his improvisation at the end of the tune is more inventive.

The Elks Lodges in Philadelphia hosted important jazz sessions. Four or five of these establishments were scattered around the city, and they were crammed with audiences eager to catch the new music in the late 1940s. Trumpeter Johnny Coles recalled that interest in the new music reached a peak during this period. "We used to play Sunday afternoon jam sessions at the Elks Lodge," he said. "Most times they would have players come from New York like Miles Davis, Sonny Rollins, people like that. But it would always be a 'battle' of the trumpeters. Sometimes it would be Clifford and I and Miles. One time it was Miles and I [at one lodge] and Clifford and Fats Navarro [at another]. We were uptown, and they were downtown—

both at Elks homes. Miles and I were right here on Broad Street. The place was packed. So we played the first set and got into a cab to go down to listen to Clifford and Fats. We stayed for the whole set! And when we came back . . . nobody had moved! Everybody was just sittin' there waitin'. That was stupendous. . . . We didn't realize the full impact at the time of how the people were so enthusiastic about the music."[12]

Many of the beboppers had good jobs playing show music in nearby Atlantic City. Coles recalled that "after the [Atlantic City] gig was over, like 5 o'clock in the morning, we used to go around to the Club Harlem [in West Philadelphia] and set up and play 'til 10 o'clock. We got hot one night, and Clifford must have played about twenty minutes. And every chorus was different. He was just in the beginning of being on his way."

Billy Root also recalled a pivotal encounter Clifford Brown had with Charlie Parker. "One time Charlie Parker was playing down in a club in Philadelphia, and somehow they invited Clifford up to play. There was an upright piano, and [Clifford] was standing behind it. Finally Bird said, 'Hey, come out here.' Obviously Bird was very impressed. He repeated: 'Come out here. What are you doing back there?' He finally got him out. Clifford was very humble."[13]

Root played an important part in the jazz life of Philadelphia at that time. His father, who was a musician, took his son to the famous Earle Theatre. "I remember when I was a little boy," said Root, "I'd go to the Earle . . . I'm talking about five or six years old. And we used to see Lucky Millinder, and I saw the old Duke Ellington band." Root began playing in jazz clubs when he was seventeen. "Philadelphia was an unusual place," he said. "When you came to Philadelphia you'd better be hot 'cause they came out after you. You had John Coltrane living there, Jimmy Heath, Benny Golson. There was one saxophone player named Mel Vines—Ziggy Vines. . . . This man was probably the greatest player I ever heard, especially an unknown player. He was an artist. When Bird would see him he'd say, 'There's my friend Mel, I wonder if he'd come up and play with me.' " Root is one of many musicians who speak of Ziggy Vines with great reverence. Unfortunately, he was one of those superb artists who never really made his mark in jazz.

Root worked as the house tenor player at the Blue Note—Philadelphia's best-known bebop club. Philly Joe Jones served as the house drummer and Red Garland, the pianist. Root recalled working at the Club with Brownie "5 or 6 times for 1 or 2 weeks at a time."[14]

Having played with Stan Kenton's and Buddy Rich's big bands, besides countless small groups, Root still had a special affection for the Philadelphia jazz clubs. "When I was in Philadelphia, there were almost six jazz clubs going, and they weren't all clubs where you had to be a star. There were clubs like Bill & Lou's, Emerson's, the 421 Club, Spider Kelly's Downtown. . . . I liked Philadelphia clubs better than Birdland in New York. The jazz fans were extremely loyal and very knowledgeable."

Four
The Brink
of Disaster

Dizzy Gillespie had lived in Philadelphia in the late 1930s and had moved on to New York in 1940 or '41. During the time of the late 1940s jam sessions and club activity, Gillespie was no longer a Philadelphia resident but a frequent visitor, very often with his big band. It is certain that when Clifford Brown began going to Philadelphia, one of his goals was to hear Dizzy play. As we have seen, because of the presence of giants like Dizzy and Bird, Philadelphia was the place that young Delaware jazzers dreamed about.

Leon Brown recalled, "You'd have to be really outstanding in those days to make it because most of the guys that weren't making it were good. You could be the best here in Wilmington and leave town and find out you were just one among many . . . but your tester in those days would be Philadelphia. If you went to Philly, made it, then you had somethin' goin' for you. . . . If you made it big, then you were on your way."[1]

Among Leon's favorite clubs was the Showboat, a small club holding "about seventy-six or eighty people," according to Johnny Coles. But the audiences were so attentive that "you could hear a pin drop. That's what I liked about the Showboat. You'd go in there and those people appreciated music. The talking stopped and the listening started when a good band came in there."[2]

The Showboat was one of the jam session sites that Brownie frequented during his year at Delaware State.

As noted before, Brown was majoring in mathematics at Delaware State. He enjoyed the logical challenges that math contained. He was well aware that it would be extremely difficult to be a successful jazz musician (as Leon had said), so his interest in math might lead to a job that would sustain him if his music career failed. When he made the decision to accept the scholarship, there can be little doubt that he intended to graduate. His sisters and Eugene before him had already distinguished themselves as students, and he intended to follow suit. So he pursued his math course of study vigorously. "He quickly earned the nickname 'the brain,'" Rella once said. "Everybody at college called him 'the brain.'"

Some of the countless tributes to Brown have used the hyperbole "math genius." It is difficult to substantiate that degree of praise, but his ability to focus and his great disciplinary habits make it clear he had great potential.

As matters developed, he lost any serious consideration in math as a profession in 1949, during the summer following his first year at Delaware State. One evening Brown and his friends met early at Brinkley's pool room. While the boys were shooting pool and exchanging gossip there was an exhilarating tension present. The guys were really killing time before they would walk from 9th and French, where Brinkley's was, to 12th and Orange, the site of the Odd Fellows Temple. It was going to be a big night—Dizzy Gillespie was bringing his big band to Wilmington. When the boys arrived at the Temple, it seemed that the entire city had turned out to see the great jazz star. Boysie Lowery was there, of course, to cheer on his old North Carolina crony, and many of Clifford's fellow alumni from the '48 Howard class were also buzzing around.

Shortly before the band was ready to play, the word got out that trumpeter Benny Harris (the cowriter of "Ornithology") could not be found. With a knowing smile, Boysie Lowery led a parade of east siders to the bandstand, where they informed Gillespie that a proper substitute for Harris just happened to be in the room. Brownie was ushered from a quiet corner up to the bandstand, where he promptly played the first set with the big trumpet section. Gillespie was amazed at his playing. "Where did this guy come from?" he screamed as the room went wild. It didn't take much to persuade Diz to allow him to take the solo on "I Can't Get Started"—a signature tune for trumpet virtuosos since it had been introduced by the legendary Bunny Berigan. "Brownie did the solo, and Diz was flabbergasted," recalled Dave Clark, who was cheering on his neighborhood pal.[3] Later, Gillespie took aside the young college student and strongly urged him to commit himself to playing jazz. Brownie was so impressed by Dizzy's advice that soon after he decided to abandon Delaware State. Within weeks he arranged for a transfer to Maryland State and its noted music department, once again with a scholarship. From now on, he would focus exclusively on music.

Encouraged by this meeting with Dizzy Gillespie, Clifford Brown sought new opportunities in Philadelphia. He had been playing at jam sessions for quite a while and had established himself strongly enough so that he thought about forming his own group. Gillespie had put the word out after the Odd Fellows Temple gig, and one of the jazz veterans he had contacted was Max Roach. Wildly excited, Gillespie told Roach, "Man, there's a cat down in Wilmington who plays piano and blows the shit out of the trumpet."[4] Such comments were extraordinary coming from the king of the bebop trumpet. Little did Dizzy realize what import those words might have for Max Roach years later.

Max Roach had established himself as the leading drummer of the new bebop school. He had played on Parker and Gillespie's classic bebop recordings and later with Miles Davis.

During this period, Roach brought a quintet of all-star musicians to a concert at the Camero Room in Mercantile Hall at Broad and Master Streets in Philadelphia. Roach's group consisted of Kenny Dorham on trumpet, Ernie Henry on alto saxophone, John Lewis on piano, and Curly Russell (with whom Roach worked on the Parker records) on bass. Fats Navarro was the guest trumpeter for the evening. Roach's ears perked up when someone told him that the group opening for him would be led by Clifford Brown.

Brownie's group at the Camero Room included the saxophonist James Young, altoist John Joyner, pianist Hasaan Ali (Langsford), bassist Steve Davis, and drummer William "Kali" Armstrong.

Once again, Clifford Brown was appearing on the same bill with his mentor Fats Navarro, and the event was properly commemorated in a memorable photograph. Charlie Chisholm, a Philadelphia-based trumpeter, had helped produce the show and taken photos as well. His photo of Brown and Navarro is touching. Navarro's normally corpulent body had become emaciated from the drug dependence that would soon kill him. Despite this, the two smiled, reflecting the great admiration and affection they had for each other.

In September 1949, Clifford went back to school on a new campus and totally new environment. Maryland State College, again an all-black school, was situated in the town of Princess Anne along Maryland's eastern shore on Chesapeake Bay. Brownie was exhilarated because the school had an excellent music department, there was an active jazz scene, and the environment brought back pleasant memories of picnics when the family visited his mother's relatives there.

Maryland State College (currently University of Maryland, Eastern Shore) had a remarkable music program that suited Clifford Brown's talents. Its jazz band included advanced players. Tom Walker, who played trombone, had played in bands while in the navy and been awarded "an automatic scholarship" at the college. Money for these awards was ostensibly provided by a combination of government, public, and private donors and various agencies. The band at Maryland State had fourteen pieces, the standard saxophone, trumpet, and trombone choirs, with a rhythm section. A sociology major who graduated in 1950, Walker remembered the young transfer student from Delaware State who jumped right into the band upon his arrival at Princess Anne and "played his ass off."[5] The band played for dances and parties, but the charts (arrangements) were heavily jazz oriented—Stan Kenton and Count Basie as opposed to Tommy Dorsey and Glenn Miller.

In this band Brown could develop his writing talent. He had been composing since the Little Dukes and Aces of Rhythm days. But now at Maryland State he had a full jazz orchestra with mature players.

According to Walker, the best musicians in the band were Brownie and Sam Turner, another trumpeter. The two hornmen assumed leadership of the band, and it soon developed a sound reputation. By the spring of 1950 the band was rapidly becoming well known regionally, due in large part to Clifford Brown's playing and arranging. Demands for their services were increasing, and the band had more and more bookings. Although not everyone in the band became famous, most of them had successful musical careers. Tommy Walker went home to Louisville, Kentucky, and became an orchestra leader, eventually claiming the title of "Prom band star of Louisville." Maryland State had, through a challenging curriculum and fine instructors, given its students the training necessary for success in the commercial music field. Ironically, like Howard High, under segregation the college had achieved high educational standards, and Clifford Brown was fortunate enough to be there during this period.

The gigs that the Maryland State Band booked took them all over the state. While they drove to their jobs, the musicians traded ideas and constantly sought new musical projects. In the spring semester, the band was busy playing more than their share of dances and parties, and on the evening of June 6, after a particularly successful outing, spirits were high. Brownie and three of his cohorts were happily motoring along when a deer suddenly sprang out from the roadside. The car swerved to avoid hitting the animal, skidded out of control, overturned and crashed. The driver and his girlfriend were killed. Brownie and the other occupant were critically injured and rushed to a hospital. As soon as Clifford's family and friends heard the news, they hurried to his bedside and learned that his injuries were so extensive that his life was in the balance. As the family waited and prayed, an announcement finally came. Clifford Brown had broken bones throughout his legs and the right side of his torso. He would need a full body cast to reset his frame and would remain hospitalized indefinitely. His music career, his college education, and all of the progress that he had made in jazz were abruptly halted. Visitors were shocked as he lay in bed broken like a china doll. Incredibly, a short time after this catastrophe, Sam Turner was killed in another car accident. The Maryland State Band had lost its best voices in one fell swoop.

As he lay in the hospital totally immobilized, Clifford Brown felt the classic sense of defeat and despair that comes over anyone who has experienced such calamity. Many cling to these negative feelings and are never the same. Some begin the struggle to establish new hope in their minds and use this to force their bodies to begin the task of rehabilitation. And a very few somehow turn such tragedies into opportunities for new challenges. Clifford Brown fell into this last group.

When it became evident that his life was no longer in imminent danger, Brownie slowly began a painful convalescence. Skin grafts produced scars that ran from his ankle up to his armpit, and the body cast was a terrible burden. The left leg was so badly mutilated that he needed a bone graft. Such procedures were difficult at best in 1950, and the pain was excruciating.

Two disparate events took place during his hospitalization. The first was the news that on July 7, 1950, Fats Navarro had died, succumbing at last to tuberculosis and heroin addiction. Navarro was gone at age twenty-six, at the height of his powers (most scholars agree that one of his finest performances was a date with Charlie Parker made just days before his death). To Brownie as he lay in his hospital bed, the news of Navarro's death was devastating. His mentor, the friend who had inspired so much of his growth as a jazz trumpet virtuoso, would guide him no longer.

While thus hospitalized Clifford Brown also received a visit from Dizzy Gillespie. "You've got to keep it going," preached Gillespie. His praise and encouragement stunned Brownie and gave him new confidence. It made him all that more determined to renew his jazz career.

As his condition began to stabilize, Brownie could plan for the day that he would leave the hospital. When it was decided that he could go, his condition was still so poor that he could be moved only as far as his aunt's house in nearby Marydel. In severe pain, he was taken there. At Marydel, a steady stream of family and friends provided constant encouragement to the nineteen-year-old patient. The old east side extended family made visits, and, according to his family, these visits played a vital role in his rehabilitation.

Ralph Morris, one of Clifford's close Poplar Street friends, became a frequent companion during the long period of his convalescence: "My mother and my sister and I all went down [to Maryland] to visit him. . . . They kept him down there for quite awhile because of the seriousness of the accident."[6] As he began to heal, Brownie determined to focus on playing jazz trumpet as his life's work. Although a college education was important, finishing his degree would take time, and because of the painful detour caused by the accident, Brownie started to evaluate the passing of time in new ways. Leaving his college career in order to concentrate on performing now loomed as a new option because of the time lost recuperating from the accident.

In Wilmington, Joe and Estella fixed up the front room at 1013, and finally, at the end of summer, their son was brought home. He was put up on a couch and soon had his east side neighbors swarming over him.

Surrounded by his family and friends, encouraged by his neighborhood jazz cohorts, and, above all, determined to realize all his potential, Brown one day reached across his bed, took his horn out of the case, and painfully put the trumpet mouthpiece to his lips.

With great emotion, Ralph Morris recalled this event. "He started playing again," said Ralph, "and you know, he never stopped. He practiced all the time." The marathon practice sessions soon became the talk of the neighborhood.

Leon Brown recalled: "When he was incapacitated, everybody in the neighborhood could hear Clifford practicing. And he would practice, I know, practically all day long, off and on." Ralph Morris recalled with amusement, "He used to get on my nerves, he practiced so much." Everyone in town who happened to be strolling in the vicinity told stories of Brownie's amazing practice routine.

The task of holding up the trumpet while he was still having difficulty with his shoulder socket proved formidable. The accident had destroyed many ligaments and much connective tissue there, so playing the trumpet practically halted the healing process and increased the pain. Against all of his determination, he was forced to stop.

Because Clifford couldn't practice his horn any longer, the entrapment and sense of hopelessness became overwhelming, so he struggled terribly. Then one day an idea occurred to him. Although he couldn't move his arm into a position to play the trumpet, he could certainly place his fingers on a piano. With renewed energy, he began to practice sitting up and moving a bit so he could position himself at the keyboard. Agonizingly, slowly, day by day he forced his body to respond to the new challenge of playing the piano. And again, the east side neighborhood came to the rescue. This time it was Deanie Jenkins, the Wilmington pianist Brownie had helped during the jam sessions in his high school days, who arrived on the scene. "I used to come down from New York," Jenkins said, "and show him stuff that I had learned from Walter Bishop and guys like that in New York, because he was in a body cast for close to a year. I was showing him different changes and extensions. The flatted fifth was a big thing to me at the time, but then Bishop introduced me to playing thirteenths and things like that. Just different variations on chord changes, like in 'I'll Remember April.' "[7] Brownie would play this tune with great success for the rest of his career.

Finally Brownie could gather enough strength to move about on crutches. Although the pain increased significantly when he began hobbling about, he somehow mustered up the courage. His family applauded his determination, and soon the news of his new mobility spread over the neighborhood; one day he was invited to play the piano in a club. Ever so gently he was carted about by his friends in their autos and soon found he could sit at a piano stool and play an entire gig.

As 1951 approached, Brownie had regained arm strength. Perhaps he had exercised his arm and shoulders enough by walking around on crutches. In any case, as soon as he could, he took out his trumpet and found he could manage to hold it long enough without collapsing from pain. So once again he began his horn exercises. Now when Deanie Jenkins came around, Clifford positioned himself on the couch in the front room, and Jenkins would go to the piano in the adjacent room and play.

Through arduous practice and careful exercise for years, Brownie had toughened the tissue on his lips so that he could produce the sound necessary for him to play at an advanced professional level. Now, because of the long layoff due to the accident, he had to begin the process anew. The task of redeveloping the calluses and tissue on his mouth was arduous, but after weeks of practice his embouchure started to come around.

His brother Leon recalled, "That's when he told me that he was tryin' to get a knot on his lip. And I said, 'What do you need a knot for?' He said, 'You can make the notes better with a knot.' So he worked on that and he ended up with one." Clifford was amused at Leon's lack of understanding of the complexities of embouchure. As he was practicing his "knot" exercises one day, Leon said, "Man, you're gonna mess your mouth all up." Clifford could only laugh quietly.

As his facility on the trumpet returned, the marathon practice sessions resumed. "Everybody could hear him practicing," said Leon, "and he would practice . . . all day long."

When he wasn't putting horn to mouth, Brownie was reflecting, planning and dreaming of his future. As he slowly regained mastery of his instrument, all other vocational thoughts melted away: The trumpet would be the only thing that mattered. Leon recalled, "He decided that he might as well go ahead and get with the trumpet all the way."

During this time his friends continued to drive him to small gigs, where he made a few dollars playing the piano. Ralph Morris remembered: "We had a short tour[once]. Clifford played the piano. I played the trumpet. The front line was alto, trumpet, valve trombone, tenor, and three rhythm. We went to northern Delaware, Maryland, and maybe Virginia. It seems that Boysie Lowery was on the tour," and Brownie managed to do some arranging. Ralph Morris recalled, "I remember one in particular he did, ' 'Round Midnight,' this time."

Brown was still in enormous pain, and, although his quiet, un-complaining demeanor betrayed none of this to those around him, they could sense the drain upon him. Just when things might become overwhelming, his friends, once again, came through. During the Christmas holidays in 1950, Harry Andrews was conducting the Howard High choir on its regular tour. Remembering his prize trumpeter and mindful of the great struggle that was going on at 1013 Poplar Street, Andrews had an idea. He promptly escorted his singers down to the Brown house, and, as Clifford gazed outside, the singers appeared and began singing Christmas carols for him. The sight and sound of his teacher and the Howard students could not have come at a better time. This moved the young trumpeter greatly and, ac-cording to his family, helped him redouble his efforts to recuperate.

In 1951 Brownie began to renew a ritual from the old days. "One of the first places that he went when he could go out of the house was the YMCA," Leon recalled. "It was about three blocks from our house." Inspired by his friends, who were ecstatic that he could once again join in the jam sessions in Room 214 at the Y, Brownie inten-sified his efforts. Summoning new willpower and drawing upon his extraordinary musical instincts, he regained his chops, and his fa-miliar sound filled Room 214 once again.

As the patient continued to get stronger in the spring of 1951, he felt the pull of Philadelphia and its clubs and the vibrant jazz scene. Brown had always known that the best way to develop as a player was to perform with the greats. Even though the popularity of Par-ker, Roach, J. J. Johnson, the Heath brothers, and others was not at the level of that of the great swing stars—Ellington, Goodman, Hamp-ton, et al.—in 1951, Brownie knew that his musical future lay with the beboppers, most of whom worked in Philly frequently.

Although the exact date is uncertain, sometime in May[8] Brownie received a call from Chester, Pennsylvania, saxophonist Tom Dar-nall. "I went up to see Charlie Parker at the Club Harlem in Phila-delphia. The band was playing without him—just a trio. He was in the next room. Just sitting in this huge room by himself. He was a little salty with the owner, who said, 'Charlie, people are waiting for you.' Bird said, 'I'm going to go out.' And the owner said, 'I wish you'd put a tie on.' Charlie Parker looked at him and told him, 'I'll take your tie.' In the meantime, I told him that I was playing and had a job that night. This was a matinee. He said, 'Well, go get your instrument. I fired my trumpet player.' I happened to mention Clifford, and he said, 'Go call him!' Which I did. I called him *from* that club and told him. [Brownie] couldn't believe it. He went up. I feel good about that. That maybe I contributed a little something to somebody being aware of him."⁹

A bandstand shared by Charlie Parker and Clifford Brown front-lining a rhythm section is almost too much for a jazz fan's imagination. Thus far no tapes or sound checks have turned up commemorating these occasions.

Brownie himself, in a 1954 interview with the critic Nat Hentoff, recalled this gig with Parker. "Benny Harris was the cause of that one too," said Brownie. (Harris, it will be recalled, was the one whose absence allowed Brownie to sit in with Dizzy Gillespie's band the year before.) "He [Harris] left Bird shortly before the engagement began, so I worked in his place for a week. Bird helped my morale a great deal. One night he took me in a corner and said, 'I don't believe it. I hear what you're saying, but I don't believe it.' "¹⁰

Two things have to be remembered here. First, Clifford Brown was so notoriously modest that it seems inconceivable that he would have exaggerated Bird's reaction. Second, Bird's comment is particularly significant because he rarely praised his fellow musicians so superlatively. More evidence of Brownie's success on this Parker date came from drummer Roy Haynes, who also played that night. "I remember that he [Brownie] played a phrase and the people went crazy," recalled Haynes,¹¹ who was playing a lot with Parker in those days. Haynes wasn't surprised, because he had heard Brownie before and recalled mentioning him in a 1951 *Down Beat* interview with Hentoff on the subject of a new talent.

Whatever Brownie did in his appearances with Bird may never be known, but it so impressed Parker that he continued his high praise of the twenty-one-year-old trumpeter. When drummer Art Blakey was assembling a band for a Philadelphia gig soon after the incident just described, Parker confronted Blakey and said straight out, "Don't take a trumpet player with you. You won't need one after you hear Clifford Brown."[12]

It is clear from these comments that Parker felt that Brownie could indeed play with the best. There is ample evidence that Bird counseled and advised Brownie during this difficult time of his life and helped him get going again when he was looking for work. Thus both Parker and Gillespie, the cofounders of bebop, played pivotal roles in Brownie's decision to abandon his academic career and focus on his horn.

As the word spread around Philadelphia that Brownie had rehabilitated himself and was playing very forcefully, leaders began to seek him out. There can be no doubt that the praise from Parker was one of the main reasons for this. Hometown hero Jimmy Heath arrived back in town during this period, after spending time with Dizzy Gillespie's band. According to one account, he immediately began looking for musicians for a booking at Pep's Musical Bar—one of the two leading jazz clubs in town. Heath was pretty well established by then, and a new band under his aegis was news. As a result, a piece appeared in *Down Beat* that mentioned "Cliff Brown" as the band's new trumpeter, the first mention of Brownie's name in a national music magazine. Along with Heath, Brownie played with pianist Dolo Coker, bassist Bob Berton, and drummer Philly Joe Jones. The date of the *Down Beat* piece is November 2, 1951. Although he doesn't deny this account, Heath does not specifically recall the gig at Pep's. "It could have happened," he says, "but I just don't recall it."[13]

According to Heath, he had first met Clifford Brown long before when he brought a band billed as the "Dizzy Gillespie All-Stars" to Wilmington. Heath admitted that he was "capitalizing on Dizzy's name" with this band and worked a club he referred to as the "Two Spot." "I had a trumpet player by the name of Bill Massey. . . . He was very good. He was the guy who introduced me to Coltrane." Heath remembered that "a very shy young man came up and asked me if he could sit in." In the ensuing encounter between Heath's star trumpeter, Bill Massey, and Brownie, "Clifford Brown just wiped him out. And he was seventeen."

Later, just before the *Down Beat* notice, Heath recalled hiring Brownie to play a gig at Spider Kelly's on Mole Street near Market Street, together with Sugie Rhodes on bass, Dolo Coker on piano, and Philly Joe Jones on drums. Heath said that "a very drunk woman came up to the bandstand where the guys were playing some hot bop tunes and said to Brownie, 'I don't know what you're playin' but you're playin' the hell out of it.' " Heath chuckled as he remembered that Clifford Brown was left speechless.

Although occasional gigs in Philadelphia aided Clifford Brown's morale and confidence following his rehabilitation, there wasn't a great deal of steady work to be had, and Brownie was certainly a victim of the economic struggle that constantly plagued all the musicians. "There's always the financial angle," he once said, "the financial angle is a tough one. There are always a lot of guys who sound very promising but what happens to them depends a great deal on economics."[14]

Because of the formidable talent that steadfastly astonished bandleaders everywhere, Clifford Brown would never be out of work very long. A few weeks after the gig at Pep's Musical Bar, he found employment, and his fattest paychecks soon began rolling in, albeit from an unlikely source—a rhythm 'n' blues pop star named Chris Powell.

Five
Rhythm
'n' Blues

There has been a tendency among writers when they analyze the work of important jazz figures to focus exclusively on their jazz music and avoid references to any other music, commercial or otherwise, that these musicians played. The truth is that many of the greats spent big chunks of time playing nonjazz jobs because they paid well, the work was easier to obtain, or because they enjoyed creating in other areas. John Coltrane, Lou Donaldson, and Milt Jackson are among many major jazz figures who spent considerable time in their careers playing music other than jazz.

During the 1950s, the black theatre and night club circuit was dominated by rhythm 'n' blues. There was an enormous national audience for this music, and as the popularity of big dance bands waned, the music also began to interest greater numbers of white audiences. By 1953, black rhythm 'n' blues performers were absorbed into the great onslaught of rock 'n' roll.

One day in late November 1951, one such group, dubbed The Five Blue Flames, and later billed as "Chris Powell and the Blue Flames," visited Wilmington for a couple of dances. The music consisted of "mostly rhythm 'n' blues, jazz, mambo and calypso,"[1] according to Vance Wilson, the tenor saxist with the band at the time. The musicians were good (many who passed through the decade-

53

long existence of the Blue Flames were beboppers), and often the music swung. The primary emphasis was on accessibility. The idea was to get some popular recordings going and start making the big money. However, despite these commercial parameters, there was substantial room for the musicians to stretch out and improvise. Indeed, if one thinks of club date gigs during the present day, it is always a pleasant surprise to hear a pianist play interesting changes or a saxophone player play a creative chorus smack dab in the middle of a carefully programmed dance set. Such has been the case with American dance music from the beginning. So it was with the Blue Flames.

One night Clifford Brown dropped into either one of the Wilmington dances or another of the Blue Flames' appearances in nearby Philadelphia. "Someone asked Clifford to play, and he came up, and we were amazed," said Vance Wilson. "The people knew he could play but we didn't. And so that's when he joined us."

In a 1966 interview, Chris Powell was more precise: "A very hip bartender named Nip asked me to let this medium-sized, homely young fella sit in with the group," he recalled. He believed that it was a Sunday night gig in Wilmington. "He [Brownie] was sitting at the bar drinking soda water," said Powell. "I invited him up, and, after hearing two choruses of 'Memories of You,' I stopped Clifford and called him over to the drums where I was playing and asked him if he could work for me like right now!"[2]

This meant the twenty-two-year-old had to pack his gear and immediately become a road musician. The Blue Flames, like so many other pop dance groups, were constantly on the move, working in dozens of cities for stretches of endless one-nighters. According to Powell, his offer "was all right with Clifford" but had to be discussed with Joe and Estella. Their son had just spent almost a year in rehabilitation, decided to drop out of college, and now was departing for the life of an itinerant rhythm 'n' blues player. Naturally, Joe and Estella had some hesitation, but they eventually said "it would be all right."

Powell recalled: "In the group at the time was Eddie Lambert, a guitarist from Philly; Jymie Merritt on bass; Duke Wells, a piano player from Syracuse; and myself playing drums. The emphasis was primarily on rhythm and blues, and of course we played the pop tunes. We were 'selling' the music." Powell's last phrase really says it all there—was no mistaking the main goal of his music.

"We all sang," said Powell, and the performances also "included a little dancing." Powell recalled that although Brownie had broken his leg in the accident, "after watching us on stage for a couple of weeks, he probably was the best dancer in the group." Vance Wilson, on the other hand, suggested that Brownie did very little dancing. In view of the circumstances, this seems more likely. Powell was known to have a penchant for the superlative—a natural inclination for all those folk who idolized Brownie.

Before and soon after Brown joined the Blue Flames, they "had done most of [their] playing in the Philadelphia area." Powell said that "after listening to him [Brownie] play night after night, the kind of music we were playing had to change. It did." This quote suggests that Brownie's work changed the repertoire, but what Powell undoubtedly meant is that Brownie influenced the quality of the playing in the group, so its performance standards rose. The pop repertoire certainly remained.

"About this time, the agency decided we were ready for the big time, so we were booked into Café Society in New York," said Powell.

The sound of the Blue Flames and the appeal that it had for large audiences was noted by pianist Billy Taylor as he recalled this period: "There were groups that I would call 'pre-bop' groups because they were playing danceable music but they were not playing rhythmically what beboppers were playing. But harmonically and melodically they were playing some of the same kind of lines."[3] At their inception, the Blue Flames were "more or less a regional group. They were very popular. They did a lot of things in the New York, Southern New Jersey, Philadelphia, and Delaware areas. They played a lot of dances, they played a lot of clubs and so they worked a lot. They worked all the time. And so it was a nice group and entertaining. . . . There were hundreds of groups like that around the country in those days. They played accessible music."

According to Taylor, Chris Powell was an ideal leader for the group. "Chris was kind of a hip musician, the kind of guy that was a leader type. I mean he would get out there, and he could get the gigs, you know, and he was a good front man. He always knew what to say on the microphone, and to the guy who was hiring him."

Brownie was unknown to Taylor and much of the New York scene at this time. "I had never heard of Clifford," said Taylor, "but he was a good musician. [Chris] was proud of the fact that he had this dynamite young guy with him. 'Hey man [Powell said to Taylor on one occasion] check out my discovery.' "

Taylor first played with Brownie at a jam session. "It was a place like Café [Society]," recalled Taylor. The likelihood is that this occasion coincided with the Blue Flames' initial booking into Café Society–at a nearby club.

Taylor clearly articulated what Clifford Brown was doing at this time. "Playing with him was so easy because . . . the clarity of his harmonic ideas just gave you something else to work with. You'd be accompanying him but his ideas were so clear you'd say, 'Oh yeah. Right. Okay,' and play something else, you know. . . . He was at that time building something new. Most of the young guys were really trying their best to play like Dizzy Gillespie. They were playing what amounted to clichés that Diz and Bird had played. . . . So for a guy at that age to be doing what he was doing, man, that was really an eye-opener."

The opening night at Café Society was a turning point for Brownie. "On the bill with us," said Chris Powell, "were Sarah Vaughan, Cy Coleman, Moms Mabley, and a folk singer. I was introducing Clifford as 'the world's greatest.' On opening night, Sarah listened to Clifford. When I came off the stand, she called me into the dressing room and said she had to have Clifford for a record date. I said I didn't mind, and Brownie got good exposure through that date." This date with Vaughan actually took place some time later.

With a group of musicians whose true love was jazz, Powell often had to struggle to keep the Blue Flames music palatable for the dancers who were his bread and butter. After Brownie came on, Powell also hired Jimmy Heath and later Philly Joe Jones for a time, and things started to get a little jazz-heavy. "It didn't help us work-wise," said Powell, "because these fellas didn't have all the talents necessary to present the kind of music to the kind of audience we faced each night." Brownie was able to acclimate, but the other boppers were soon gone.

Clifford Brown impressed Powell in ways that he had impressed many people before. "As a musician with the ability he had, I always thought he was too humble," said Powell. "It would always seem that someone was trying to take advantage of him because of his humbleness. But he was a family musician who worried a great deal about how his father and mother were making out. He'd send money and call them more often than most musicians. . . . Clifford was courteous and gentlemanly . . . almost too good to be true."

Clifford Brown settled into life on the road with few complaints. He handled the topsy-turvy life of the one-nighters equably. Unlike some, he was not drawn into the bad habits so often associated with musicians on the road. He socialized with his bandmates, had an occasional drink, and casually smoked a cigarette or two. He even dealt with the groupies who are always around musicians. "About women," said Powell, "he was probably more capable than men who looked a great deal more appealing than he did because he had a stick-to-itiveness that comes with honesty."

Up until this time Brownie did not have a steady girlfriend for many reasons, not the least of them the enormously busy schedule he had kept since his early teens. Although he encountered local girls back home during his school days and at the various gigs he played there, in Philadelphia, and elsewhere, he hadn't focused on anyone in particular.

Perhaps because of the lonely existence on the road and because he had met an interesting girl who hailed from back home, things changed during this time. Ida Mae Thomas, originally from New Castle, Delaware, was a Howard High graduate, a church organist, and a schooled musician. She came from a family with substantial means and very soon could be seen driving Clifford around in her Cadillac. Considerably older than Brownie (she said in an interview that she graduated from Howard with Eugene Brown's class, which could make her as much as seven years older than her beau) she was not unattractive and had what many remember as a curvaceous figure.

As soon as they were together, Clifford naturally brought her to 1013 Poplar, while on a break from the road and introduced her to his family. During an interview with Alan Hood in 1996, Ida Mae brought out pictures of Eugene, Clifford, Margaret (Brownie's sister-in-law) and some of the neighbors on Poplar Street, including Ruth Burton. It was evident that she had adjusted comfortably into the comings and goings of the Brown household.

Because of the Blue Flames' regional schedule, the musicians had the option of traveling with the band bus or, if it was more convenient, to proceed by car and catch up with the group at the next gig on their own. It is apparent that Brownie took advantage of this option a lot because several people remembered him being driven quite often from gig to gig by Ida Mae. This allowed him to spend as much time as possible at home between gigs, which pleased his parents. "Estella Brown knew I drove Clifford everywhere," recalled Ida Mae.[4]

The couple spent a great deal of time together. "I knew her just like a sister," recalled Vance Wilson, "because she was always with him." Wilson specified, "That was his first love."

After a successful New Year's Eve date at the Club Harlem, 1952 promised to be a big year for the Blue Flames. The bookings were coming more heavily, and Powell could hardly keep up with the demands for his music. Decked out in "white suits, blue bellhop pants and green cowboy string ties," the group went everywhere—"Louisville, Las Vegas, Miami, Reno, Arkansas, New Orleans," etc. They had theatre dates at some ninety venues all over the place, including the venerable Earle Theatre in Philadelphia, the Royale Theatre in Baltimore, and the Apollo in New York. Initially, they played local college dates, but soon schools far away were requesting a Blue Flames dance party. Vance Wilson recalled that "we played the Earle Theatre—five shows a day and a fire engine came to escort us to the club." Another club, The Click, had a revolving bandstand, "and we had to jump quick to get on."

The musicians loved the colleges. At Dickinson College, "the students gave parties afterward and they had more booze than the bars." At Bucknell, "we spent the night there and they asked us if we were hungry. . . . The cook opened the kitchen and we took all the legs off all the turkeys. Clifford said, 'What are they gonna say about all the legs tomorrow?' The guy [cook] said, 'Don't worry about it.' " Typical stories of young musicians on the road having fun.

By the early spring, the Blue Flames had indeed succeeded in "selling" their music well enough to start recording. Powell's ebullient personality and his ambition to establish a national following was beginning to pay off. During a particularly successful stint in Chicago in March, negotiations were quickly made to record some sides. It certainly was an exciting time for the band, and Clifford Brown was at the center of attention.

Suddenly tragic news arrived from Wilmington—Brownie's sister Marie had died at age thirty-four. Marie Vendetta Brown had been among the most precocious of the Brown siblings, and her death came as a great shock. Clifford rushed back home for the funeral. Ralph Morris recalled the sad time: "I went to the funeral, and Clifford was more emotional than anybody."[5] The Brown family had always been extremely close, but, although they drew support from each other, the specter of Marie's death dealt a heavy blow to the youngest child—Brownie was devastated.

Unfortunately there was little time to share his grief with his family. Calls came from Chicago, and he was told that a record date had been set. The Flames had signed a deal with Okeh Records, and the session was to be held on March 21.

Powell quickly put together some charts to prepare for the session. As is always the case, the studio time had to be crammed into the heavy performance schedule. In view of this it is perhaps curious that Powell wrote a novelty number, "Ida Red," for the group of four tunes recorded. "They wrote 'Ida Red' about me," recalled Ida

Mae. "I think it had something to do with my clothes." This quote makes sense because Ida Mae was often flamboyantly attired in form-fitting dresses that emphasized her figure. By her own admission, Ida Mae enjoyed the attention paid her because of her sexy appearance.

The session contained four tunes—two ballads, "Blue Boy" and "Darn That Dream"—and two up-tempo pieces featuring solos by Brownie. The first, "I Come from Jamaica," is a simple calypso tune with the group singing, "I come from Jamaica, Jamaica she's my home." After an eight-bar rhythm intro, this single lyric continues for a full chorus. Next comes an acceptable guitar solo alternating with a piano solo followed by Brownie's solo—a bright upper register affair lasting a full chorus. Jungle sounds and noises follow to a fade. The 2:36 time follows the norm established by the record companies for 78s—a quick hummable tune with danceable rhythm. Such recordings often achieved high numbers on the charts.

"Ida Red" has a calypso intro with equally simple and contrived lyrics. Brownie's solo is the only one on the cut. The forgettable lyrics assured oblivion for this tune: "I'm tellin' you late, but I'm tellin' you straight, you can't catch no fish if you ain't got no bait."

Brown's solo has a bluesy feel, but the sequences of triplet figures belie the bebop ideas that were certainly buzzing in his head.

The personnel listed for the date are: Clifford Brown, trumpet; Vance Wilson, alto and tenor sax; Duke Wells, piano; Eddie Lambert, guitar; James Johnson, bass; Osie Johnson, drums; Chris Powell, vocal, percussion. Although this session had little success, it did boost the group's prestige in its already popular regional markets. It was a start, and one day there would be some sessions that did produce hits of a sort. According to Wilson, none other than Mitch Miller was the producer for some of these later sessions. Miller would later have enormous success with innocuous novelty tunes of the 1950s. A Flames anthem titled "Man with the Horn" was a "pretty big seller," said Wilson, as was "Sandman Mambo." By this time, however, Clifford Brown had long since left the group.

After the March 21 recordings the Flames marched themselves once again into the parade of one-nighters. Traveling through the South for a black band could, of course, have many pitfalls, and the

Flames had the usual troubles with hotels, restaurants, and hostile police officers. The latter, on occasion, could also be a problem in the North. One time in Providence, Rhode Island, they were booked into a "big club" called The Celebrity. They had been there several times before, and a local girl had become friendly with Brownie and Vance Wilson. One evening the musicians got into a car and picked the girl up "on the hill." "The cops saw the white girl and pulled us over," recalled Wilson. "The cop said, 'We got to take you guys in,' and we told him we were playing the club. They took us to the police station. They interrogated us separately to see if our stories matched. They kept us there all night, then they let her go, and they finally let us go." Although Wilson was frustrated by this harassment, Brown "was just sittin' there with his legs crossed [because] there was nothin' to it. They were just tryin' to scare us."

Another time, when the band route took them from a club in Atlantic City to places like the Showboat or Pep's in Philadelphia, "there'd be lines of people around the corner" because the band was really successful. At one such club, Wilson recalled, "I told Clifford I had to go to the bathroom. Our uniforms were upstairs. He and I went upstairs. The lights were out so when I put on a light the door slams in back of us, and the cops had us circled. They said, 'Where's your clothes?' and we pointed to the clothes. The cops sent Clifford downstairs to bring the whole band up. The cops asked everybody where their clothes were. Then they searched the clothes and got to Chris's. They said, 'Whose clothes are these?' They produced cocaine and asked if it was Chris's. He said, 'I've never seen that before in my life.' So they let everybody go and said the Captain and the Lieutenant were gonna sit downstairs until the last show. And they took him [Powell] with them . . . he was out the next day."

Wilson has a considerable amount of memorabilia from his days with the Flames, and strewn about his house are various arrangements he attributed to Jimmy Heath and others to Brownie. One tune called "Commercialized Utensils" he specifically attributed to Brownie. Thus it is apparent that he spent at least some time on the road writing—a preoccupation that continued to grow. Wilson's collection of Clifford's arrangements has yet to be available publicly.

Despite the popularity of the band and the new musical horizons that were opening up for Brownie, he was still suffering from his auto accident injuries. Wilson recalled a time when the band members were riding in a limousine that "sat about nine people. He and I were sitting in the middle seat," and the doors opened the opposite way. The door came open on Brownie's side "so he went to yank the door closed with his bad arm." The arm went out of its socket, and Wilson "grabbed him 'cause the wind grabbed the door and we were moving pretty fast. I grabbed him and kept him from goin' out." The pain was excruciating, and this kind of thing happened repeatedly. The agony that Brownie went through putting his arm back in its socket and adjusting the limb with a sling was shocking to his fellow musicians.

On another occasion in Lancaster, Pennsylvania, Brownie was untypically late for the job. The Flames were wondering what happened to him. He telephoned to tell them that he was driving Ida Mae's Cadillac, hit a patch of ice, and spun around. It appears that he had difficulty driving because he was still weak from his accident. He maneuvered the Cadillac and finally arrived at the job, but, once again, the pain must have been severe. "He always kept a cane around," said Wilson. "Sometimes his arm would jump out of the socket. . . . It would come out at the least little thing."

Clifford Brown and Vance Wilson were quite close and got the kind of education that only comes from being on the road. One time, recalled Wilson, "We were in Wildwood [New Jersey]. Clifford had never eaten raw clams and neither had I. So we dared each other. We went over to this counter where they were serving them, but we didn't know how to eat them."[6] They proceeded to put sauce on the clams and started to chew them, failing to notice other eaters who were "slurping" them. Their exaggerated chewing made everyone laugh.

The Flames often crossed paths with beboppers as they moved about. Vance Wilson recalled that a young Freddie Hubbard was eager to hear Clifford Brown when the Flames were in Philadelphia. And, another time when "we were in Atlantic City at the Paradise, Bird came in there soakin' wet one night. He had been on the beach.

He had on a pinstripe suit, and he came up to me and asked if he could sit in. I said the leader's over there [pointing to Powell]. Once the OK was given, Bird played with us all night." The R&B sound and bebop were thus not such strange bedfellows, for musicians continually crossed over.

Wilson recalled that saxophonist Stan Getz "would hang around us a lot. Him and Chris were close." As has been widely reported, this was a period of serious drug use for Getz. Powell also was a user, and this eventually caused the Flames to disband. During this time, Getz's wife, Beverly, was arrested for heroin use, and he was scuffling for money. Much has been said (by people like Art Farmer) about how Brownie quietly organized a benefit concert and raised about five hundred dollars for Getz. The incident seemed to receive special attention because a black musician was coming to the aid of one of his white peers. Scenes like this were rare, and Clifford Brown gained much respect for his initiative. Wilson was one of his greatest admirers. "You could always count on what he said because he was an honest guy. . . . He had no bad habits . . . I never heard him curse. He was the perfect human being," Wilson remembered.

Despite the rigorous road schedule, Clifford Brown didn't spend very much time resting between gigs. If anything, his practice habits intensified, and even when he went back to Wilmington, he practiced constantly. When he was home there would still be sessions at his Poplar Street home with his old friends Deanie Jenkins, Bop Wilson, and others. During that time Ida Mae was present on some of the occasions. Because of her exposure to Brownie's music, she recalled having playfully added some interesting chords to the standard changes of her liturgical music. Ever the teacher, Brownie tutored her often. "One time," she recalled, "he showed me how to play the upright bass."

Whenever possible, Brownie eschewed the band bus for Ida Mae's Cadillac. One of the things she enjoyed the most about the gigs was meeting new people. In an interview she had fun rattling off the names of the people she'd met when she was driving around with Brownie: "Dizzy Gillespie, Sarah Vaughan, Harry Belafonte, James Moody, Jimmy Heath." Her church organ work was her primary performance outlet. "I think I'm pretty good . . . I play by ear and read music so I'm kind of gifted." She said that "people from the white church would ask about my playing . . . I would improvise . . . but I didn't tell them my secrets."

As 1952 ended and the new year began, the Blue Flames would run into increasing numbers of beboppers in their travels. The clubs in Philadelphia, Wildwood, New Jersey, and Atlantic City were teeming with them. Outside of the bassist James Johnson, who had once recorded with Fats Navarro, no one in the Flames had anywhere near Brownie's feel for bebop, so each time the Flames encountered boppers, Brownie was eager to stretch out and jam. In addition to the Atlantic City story about a soaking wet Charlie Parker, Chris Powell recalled meeting John Coltrane in a Wildwood club. More and more figures like Benny Golson, the Heath brothers, Sonny Stitt, Gene Ammons, and Red Garland showed up at the Flames' dances or were playing in clubs close by. As a result, Brownie had more encounters with these major musicians, and so his bebop education evolved steadily.

Powell remembered one other meeting that was important for Clifford Brown. "One day in Washington, D.C., Raphael Mendez [an internationally known classical trumpeter] visited our rooms and wanted to meet Brownie. They shook hands as Mendez said he heard a lot of nice things about him. Mendez had one of his books with him. Clifford asked to see it, and before an hour had passed, Raphael Mendez and Clifford Brown were playing duets from Mendez's latest book. He gave Clifford the book and his instrument because he appreciated his musicianship." That this incident ever occurred is the subject of much doubt.

Two things should be noted here. That Mendez may have heard of Clifford Brown by late 1952 or early 1953 suggests that by this time word of Brownie's artistry had spread far beyond the world of the northeast jazz clubs. The twenty-two-year-old sensation had really begun to make waves, and because of this his days as a rhythm 'n' blues sideman would be numbered.

(Previous page) Clifford Brown. (LARUE BROWN-WATSON COLLECTION)

(Top left) Perhaps the most enjoyable moments for Brown's father, Joe, were those spent around musical instruments. He loved the piano, but his talent was limited. (LARUE BROWN-WATSON COLLECTION)

(Top right) Brown's mother, Estella, was a bright, industrious woman who made an early contribution to the history of Howard High School as a lyric writer. (LARUE BROWN-WATSON COLLECTION)

(Bottom left) Clifford Brown was a junior playing in the band at Howard High when this photograph was taken in front of the school. His teacher, Harry Andrews, was proud of Clifford's rendition of "Carnival of Venice." (LARUE BROWN-WATSON COLLECTION)

(Bottom right) Always a close family, the Browns have enjoyed many celebrations through the years. Brown's siblings, from left: Harold Brown, Rella Bray, Leon Brown, Geneva Griffin, and Elsworth Brown. (LARUE BROWN-WATSON COLLECTION)

(Top) The pupil and the teacher: Clifford Brown (right) and Fats Navarro in the Camero Room of the Mercantile Hall, Philadelphia, 1949. When asked about trumpeters who influenced his style, Brown listed only one name: Fats Navarro. (NORMAN SAKS COLLECTION)

(Bottom) As a college freshman at Delaware State, Brown had become well known enough to lead groups in nearby Philadelphia. He appeared there with Miles Davis, Charlie Parker, and other bebop legends. In the Camero Room of the Mercantile Hall, Philadelphia, 1949, Brown performs with alto saxophonist John Joyner, drummer William "Kali" Armstrong, and tenor saxophonist James "Sax" Young. Also performing that evening, but not shown here, were pianist Hasaan Ali and bassist Steve Davis. (NORMAN SAKS COLLECTION)

(Top) After working as a blues sideman, Brown got his first chance to record with important jazz players in June 1953. Lou Donaldson (left) was the leader of the quintet on this June 9 date for Blue Note Records. Elmo Hope joins Brown and Donaldson. (FRANCIS WOLFF PHOTOGRAPH, COPYRIGHT MOSAIC IMAGES)

(Bottom) Jimmy Heath marveled at Brown's improvisational designs during the June 22, 1953, sextet session with J. J. Johnson. The producers were awestruck and stopped the session to sign Brown to a Blue Note contract. Shown: Brown with J. J. Johnson (left) and Jimmy Heath. (FRANCIS WOLFF PHOTOGRAPH, COPYRIGHT MOSAIC IMAGES)

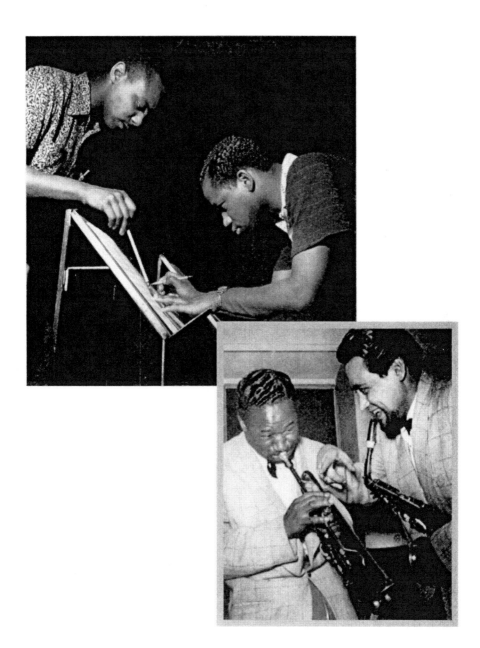

(Top) Brown shows little sign of the crippling accident that had forced him to remain in a body cast for most of 1950. His arms continued to become dislocated throughout his life due to weaknesses incurred from the accident. Shown: Brown and J. J. Johnson, June 1953. (FRANCIS WOLFF PHOTO-GRAPH, COPYRIGHT MOSAIC RECORDS)

(Bottom) Clifford Brown and Anthony Ortega blowing horns together on Lionel Hampton's tour of Europe in 1953. As a result of many clandestine recording sessions during the tour, Brown would return to the United States as a jazz celebrity. (LARUE BROWN-WATSON COLLECTION)

(Top) On August 28, 1953, three days before he left to tour Europe with Lionel Hampton, Brown recorded his first session as a leader. He wisely chose Charlie Rouse (left) and Gigi Gryce to play alongside him at the Clifford Brown Sextet date. (FRANCIS WOLFF PHOTO-GRAPH, COPYRIGHT MOSAIC IMAGES)

(Bottom) The two "boppers" Brown and Gigi Gryce became lifelong buddies in 1953. Gryce's genius as a jazz composer/arranger has never been properly acknowledged. (FRANCIS WOLFF PHOTOGRAPH, COPYRIGHT MOSAIC IMAGES)

(Top) In February 1954 Clifford Brown recorded live at Birdland in a session that became a milestone in jazz history. From left: Brown, Curly Russell, Lou Donaldson, and Art Blakey. Horace Silver is hidden at the piano behind Clifford. (FRANCIS WOLFF PHOTOGRAPH, COPYRIGHT MOSAIC IMAGES)

(Middle) Horace Silver, Curly Russell, Art Blakey, Lou Donaldson, and Brown at Birdland, with the club's emcee, Pee Wee Marquette, in front. Marquette's voice can be heard introducing the band on this legendary recording. (FRANCIS WOLFF PHOTOGRAPH, COPYRIGHT MOSAIC IMAGES)

(Bottom) Brown and Zoot Sims rehearsing for a Pacific Coast recording, 1954. Shortly after his wedding Brown plunged into a whirlwind of recording sessions that would leave him time for little else. This Pacific Coast jam session saw the first recordings of "Joy Spring" and "Daahoud," two of Brown's best compositions. (LARUE BROWN-WATSON COLLECTION)

(Top) Clifford and LaRue Brown with Father Mathews. The photo commemorates the various weddings the young couple had due to scheduling conflicts and recording dates. "I am much married," said LaRue. (LARUE BROWN-WATSON COLLECTION)

(Middle) Clifford and LaRue toasting each other on June 26, 1954, the date of their marriage. "If you marry me you marry my music," said Clifford. LaRue was overjoyed to unite with "the most beautiful person I have ever met." (LARUE BROWN-WATSON COLLECTION)

(Bottom) Brown managed to spend time with his newborn son despite an exhausting recording and touring schedule in early 1956. At this time Brown and Max Roach were recording their "Basic Steel" album, which would become a jazz classic. (LARUE BROWN-WATSON COLLECTION)

Six
The Month
of June

       In 1952, Clifford Brown met a figure with the unlikely name of Tadley Ewing Peake Dameron. Born in Cleveland in 1917, Dameron had studied medicine at Oberlin College before embracing music as a career. During the heyday of the swing bands in the 1930s he wrote arrangements for Harlan Leonard, Jimmie Lunceford, and Coleman Hawkins. Compositions such as "Dameron Stomp," "A La Bridges," and "Half Step Down, Please" date from this period. With the arrival of bebop in the 1940s, Dameron's compositions and arrangements did as much to advance the music as did the virtuosity of the instrumentalists. He wrote arrangements for Dizzy Gillespie's big band, and his major orchestra piece, "Soulphony," was premiered by the band at a Carnegie Hall concert in 1948. That same year, Dameron led a group in New York that featured Fats Navarro. By then he had composed "If You Could See Me Now" for Sarah Vaughan, who was by this time a famous vocalist. In 1949 Dameron was featured with Miles Davis at the Paris Jazz Fair.

    In 1952, Dameron was involved with various groups in the New York–Philadelphia area and had become an important figure for jazz record producers. During the spring of 1952 Brownie was supposed to record with one of the Dameron groups, but the date was canceled, apparently because of Dameron's continuing struggle with heroin.

In the last weeks of May 1953, Clifford Brown became suddenly more active on the bebop scene. He was being besieged by leaders to record and appear with them, but it was Dameron's band that interested him the most. Once recovered from his addiction episode, Dameron began rehearsing his nonet, and a recording date was rescheduled for June 11. Meanwhile, altoist Lou Donaldson, under contract to Blue Note Records, had long sought out Brownie for a record date, slated for June 9 in New York.

At long last, after a near-fatal accident, agonizing months of rehabilitation, and sixteen months of playing R&B dances, Clifford Brown was about to get the opportunity that he had longed for since his high school days—a chance to record with important beboppers.

Chris Powell had known for a long time that his star trumpeter would move on one day. When the time arrived, he wished Brownie the best, but there were no sad good-byes. Brown always stayed in touch with the man who had "discovered" him, as Vance Wilson said. Later, when he became a major jazz player, he still sought advice from Powell.

Brownie arrived in New York and immediately walked into the WOR studios to record his first jazz record. Lou Donaldson was the leading Charlie Parker clone of the hour. Born and raised in the Bronx, Donaldson stood as a truly gifted player who understood the bop literature and would make important contributions to it. He never did receive proper credit. To the present day, he admonishes those who lionized the headline-making, heroin-addicted beboppers and ignored the straight establishmentarian musicians who avoided drugs and scandals. Alas, in the American way of things, it is usually the notorious who receive attention. When this habit filters into serious music criticism, great injustices are committed. At this writing, Lou Donaldson is still playing brilliantly, living quietly in the Bronx, happily married to the same woman, and largely ignored by critics.

To the musicians (who are always the ones who know), Donaldson has always been a true heavyweight. That June day Brownie knew he would be performing with a master. And so it was.

The Blue Note session was organized by Alfred Lion, who had become one of the most prominent bebop record producers; the group included Elmo Hope on piano, Percy Heath on bass, and Philly Joe Jones on drums—a formidable crew. Brownie was asked to contribute a composition and brought "Brownie Speaks," one of many tunes he had been working on during his R&B hiatus. The session features original music—tunes by Hope and Sonny Rollins, "Cookin'" by Donaldson, "Brownie Speaks," and the standard "You Go to My Head." In "Brownie Speaks," Brownie utilizes the "turnback"—a chord pattern at the end of the final phrase of a chorus—that he had developed under Boysie Lowery. Few who listen to the music would ever guess that it was his first jazz date. From the medium-tempo "Bellarosa" to the hot Rollins opus "Carvin' the Rock" (referring to the prison on Riker's Island), Donaldson and Brown are one voice in the front line. The solos are crisp and economical. There are no unnecessary blowing choruses to fill out the time. Of "Rock," one writer said: "Brown attacks it head on, combining tight arpeggios with tricky bebop phraseology to deftly outline the changes." Above all, his inimitable fat sound seduces the listener in "You Go to My Head." As Benny Golson would note years later, Clifford Brown can never be heard on records as an amateur or sideman.

So on a hot summer day in New York (photos show the musicians sweating in their light sport shirts) the jazz recording career of the twenty-two-year-old Wilmingtonian began. Years later Donaldson (who would record again with Brownie) would remember him in the context he (Donaldson) held most important. "Back then, a lot of guys were strung out. But Clifford was strong. There was nothing to get in his way. He was powerful, the guy who could play all night and never split a note." This comment contains the prescience of a master player who knew, more than most, that many of record dates of the time were often hastily organized jam sessions.

When "Brownie Speaks" was released in 1953, Leonard Feather wrote, "Clifford's melodic contours at times are reminiscent of Miles Davis's, yet his tone and attack are blunter, more emphatic, and his harmonic imagination is in a class with that of the late great Navarro.

The continuity of his solo line is astonishing, placing him at the very top rank of contemporary trumpet stylists."[1]

Two days later, Clifford Brown went over to the Prestige studios to record with Tadd Dameron's nine-piece group. He had already done some live break-in dates with Dameron a couple of weeks prior to this. The band had just finished playing an engagement at the Apollo Theater, where the rumors of Brownie's brilliant horn-playing had created quite a stir.

A year before, Dameron told St. Louis disc jockey Henry Frost about a young horn player he was planning to use for an upcoming recording session. "I want to have a fellow named Brownie," said Dameron. "He's in Wilmington, Delaware, and he's another Fats Navarro, but he's a little smoother than Fats was, I think. He has a lot of drive, he's just beautiful."[2]

As the session approached, Dameron kept up the hype. He told critic Ira Gitler, who was to oversee the date, that he was going to reveal a great new trumpeter. Gitler had already heard of Brown from the musicians who had played around Philadelphia.

On June 11, Brownie hopped over to Rudy Van Gelder's studio in Hackensack, New Jersey, with the rest of the band. Like Donaldson, Dameron had collected an excellent group of players: Philly Joe Jones on drums; Percy Heath on bass; a reed section of Benny Golson, Gigi Gryce, Oscar Estelle, and Herb Mullins; Don Cole on trombone; and Idrees Sulieman, Johnny Coles, and Brown on trumpets. Dameron played piano.

The tension might have been a bit thick for Brownie, who certainly was aware of the explosive hype that had surrounded his arrival on the New York scene. Whatever reservations Ira Gitler might have had following Dameron's touting of Brownie disappeared quickly.

"When Brownie stood up and took his first solo on 'Philly JJ,' I nearly fell off my seat in the control room," wrote Gitler. "The power, range, and brilliance together with the warmth and invention was something I hadn't heard since Fats Navarro, but Brownie, although influenced by Fats, was not just a reincarnation of Fats—he was a new trumpet giant. . . . There was a terrific lilt to Brownie's playing. It was an inner drive that carried his ideas cascading with a power much like the overdrive in a big sedan. His sound was hard and brilliant when it had to be but usually encased a large warmth the size of his soul."[3]

Such extravagant praise was rare from critics such as Gitler and Leonard Feather. But these sorts of comments became a routine when people heard Brownie for the first time.

After Clifford Brown wailed away on "Philly JJ," he soloed cleverly on "Choose Now" and then contributed a muted improvisation on "Theme of No Repeat." Dameron's band had played a memorable session.

The date gave Brownie a chance to show his wares and, particularly, to whet Dameron's theoretical palate. The veteran composer/arranger had, for years, advocated the use of turnbacks. He had once said, "When you play a solo, you're going from your first eight bars into your second eight, that's where you really play those turnbacks. ... There's where you can tell whether a man can really blow—when he starts playing that eighth and ninth bar and then when he comes out of the middle into the last eight. Those turnbacks mean so much."[4] Brownie had long since worked on this technique, dating from his time with Boysie Lowery, and Dameron continued to develop this approach with him in the time they were together.

No sooner was this Prestige session over than the band rushed back to Atlantic City and their club work. They had scored well at the Apollo Theater gig, and word spread quickly about their success. Beboppers had long admired Dameron's work, but his new band, with its strong horn section and Dameron's inspired writing, brought new attention to him and the band. Meanwhile, Brownie's success at the Blue Note date with Donaldson was attracting attention in the record industry. Whenever a trumpeter's name came up, the producers kept thinking of that great session, and soon Brownie was summoned for another Blue Note session—this one led by J.J. Johnson.

Johnson had established himself as a virtuoso bebop trombonist. He had teamed up with Fats Navarro and created quite a stir at a time when the bebop revolution was still in its infancy. But in 1952

Johnson had decided to retire from the scene, and he actually worked for a while as a blueprint inspector for Sperry Gyroscope. Ever on the watch for quality beboppers, Alfred Lion had convinced Johnson to return to the scene and signed him to what would be his first date as a leader since October 1949. Later on in 1953, Johnson would team up with trombonist Kai Winding to form the J&K group, which had enormous success on records.

On Monday, June 22, the musicians assembled at the WOR studios in New York. For this date the group was billed as the J. J. Johnson Sextet and featured familiar faces for Brown: Jimmy Heath on tenor and baritone, John Lewis on piano, Percy Heath on bass, and bebop pioneer Kenny Clarke on drums. This rhythm section constituted three-quarters of the Modern Jazz Quartet minus vibist Milt Jackson.

The first cut was "Capri," a Gigi Gryce opus. In the alternate cut, Johnson took the first solo followed by Heath and then Brownie, who triple-tongued his way through a bright upper register solo that soared. On the master he worked out new variations at the lower part of the horn. This time he swung even more. At the finish, heads in the studio were shaking.

Next came a piece by J. J. Johnson himself, dubbed "Turnpike" and based on the changes of "I Got Rhythm." "J. J.'s music was great," recalled John Lewis, "but it was very difficult. I remember thinking that things would have been better if we had had a rehearsal. But there were no rehearsals on these record dates."[5] Lewis, however, was glad to be on the date. He had played in Philadelphia clubs such as the Blue Note with Lester Young and Charlie Parker and was happy to be included with the Heath boys on a label that was recording his type of music.

Jimmy Heath remembered what happened then. "J. J., being a perfectionist, had already 'worked out' the ideas that he wanted to get on the record. And if he would miss a note, we'd make another take. And every take, Clifford was playing a different solo on that cycle of fourths sequence that was in that piece." Heath's comments were pivotal. He was not as impressed by Brownie's technique (as was the case with the everyone else at the session) as he was by the richness and variety of his improvisational designs. Many veterans like Heath had heard players who could deliver rapid fire solos but were limited in their ability to construct inventive lines. So when Brown kept coming up with new bursts of creativity, Heath was greatly impressed. The studio personnel were simply mesmerized by the young phenom. According to Heath, everybody just dropped everything. "At that point," said Jimmy, "the Blue Note people [Alfred Lion] asked him to sign a contract."[6] Evidently, there was no point in waiting. Lion could simply not believe what he was hearing and wanted to sign Clifford before someone else did.

As soon as the session ended, Brownie motored back down to Atlantic City to rejoin Tadd Dameron. That summer the band played at the Paradise on North Illinois Avenue, a club in a black neighborhood of the resort city. It was separated from the affluent white hotels on the other side of Atlantic Avenue.

The personnel in the band had changed somewhat from the Prestige record date group. Jymie Merritt was the bassist, and Cecil Payne joined the reed section on baritone sax, replacing Idrees Sulieman. Johnny Coles described the job: "This gig was about playing the show; it wasn't about playing jazz. The band was made up of all jazz musicians who have since become famous. . . . Oh, man, that was a poppin' little band! It was a complete show. We must have had maybe ten dancing girls and then maybe twelve show girls. We had male dancers in the chorus line. And then we had a star singer. Sometimes the show would be built around a comedian like Redd Foxx or Slappy White. It ran every night, seven days a week. We'd get a chance to do maybe a jazz tune or two before the show started."[7]

In the early 1950s Atlantic City provided a showcase for many black entertainers. Kelly Swaggerty, one of the musicians associated with the Dameron gig, recalled that Sammy Davis Jr. was headlining the show at Skinny D'Amato's 500 Club on South Missouri Avenue during the time that the Dameron band was playing the Paradise.[8]

After playing all night long for the show at the Paradise, the band wound things up with "a breakfast show" in the dawn hours. Swaggerty recalled Sammy Davis coming up from the audience as he was introduced by M. C. Larry Steel, then sitting in on drums with the band. In addition, musicians from name bands such as Basie or El-lington, who were featured at the Steel Pier in Atlantic City, would hop over to the Little Belmont or the Paradise to jam after their show was finished.

The show that the Dameron band played for at the Paradise was essentially a revue. According to Swaggerty, Dameron wrote all the specialty charts for the performers, and, after the usual breaking in period, the band soon picked up the rapid tempo changes and quirky little spacings that are the metier of all such stage shows. Among the performers were singer Anita Eckles; Princess Dequar, a Haitian voo-doo dancer; and, of all people, Betty Carter (known as Betty Bebop), singing "Moonlight in Vermont." There were comics like "Stump & Stumpy," another singer, Janet Sayres, and even some jugglers.

After the show there was always the nightly jam session. Swag-gerty recalled one in early July that saw Brownie playing alongside Art Farmer and Joe Gordon. The session was so wild that after the musicians left the Paradise they moved the party to the Club Harlem to continue jamming. A private recording of this session has surfaced recently.

In late July Lionel Hampton's band was working in neighboring Wildwood, New Jersey. One of the trumpeters in the band was a young musician/arranger named Quincy Jones. Swaggerty men-tioned that Jones came over to Atlantic City to "persuade Brownie to join Hampton." This statement has been corroborated by other sources. Swaggerty then said that Dameron proceeded "one Sunday morning" to "fire Clifford, myself and somebody else right after the breakfast show." In addition, it appears that this same weekend there was a big drug bust, which, according to Swaggerty, may have played a role in unsettling Dameron. And he may have resented Jones's attempt to lure Brownie away. In any event, the fact that musicians were battling for Clifford Brown's services indicates what a hot property he had become.

The Hampton band had been booked into the Surf Club in Wild-wood on July 7, 1953. The Dameron band had ended its stay at the Paradise the previous week. During this time Clifford Brown left the band and signed on with Lionel Hampton. Hampton's band had been booked for its first European tour, which would include virtually every important city in Europe over a three-month period. By now Brownie had become quite close to Gigi Gryce, who had joined Hampton at the time. The two young musicians were excited to be going together on the European junket.

Clifford Brown also was about to make his debut as a leader on a recording session. Alfred Lion had indeed signed Brownie to a Blue Note contract, and the young trumpeter had much work to do. In addition to hiring musicians, there were decisions to be made about compositions, arrangements, and rehearsals. It was a frenetic time, but Brownie's remarkable maturity served him well. Rarely has a musician been so prepared at such a young age to assume the responsibility of a bandleader.

Clifford Brown put together a band that included many of the cohorts he had worked with earlier in the summer; Gigi Gryce headed the list, followed by Percy Heath and John Lewis. Alongside himself and Gryce, he obtained Charlie Rouse, a shy, serious tenor player who had played in the orchestras of Gillespie, Ellington, and Billy Eckstine. He would record for the first time with drummer Art Blakey, with whom he had previously jammed in Philadelphia. In addition, Quincy Jones would compose two tunes and Gigi Gryce one. Probably due to lack of time, Brownie himself would contribute only one composition.

Brownie had a bold idea to record the Ray Noble standard "Cherokee." The song had become a signature tune for Charlie Parker under the title "KoKo," and so all subsequent jazz performances of the tune would be compared to Parker's legendary recording session.

The first tune recorded at Brown's session was Quincy Jones's slow swing, "Wail Bait," with Brownie soloing sweetly, followed by Rouse. The harmony of the three horns is rendered delicately, suggesting careful rehearsal. The tune is short, but everyone gets solo time. The sixteen-bar length of the solos provided a refreshing departure from some of the marathon solo sessions of this period. Gryce's "Hymn of the Orient" follows. Brown solos for three choruses, establishing his leadership; Rouse and Gryce divide one; and then comes Lewis. Clifford leads the trading of fours with Blakey, and once again the harmony of the horns is played evenly. Leonard Feather singles out Brownie's solo on this tune for special praise: "The second and third choruses of this minor-key work illustrate strikingly Brownie's capacity for creating long, flowing phrases and executing them impeccably. This passage, 65 seconds long, was to us a major highlight of the entire LP."[9]

What follows next is remarkable. On Quincy Jones's ballad, "Brownie Eyes," and the standard "Easy Living," Clifford Brown's fat sound soars brilliantly. On "Easy Living," the gorgeous smoky sound of his lower register takes the instrument in a new direction. Interestingly, a year later, when Brownie was interviewed by Feather for his entry in Feather's *Encyclopedia of Jazz*, he selected that solo as his best.

To those fans who recall the recording of "Cherokee" that Brown made later with Max Roach, Harold Land, and their group, the Blue Note performance will not turn too many heads. But on two takes (the alternate has some of Brownie's sloppier runs) of the tune he flies along at a speed and a clarity that certainly surpass any other recorded trumpet interpretation of the tune up to that time. What is notable are the explosive exchanges that he has with Blakey. If he had never recorded the tune again, this performance would stand as a milestone.

Brown's own "Minor Mood" has an unusual melody set in a familiar rhythmic framework. His solo sparkles, with Gryce playing a smooth interlude and Rouse following somberly. Lewis's sparse single-note piano lines are a little puzzling, but against the crowded front line of horns the contrast works adequately.

Clifford Brown's Blue Note debut as a leader was thus a resounding hit. It made Quincy Jones a major Brown booster. During the ensuing Hampton tour, Jones was interviewed about Brown: "About Clifford Brown, I'll put it like this. If any musician of the present day can be compared to Parker, it's Clifford. I can honestly say that his is the most unblossomed talent of this generation. He should not only be judged by his present talent (which is still of superior quality) but by its potentialities. Charlie Parker and Dizzy Gillespie and all the other influences were not judged until they reached maturity. It takes a young musician many years to rid the mind of clichés and to unscramble the millions of young ideas into what it takes to make a mature and original musical influence. By knowing Clifford very well, I'm aware of his sensitivity and superior taste; he will never lower his standards and play without sincere feeling, whatever the mood. He is a young musician in age but already a comparatively mature one in ideas. When he matures in his own standards, I do believe he will be a major jazz influence. He is the kind of person who would excel at anything attempted. (He plays as much piano now as he does trumpet.)"[10]

Art Blakey had also become a fervent admirer of Clifford Brown. A long time before the August record date, he related the following incident. "When I saw Clifford Brown, I said, 'Well, Jesus, I need a trumpet player,' so Charlie Parker said, 'When you get to Philadelphia and play in the Blue Note on Ridge Avenue, your trumpet player will be there.' And we get there and in the dressing room somebody's back there blowing. This guy had a stocking cap on, suspenders and blowing his horn, warming up. He sounds beautiful. So Ike Quebec was with me at the time, he said, 'Man, why don't you tell me you're getting a farmer to play trumpet.' [Laughter] I say, 'Well, I don't know, Bird tells me. . . . ' He said, 'Man, Jesus Christ, man, plus he ain't nothin' but a kid.' And he [Clifford Brown] had a very high voice and was very sweet. So I said, 'Well, come on, we're going to hit.' He [Brown] came out and played the first chorus, and after he played the first chorus Ike turned around and cussed me out. 'Dirty so and so, how come you didn't tell me the kid could play like that?' [Laughter] That's what happened, he upset everybody."[11]

All this praise from his peers didn't unsettle Brown. He remained the same modest person he had been since childhood.

The Hampton Band, his new home, had been playing The Band Box in New York since August 18. After the recording session on Friday the twenty-eighth at the Blue Note, Brownie had barely enough time to prepare for the trip. The Hampton band was about to fly to Europe.

Seven
European
High Jinks

Lionel Hampton's 1953 European tour was his first overseas, but he followed a pattern that he had established well before and continued with for decades to come. The band was a well-organized machine whose music was carefully targeted to please an audience that had grown up on the Jazz at the Philharmonic formula of Norman Granz. Hampton had of course made jazz history with Benny Goodman some fifteen years before. His small group recordings with Goodman alone would have been sufficient to ensure his reputation. But in addition Hampton had a rigorous business sense. Few were as adept at running a band with such financial success as were Lionel Hampton and his wife, Gladys.

During a gig at The Bandbox in New York, Hampton had to use time most effectively to prepare for the European tour. Because he was well aware of the success of bebop and how popular it was among jazz fans in Europe, he hired as many young boppers as he could jam into the available chairs in the band. At the time he was planning a bebop album, so it was a natural move. Then, to show off the band, he decided to outfit his men in costumes. He and Gladys outfitted the musicians with little Tyrolean hats, Bermuda shorts, and purple jackets. Also, in order to prepare for Europe, he decided to parade his merry band of elves out onto Broadway during the stint at the Bandbox in August. Quincy Jones remembered how embarrassed the musicians felt. "I was so hip then it was pitiful," Jones recalled, "and Brownie and I would stop to tie our shoes or something, because outside Birdland in the intermissions there'd be Monk and Dizzy and Bud Powell, all the bebop idols saying, 'What is this shit? You'd do anything for a gimmick.' " The guys explained that it was Hampton's idea, but they still had to take a lot of kidding about their attire.

On Wednesday, September 2, the band and their entire entourage, costumes and all, boarded a plane for Oslo, Norway. They were to play a benefit for the Norwegian Red Cross (although Art Farmer disputed this). The personnel of the band had changed almost up to the minute that the plane departed. Veterans of the Hampton band included guitarist Billy Mackel, trombonist Al Hoyse, alternate drummer and dancer Curley Hamner, and lead trumpeter Walter Williams. Together with road manager George Hart, they had been with Hampton through the various bands that he led in the 1940s and early 1950s. The new personnel included Clifford Brown, Gigi Gryce, and baritone saxophonist Oscar Estelle, who had been hired away from Tadd Dameron's band. Joining Brownie, Quincy Jones, and Williams in the trumpet section was Art Farmer, who by this time had gained a respectable reputation as a bebopper. Alongside veteran Hoyse in the trombone section, Hampton had hired George "Buster" Cooper and Jimmy Cleveland. Next to Gryce and Estelle in the saxophone section was bopper Anthony Ortega, another Hampton veteran, and tenormen Clifford Scott and Clifford Solomon. The rhythm section included Monk Montgomery, who brought along a Fender electric bass (seldom used in those days), and drummer Alan Dawson. Sonny Parker tagged along as a vocalist.

The two last-minute performers whom Hampton rounded up were singer Annie Ross and bebop pianist George Wallington. Annie Ross recalled the circumstances. "I was appearing at the Bandbox, and Hamp came in and saw me there. I was with Max Roach, Tommy Potter, George Wallington, and Ernie Henry . . . Hamp came in and heard me and asked me if I wanted to go to Europe."[1]

She recalled that Clifford Brown "was a very introverted quiet guy
. . . but he would smile and his eyes were warm and nice."

On Sunday, September 6, the band played two concerts at the
Coliseum in Oslo, and immediately following the shows some trouble developed. The beboppers had quietly conspired to further their
careers and their income by making some recordings. I say "conspired" because Lionel and Gladys Hampton, evidently aware that
European producers were eager to record bebop, had established an
ironclad rule before the group left the States: No one in the band
would be allowed to record independently in Europe without Hampton. Anyone caught doing this clandestinely would be fired immediately and would not receive any money for passage back to
America.

The conspirators, led by Quincy Jones, had no intention of obeying the edict. There were scores of record producers mobbing the
musicians and begging to record the new generation of beboppers,
so after a performance on the 13th at the Lighthouse, as soon as the
band arrived in Stockholm, plan A went into action. On September
15 Jones went to the Europa film studios in Stockholm to record
some sides for the Swedish label, Metronome. After recording during
the day, he had to go back to perform with the band at an evening
show. Jones promised Metronome to return at midnight, after the
band's job, and to bring Clifford Brown and Art Farmer with him.
The plan was to feature the young trumpeters Brownie and Farmer
in a group called the Swedish All-Stars. According to Art Farmer,
George Wallington had "naively" mentioned the recording that had
occurred during the day in the hotel lobby, and Hampton "hit the
ceiling."[2] So frustrated was the leader that he took hard measures,
although he didn't fire them. It was, after all, early in the tour. Writer
Raymond Horricks described what happened next: "When the men
went back to their hotel after the concert, they found George Hart,
the band's road manager, posted in a large armchair in the foyer
with orders to stop any musicians leaving the premises that night
with their instruments. Quincy, Clifford and Art complained of
tiredness and went to their rooms. There they sat in complete

frustration until nearly midnight; and still the road manager, as reported by other bandsmen, hadn't moved. A solution was found when one of them thought of the fire escape, which ran by a window at the end of the corridor. Delighted, the three felt their way down in the darkness and were off to the session."[3]

According to Art Farmer, the fire escape window part of the story is a fabrication. "We just went out the back door," he said, "and that's when we went to the studio and spent most of the night."

The Swedish All-Star group included trombonist Ake Persson, alto saxophonist Arne Domnerus, baritone saxophonist Lars Gullin, pianist Bengt Hallberg, bassist Gunnar Johnson, and drummer Jack Noren. For the date, a couple of standards—"Lover, Come Back to Me" by Sigmund Romberg and "Falling in Love with Love" by Rodgers and Hart—were chosen. Quincy wrote two charts: " 'Scuse Those Blues" and "Stockholm Sweetnin.' " "Falling in Love with Love" is a closely harmonized affair, with brass over saxes, where everyone solos. A dreamy solo by Farmer leads the way for solos by Domnerus, Brown, and the others. The harmonic layering smacks of Jones's writing, but no arranging credit is noted. On "Lover, Come Back to Me" Brownie flies through a solo with long smooth lines followed by Hallberg's piano, Domnerus, and Gullin (the latter two blowing pleasant if broken lines). At the end, Farmer solos, trying Brownie's long-lined approach, but is forced to break things up a bit.

"Stockholm Sweetnin' " is Jones's medium swing affair. Solos begin with Farmer, who is truly at home in this tempo. Domnerus's alto follows, his tone rich and Desmond-like (so much for the Parker craze). Hallberg continues with almost exclusively right-hand thin lines. Gullin follows, and again we hear the muted reed sound so well established in the "Birth of the Cool" period of four years previous. Brown's solo works well with the others, but he cannot resist the temptation to double up some phases in order to liven things up.

" 'Scuse Those Blues" is a medium-up tempo affair with a long piano intro by Hallberg and then hard solos by Persson and Domnerus. The heart and soul of the tune are muted choruses by Farmer and Brown and then four bar trades between the two that flow very well. Gullin wraps things up, and the tune ends with a Dixieland parody.

This session has Quincy Jones's stamp all over it, underscoring once again the suggestion that he had been preparing for these recordings long before the Hampton tour commenced. Jones loved Brownie's solo in "Stockholm Sweetnin'" so much that he transcribed it for a big band version of the tune in a later album, *This Is How I Feel About Jazz*. In the liner notes to this album he said, "I consider this one of Brownie's best-constructed solos on records and it serves as a stimulating, inspired composition." Leonard Feather's *New Edition of the Encyclopedia of Jazz* contains a sample of Quincy Jones's arrangement of Brownie's solo, followed by an analysis.[4] Just a few years ago, Quincy Jones once again recalled this occasion when he said: "I love the way Brownie played, and I [Quincy] said, 'To play like you I would have to play all the time.' But he loved the way I wrote, and he said to write like that [he] would have to write all the time. I had always loved the idea of arranging, right since I was a small kid, but that was when I decided to concentrate on it."[5]

Two days after the Stockholm session, the band traveled to neighboring Denmark, where on September 17 they appeared at KB hall. After another day of traveling, they landed in Amsterdam and played the famous Concertgebouw Concert Hall, where, it has been reported, some "chop problems" were encountered in the band's performance. But a bigger problem was developing, involving Annie Ross and George Wallington.

Ross recalled that as the tour moved around Scandinavia, squabbling developed between the beboppers and the older Hampton veterans. She has noted that this was not uncommon in traveling bands—cliques would develop most of the time. To complicate matters, the Scandinavian audiences would have a contingency of troublemakers, who booed when Ross got up to sing. The reason: she and Wallington were white performers in a black band, which created a problem for some European listeners during those days. In Scandinavia the disruptions weren't so terrible, but in Brussels things began to get out of hand.

The day after the Concertgebouw gig the band went to Brussels, and, according to Ross, that's where the real fireworks began. The show was at Palais des Beaux Arts. Ross said: "This is what I was told. When Hamp was going to bring the band over, he was told to bring a very heavy black lady who could sing the blues. I really didn't fit that bill. So the contingent [of racist fans] would go and boo and make noise to disrupt the concert."

In addition, there was trouble with the media. Art Farmer recalled that when Annie Ross came up to sing, "it didn't go too well because all that time there was still a great amount of prejudice in Europe as far as jazz was concerned and the stupid critics and the people who were supposed to know what was goin' on and the audiences in general felt that only black people could play and sing jazz. When she [Ross] came on, she had some trouble with the audience. And George [Wallington] too. We played this one event, and the critics said that Lionel Hampton must be goin' crazy bringing these [white] people over here." Farmer continued, "Annie Ross was not allowed to stay on stage long enough to receive her bouquet after she sang two or three tunes."[6] Farmer alluded to Hugues Panassié, who wrote negative things about Ross and pressured Hampton to fire her. "Look, if you bring her to Paris, they're gonna throw her off the stage," said the critic.

After a day off, the band played at "La Libre Belgique" on Tuesday, September 22. Tension had gotten pretty bad by now. In addition to the audience and media, Ross had also fallen into disfavor with Gladys Hampton because of her behavior. "I was wild" in those days, admitted Ross, who was socializing with the beboppers. This helped widen the breach between the old guard and the new. The day after the second Brussels gig (September 23), Hamp and Gladys decided to fire her. Ross was frustrated. She pleaded that she could not go back to the United States at that point because she wasn't a U.S. citizen and had made special arrangements to be in Europe for the entire length of the Hampton tour. Immigration would not let her return until that time. At that point Gladys Hampton stepped in and said, "Okay, we'll just keep your plane ticket until you *can* go back and then let us know, we'll send you your ticket." George

Wallington, also feeling the social pressure, and having incurred Hamp's wrath over the Swedish record session, made a decision to leave also. "His wife was Annie Ross's manager at the time," said Farmer, "so to show some sort of protest unity, he quit, too, at that time, which was before they got to Paris."

Ross never did receive her plane ticket back home. "My return ticket was supposed to be waiting for me in Paris and it never was," she said. "That was the reason I spent yet another long period of time in Paris." She finally managed to get "into a show in London after a long time," and, when she eventually did get back to New York, it was to start Lambert, Hendricks and Ross, the jazz vocal group that would achieve great success.

Art Farmer had first met Clifford Brown in Atlantic City when the Hampton Band was at the Wildwood, New Jersey, gig, and Brown was still with Dameron. Farmer, Quincy, Jimmy Cleveland, and other Hampton sidemen had driven over to Atlantic City to hear Tadd Dameron's band. Although the Club Harlem was officially closed, a jam session got under way there. "There were a lot of trumpet players there," recalled Farmer, "Blue Mitchell, myself, Brownie and Joe Gordon. We played for the rest of the night." Clifford truly impressed Farmer that night. "Brownie was really pushing," Farmer told *Down Beat* in one of his many recollections of the evening.

When Brownie began playing alongside Farmer on the European tour, Hampton gleefully prodded the young boppers by pitting them against each other on stage. "Hamp goes for battles," said Farmer, "so this was his chance for a never-ending trumpet battle between Brownie and me. He would send Brownie out front after me and then we would play choruses, halves, eights and fours. The pressure was something painful, but more often it was a pleasure for the give and take of the thing. I must admit that I was more than a bit jealous of his ability to play so well. However, he was such a sweet and warm human being, I was forced to like him, even though he made things very difficult for me as a trumpet player. Although I felt that Brownie was the better player, I couldn't just be content to let him make a fool of me. So I think there were some very interesting nights.

In fact, every night was very interesting. Brownie and I received our primary inspiration from the same source [Fats Navarro], and I think at one time we sounded somewhat similar, but he was always the more capable for being able to move around the horn."[7]

Very often during the tour Hampton would call for Brown and Farmer to trade off against each other. Farmer felt "like I was fighting for my life."[8] He was marvelously candid about his inability to keep up with Brownie. "He was doin' what I wanted to do," he said to me, "and doin' it very well. He was no doubt far advanced. We were around the same age, I guess, but he was far advanced as a trumpet player. And so Lionel, to his credit, didn't take any solos away from me and give them to Brownie. He just opened up the arrangement, and, where I had a solo, at least a lot of times where I had a solo, he would let Brownie come after me. So every time I went out to play I felt I'd better really do my best because this guy could come behind me and murder me. That's the way it was." Even though Farmer was under such terrific pressure, he did admit that, despite that pressure, "it was great to hear someone who really was able to do what I wanted to do."

In addition to the underground recording session in Stockholm, the band had been recorded in a radio broadcast, which was taped and later released in 1981. Brownie soloed on "Blue Boy" and, as Phil Schaap notes, has the second solo in "I Only Have Eyes for You."[9]

On September 24 the band played a concert in Zurich, Switzerland. There exists a private recording of the show, but there are no solos by Clifford Brown. The next day the band left for Paris, where they would be for five days but would only play two concerts each day, September 26 and 27, at the Palais de Chaillot. It was a perfect opportunity for more surreptitious recording, and the beboppers wasted no time. Because Hampton still had George Hart keeping an eye on the youngsters (particularly Brownie), they had to seek help. According to one writer: "The musicians who wanted to showcase their playing and at the same time augment their salaries enlisted the aid of the French Vogue recording staff, in whom the cunning of a wartime underground and a natural American business acumen still flourished. These men (and women), by an elaborate system of decoys, ensured that the musicians made the sessions."[10]

After the last shows at the Palais de Chaillot, the Hot Club de France invited Hampton to a party on Monday, September 28, at the Ecole Normale de la Musique Superieure. Anticipating that he would be asked to play, the people at French Vogue had asked if they might tape the music. Apparently they were given carte blanche. Gleefully, the Vogue producers rejoiced. Not only would they get an LP from the great Lionel Hampton in a jam session, but, while this activity was taking place, his spies would be preoccupied at the party, thus permitting Brown, Gryce, and half of Hampton's sidemen to hustle over to the other side of town, where other Vogue producers were waiting to record them. What is particularly amusing is that even though Hampton had intensified his efforts at preventing the clandestine recordings, some sidemen who had been obeying his edict now decided to hell with it, and so joined Brownie and Gryce in what was tantamount to a great escape. People like Anthony Ortega, Clifford Solomon, Al Hayes, and Alan Dawson thus became new members of the renegade contingent, which now contained practically the entire Hampton band.

In a further irony, Hamp, knowing there would be a jam session at the Ecole Normale party, asked Walter Williams, Jimmy Cleveland, Billy Mackel, and others to accompany him. After the party and liquor got rolling and they had played for a while, Williams and Cleveland looked at each other, nodded, sneaked out, hailed a cab, and roared over to join the rebels at Scola Centorum—the Vogue recording site. Imagine the hilarity there as practically the whole Hampton band would be recording as The Clifford Brown Big Band in Paris.

The producer of the Paris rebellion—there would be a total of four sessions recorded over a three-week period—was pianist Henry Renaud, now a legend in French jazz circles. This is his recollection of events leading up to September 28 and the sessions that followed: "George Wallington was the first one who told me about Clifford Brown. Even though George was so enthusiastic about Clifford, I did not expect the tremendous surprise I was going to have in hearing Brownie for the first time. This happened a couple of nights later when the Hampton Band arrived in Paris. One night, some of the soloists came down to the Tabou where we—guitarist Jimmy Gourley, drummer Jean-Louis Viale and myself—were working. Farmer, Gryce and others played some very good things . . . but, suddenly, real fireworks exploded from the darkest part of the stage! That was Brownie who started playing! Everybody was just knocked out, musicians as well as listeners. Mr. Cabat, owner of the Vogue Company, was there. At the end of Brownie's solo, he came to me on the bandstand and said, 'We start recording tomorrow. You take care of the rhythm section.' So I asked Pierre Michelot to join my trio, and during the following weeks we had the wonderful pleasure—and the great honor—to play with Brownie on several recording sessions."[11]

Obviously Clifford Brown was more than just a naive onlooker while all of this clandestine activity was taking place. It is interesting to note that his ambition and sense of opportunism subsumed any misgivings he may have had about violating Hampton's arbitrary edict. All of the jazz world in Europe was talking about him, and such opportunities to record under his own name would not be available too often. So he did not hesitate to strike out boldly to further his musical career.

By the time Cleveland and Williams got over to the Vogue studios, the band was just about ready to record. First was a big piece by Gigi Gryce (he understandably uses an alias for his arranging credit—"Basheer Quism"), whose writing flows as if he couldn't wait to compose for Brownie. "Brown Skins" starts with a lengthy rubato passage that introduces Brownie (the only soloist) and the rich harmonic textures of the band. The melody utilizes the changes of "Cherokee," and as it launches into a bright tempo, Brownie, despite a couple of muddy triplets, solos splendidly. Most of his work is in the upper register—forced there by Gryce's massive brassy writing. The band sounds very crisp, despite the high jinks surrounding their presence. Gryce wrote for five trumpets (in addition to Brownie as soloist), so Renaud recruited Fernand Verstraete and Fred Gerard to supplement the Hampton brass rebels—Brownie, Farmer, Jones, and

Williams. In addition to bassist Pierre Michelot, Renaud imported a French connection of tenorman Henri Bernard and baritone saxist Henry Jouay.

"Keeping Up with Jonesy" is a Quincy Jones chart. Utilizing the Farmer-Brownie trades that had been developed during the Hampton performances, the tune is a slow swing chart showcasing Renaud at the opening. The saxes play the lead (the changes are from the tune "Moonglow"), then Brown and Farmer trade eights and fours through two choruses, with Brownie doing some doubling for fun. Jimmy Cleveland solos, also doubling nicely on the bridge, followed by the altos who trade with the band shouting under them. Cliff Solomon is heard, beginning with a comic quote from "The Last Time I Saw Paris." The alternate takes of these two charts are useful because they illustrate the careful preparation taken by the rebels despite the hurried, furtive circumstances. The session also had another Gryce original, "Deltitnu," that contains no Brown solo, and "Strike Up the Band," which features Farmer and the other Hampton rebels.

One further note. It is amusing to speculate what the expression on Hampton's face might have been, had he heard his group of Tyrolean-clad swing-shouters transformed into a cerebral bebop orchestra playing melodies as abstract as "Brown Skins." At any rate, it surely was a welcome respite for the rebels lucky enough to have been there.

In the tune "Brown Skins" we get a good insight into the writing skills of Gigi Gryce. Gryce had studied composition with Daniel Pinkham and Alan Hovaness at the New England Conservatory of Music in 1948 and then made his initial trip to Paris on a Fulbright scholarship to study with Nadia Boulanger and Arthur Honegger. He was a brilliant writing talent, but, as so often happens with someone who is far ahead of his time, Gigi Gryce's work remains neglected to the present day.

During the "French revolution" of September, however, Gryce and Clifford Brown became very tight friends. Their mutual respect and genuine liking for each other greatly increased. Brownie would one day be godfather to Gryce's child, and the families would remain close.

On Tuesday, September 29, the rebels sneaked out again and went back to the Vogue studios. This time Brownie and Gryce would represent The Clifford Brown Sextet, with a rhythm section of guitarist Jimmy Gourley and the three musketeers—Renaud, Michelot, and drummer Jean-Louis Viale.

The first tune is Brown's own "Goofin' with Me." The composer starts things off with a muted solo on the melody (changes from "Indiana") more than amply supported by the rest of the group. Gourley follows quickly, and then Gryce manages his most creative effort of the Paris rebellion leading into an exchange of fours between the three soloists and Viale. Next comes "All the Things You Are," with Brownie playing the melody and Gryce simultaneously playing a countermelody. Gryce and Gourley then solo, followed by Brownie. The alternate take utilizes the Hampton chase formula, with Brownie referring briefly to "Jeanie with the Light Brown Hair" in the bridge—not a common habit for him.

Gryce's "Blue Concept" employs augmented blues changes that were popular after a fashion during the 1950s. It is a swinging affair, beginning with Gryce and Brown playing the melody. Gryce once again reveals some compelling ideas. On the alternate take Brownie's solo shows how comfortable he was at this tempo.

"I Cover the Waterfront" again has Clifford Brown in brilliant ballad form, but the rest of the group doesn't seem relaxed enough. Michelot and Viale are very mechanical. Gryce's solo excels, while Gourley lays out on the tune.

This sextet session and its companion on October 8 went a long way toward establishing Gryce as an important alto voice in bebop. He plays with inspiration, and his writing explores the bebop idiom with fresh imagination.

This session had to be abbreviated because the Hampton band, by now an annoying distraction to the creative boppers, had to play in Germany with a concert in Dusseldorf on the following day—the last day of September. The band then went to Munich, Frankfurt,

Hamburg, and a concert at the Berlin Sportspalast on Sunday, October 4, that was broadcast on Armed Forces Radio. Brown soloed on "Airmail Special" here. Some unissued recording was done on this date, but there were apparently no German record producers ready to utilize the rebels as had been the case everywhere else.

After a day off on Monday, the band scooted across the German heartland to Mannheim for a show on Tuesday. Some private recording was also reported that night.

The band traveled back to Paris for what would be an important concert series at the Theatre de Paris from Wednesday the seventh until Sunday, the eleventh. Some private recording was also done here. Exhausted from the weary crisscrossing of Germany, the musicians looked forward to a nice rest for five days. Well, not *all* the musicians. The very next day, the rebellion resumed as Brown and Gryce slipped over to Vogue, eager to continue their sextet date. The site had shifted to the studio on 6 Rue Souvenet, but the musicians looked over their shoulders, gave the password, and went in. The three musketeers were in their chairs, smiling as if they had been frozen in time waiting for their heroes to return from their German hiatus.

It was to be an all-Gryce affair as he presented four more of his originals. The first is a haunting ballad. Gryce had become bedazzled by the Brownie magic, starting off his friend with another melody that is simply lovely.

"Minority" is one of the better-known Gryce tunes of the period. A sixteen-bar theme in a minor key, the tune opens with a relaxed Gryce solo played in the middle register of the alto. Clifford Brown goes through the changes well but, following Gryce's lead, stays in the middle of the horn. Gourley's guitar solo is uninspired, but Renaud finds the minor key changes to his liking, and his brief solo is more daring than his other tunes on the date. In "Take Two" the tempo quickens, and the solos become more interesting, with Brownie doubling here and there, leading the pack. "Baby," another Gryce effort, swings nicely from the start, with Brownie working through long lines that really glide. At the end of his solo he plays a couple of novel climbs in the turnback bars that are quite inventive.

Gourley gets into the spirit after a brief Gryce solo and works through triplet figures in fine fashion. Michelot takes a half-chorus solo—his best effort—and the tune ends with brief exchanges between Brownie and Viale, then Gryce and Viale. Economical and delicious bebop.

"Salute to the Bandbox"—the club next to Birdland where the Hampton band worked before leaving on the tour—is easily the most lyrical Gryce composition of the date. A bright-tempoed affair with an infectious head and an inspired bridge, the tune showcases the smooth harmony of Gryce and Brown playing together. The melody has that playful quality that Tadd Dameron captured in "Gertrude's Bounce."

Although these dates have been remembered more for the humorous irony of how they were recorded, they enabled Gigi Gryce to contribute a significant amount of important material to the bebop literature.

On Friday, October 9, the rebels convened again en masse to finish up some big band charts by Gryce and Jones. The band did three takes of Gryce's chart, "Quick Step," on which Brownie played no solos, and Jones's piece, "Bum's Rush," on which he did. The latter chart is a screamer from the start. Brown is the first soloist to join the fireworks, followed by the altos.

The next day, an octet date, saw Jimmy Cleveland and Clifford Solomon share the bandstand with the sextet musicians of October 8. On "Chez Moi"—a French pop tune—Gryce opens alone, followed by the horns on melody. After a rhythm break, Brownie pounces in with an interesting solo played all over the horn. Clifford Solomon wails away for a while, followed by André Dabonville, a new, untested member of the French forces. Jimmy Cleveland then sparkles with an outstanding, clearly articulated solo—his best of the tour—followed by Gryce, Gourley, and Renaud. The nicely harmonized head returns again at the end. "No Start, No End" is just what it sounds like—actually just a recording of another Brown solo from "Chez Moi." It is a long-lined affair. At the end Brown retreats to the lower register and breaks up his phrasing a bit, indicating he may have finally become a bit fatigued after all this continuous blowing.

The following day there was a nonet session. This Sunday session is devoted to takes of "All Weird," an original composition and arrangement of Clifford Brown's. Here his writing illustrates the harmonic influence of Dameron. The composition has some tricky chord changes, which Brownie worked through nicely in his solo. The arrangement reflects some new thoughts, even though Brown has not quite fully developed them yet. In the fragment of a second take, all that remains is the Brownie solo, this time in slower time and not nearly as enthusiastic as the solo on the master.

Where these rebels got all this energy to write and play around the clock the way they did remains an enigma. Yes, they were young, but ask any trumpet players that you know about all this, and they are bound to shake their heads.

After a few days in places like Bordeaux, the Hampton band returned for their last day in Paris to rest before departing for some hastily put together dates in Africa. But rest was not what Clifford Brown had in mind—it was his last shot during the French part of the tour, and he was determined not to waste it. Once again he went over to the Jouvenet studio, this time alone. By now the other band members had finally blown themselves out. Henri Renaud recalled the circumstances: "The quartet date was the very last session Brownie made in Paris. It was absolutely unprepared and we did it in three hours one afternoon which turned out to be his final day in Paris. Brownie did not have a lot of time because he had to take a plane or a train with the Hampton band."[12]

There is one new face—Benny Bennett, an American drummer who had remained in France after the war. He had picked up many dates with the French jazzmen and had also recorded with Don Byas.

The first tune of the session was a Brown composition, "Blue and Brown." Clifford certainly sounds refreshed as he opens the date with some energetic blues improvising and seems to react well to Bennett's ride cymbal. The rest is bare bones comping from Renaud and a fade at the close. For 3:13 the cut is all Brownie.

"I Can Dream, Can't I" is the first of the standards on the release. Three takes are included. A refreshed Clifford Brown solos splendidly, even including a triplet figure quote from "Flight of the Bumblebee." The quartet format allows him greater freedom, for he is the only soloist. In take two, he again refers to "Bumblebee," and there are double-time figures everywhere as he really stretches out. Despite these rapid-fire sequences, the mood is relaxed, as the composer intended.

On "It Might As Well Be Spring," his smoky lower register comes prominently into play. "The Song Is You" is played in a bright tempo. Brownie's tone is quite smooth, although there are a couple of clams heard as he plays the head. The improvised choruses really move, inspiring a split-second stop-time break by the rhythm section. The song ends abruptly after Brown's solo. On the second take, strangely, he misfires once again on the head. But the improvisation choruses are full of the triple-tongued passages that were becoming a trademark of his.

The Chaplin-Cahn standard "You're a Lucky Guy" is next. After a four-bar intro, Brownie roars out with the lead, followed by a very adventurous improvisation that evidently pleases him. Take two draws on the take one ideas but incorporates more triple tonguing. He works through all the changes and is all over the scale in the last chorus. His tone is spectacular. After a brief solo, Brownie takes it home and ends with a conventional major seventh chord. Take three is played at the same tempo, and the articulation is as clear as the first two takes. He plays one figure that will become legendary in "I'll Remember April" much later. There is a greater ease and dexterity in his playing than in any other of the Paris sessions.

"Come Rain or Come Shine" is a medium swing and, once again, Brown dominates the entire piece. The rhythm players are definitely in the background. The final chorus is practically a reworked melody. Take two is another relaxed adventure. Brown plays with enormous confidence and launches into new harmonic areas. His "chops" are in superb shape, despite the amount of playing he had been doing.

This quartet date reveals so much technique and so much originality. As liner note writer Mark Gardner said, "If you want to know where Lee Morgan, Freddie Hubbard, Charles Tolliver, Carmell Jones, Woody Shaw, Randy Brecker and a whole lot of other cats come from, it is all right here."

Henri Renaud would spend the rest of his life marveling at what happened during Clifford Brown's stay in Paris. Renaud said of him: "He possessed the highest qualities anybody could ask for: a world of technique, a real trumpet sound, big and strong, a fat, fat sound, a wonderful ear and much facility for improvising. Brownie could play the most complicated tunes by Gigi Gryce, just as easily as if he had been playing the blues. As a human being, Clifford was all kindness, warmth and simplicity."[13]

The rest of the tour was somewhat fragmented, as the band picked up dates where they could before returning to Scandinavia. Meanwhile, back in France, Vogue began releasing the recordings that Brown and his colleagues had made. The records created a sensation as soon they were released, and by the time the band got back to Scandinavia in early November there weren't many musicians or producers or jazz fans in Europe who didn't know about the rebels and their feats.

Jimmy Cleveland remembered graphically what a media blitz had taken place in just a few weeks. "All the guys were on the front pages of all the European publicity papers and magazines and jazz papers," he said. "Clifford was all over the covers and the whole bit that we had been recording. And these recordings were major hits in the jazz world."[14]

One can just imagine the reaction of Lionel and Gladys Hampton to the stir caused by these records. After taking great pains to prevent it, after threatening to fire them if they even dared, putting them under virtual house arrest, Hampton had stood by while his musicians had flown the coop and become famous for doing it. "Hamp was just put out by the whole thing," said Cleveland. "The scene with Hamp's entourage became so obnoxious that they finally said they were going to fire Clifford."

On November 10, Clifford Brown was scheduled to record again for Metronome in Stockholm, together with Farmer, Dawson, Cleveland, and the Swedish All-Stars. But shortly before the session was to take place, Brown received a telegram from the American Federation of Musicians officially forbidding him to violate Hampton's edict against recording in Europe. "Rather than risk losing his return passage to America as a member of the band, Clifford stood down," said the critic Alun Morgan.

Jimmy Cleveland got into a shouting match with Hampton over his intention to fire Clifford Brown. Cleveland recalled: "Hamp said, 'Well, he didn't get permission to record!' I said, 'None of us got permission to record. We don't have to get permission to record. We're out of the continental United States. But the contract spells out what we can do and what we can't do, depending on the deposit. Now, in your case, you didn't pay the deposit before you left. So what you have to do is *pay* the deposit and *then* your contract will be binding. Until such a time, we can quit right now.'

"He said, 'Well, talk to Gladys.' I told her, 'I just spoke to Al Jaffe in New York and he told me that if you guys don't give us our return ticket, the union will send us our tickets and you guys will have to pay for them, and then they'll sue you. We'll all come in and file charges against you, and you'll have to pay us for this trip, pay us all a deposit and pay us for the time lost.' Gladys said, 'Can you come over here to the Stockholm Grand?' I got there, and Hamp says, 'Look, here, Gates, can we . . . ?' I said, 'No, Hamp. You're talking about trying to export this man—one of the great trumpet players in the world! We're all brothers, we've got to be good friends and we *know* he's playin' *your* music, man! This whole thing is because these people didn't want to record you. This is just professional jealousy, and this is totally ridiculous and you really shouldn't be that small.' I told him face to face.

"Gladys said, 'Jimmy, can we solve this?' I said, 'Yeah. Clifford stays. And all the rest of us—we stay. And from now on we want to get an advance. Otherwise tomorrow we'll be on the plane.' Just to make a statement, Hamp got angry at us and cussed us out and called us a whole bunch of names and choice words."

This part of the account has undergone several different versions over the years. But it seems clear that a truce was achieved. Clifford Brown remained, but tensions on the rest of the tour got worse.

Actually, Farmer, Cleveland, and the others sneaked away on that Tuesday, November 10, and recorded without Clifford Brown. They played "Pogo Stick" (which Quincy Jones wrote in tribute to Brown), "Liza," and "Sometimes I'm Happy."

The next day, the Hampton band played a date at the Storyville Club in Copenhagen as the tension rose among the band members. Some of the older members were commiserating with Hampton. There was, naturally, some jealousy about the attention being paid to the rebels.

On Thursday, November 12, the hostility abated somewhat at a jam session with Hampton, Brown, and the other band members, together with some Danish musicians, at Forvarsbrodrenes Hus in Copenhagen. On "Perdido" and "All the Things You Are" there are no Brownie solos, but he did solo on "Indiana," and the performance was recorded privately. The Xanadu label later released the material in the United States, France, and Japan in 1976, under the title of *International Jam Sessions.*[15]

It has been suggested that the only reason Lionel Hampton was in on this particular jam session is that he wanted to make sure that there were no more outlaw sessions by the rebels.

The tour began to wind down. The original plan had been to spend three months away; now it was mid-November, and all that remained on the band's schedule were some dates in Algeria. These may or may not have been on the original route, but in any event the band packed up and left for Africa.

When the musicians arrived in the capital, Algiers, they were met by Louis-Victor Mialy, a producer who would oversee the band's activities there. He became quite friendly with Clifford Brown and was photographed with him. Mialy was established in radio there and was a close friend of George Wallington, who was back in Paris, scratching for gigs after leaving Hampton. Mialy showed some of the young musicians the sights of Algiers and remembered taking Brownie to the Casbah. He noted the almost threadbare clothing that Brownie wore. Although he couldn't afford many clothes, he did managed to acquire quite a few pairs of shoes. "He loved shoes," said Mialy.

From the time of their arrival, the week before Thanksgiving, to their departure on December 1, there were six concerts in Algiers and two in Oran. In addition to these performances by the Hampton Band, there seems to have occurred one tiny last uprising: From November 24 to 26 there were jam sessions at the Hotel Aletti. Although tapes made privately of these sessions have never been released, it has been reported that certainly Brownie was in the midst of things, with some other rebels and some French musicians from Algiers. There were six tunes taped: "Indiana," "Midnight Sun," Keepin' Up With Jonesy," "Come Rain or Come Shine," "Minority," and "You're a Lucky Boy." The repertoire taped makes sense because, as we have seen, it reflects material that had been worked on in previous group recording sessions in Europe.

When the news of the activity reached the Hampton hierachy, a terrible incident resulted, reported by Mialy: "There was, in the band, a kind of road manager, a valet. A tall guy–George Hart. He hated Clifford Brown! And in Algiers, next to their hotel, the Hotel Aletti, there was a small street. One day I went there around three in the afternoon, and I see all of these black musicians outside. And there was an argument going on between George Hart and Clifford Brown, and then there was a fight, and he pulled a knife on Clifford Brown! And of course, it was like a riot. People trying to separate them. He wanted to knife Clifford Brown. He wanted to kill him! And Clifford fought and in fighting he dislocated his shoulder. Oh, he was in pain! So we took him to his hotel room, and I called the doctor, but he didn't come right away. I thought he wouldn't be able to play that night. That's it. And Quincy Jones started to slowly move his arm and massage it. And he put back his shoulder. Painful. He screamed–crying and crying. That same night he was playing trumpet! I wish you could have seen the faces of the musicians in the room when Clifford was in pain and Quincy was trying to put back his arm. They were *defeated!* Art Farmer was white as a bedsheet. There were ten or twelve people in the room looking at

Clifford Brown, thinking, 'Oh, what's going to happen?' That fight could have been the end of his life."[16]

"Clifford Brown was tough, man," Jimmy Cleveland said. Indeed it took a lot of toughness for Brownie to recover from his injuries and play the show that night. Once again, he was haunted by what the auto accident had done to his body. Once again, he had to endure terrible pain. But, once again, he gathered his strength and made the music happen.

In the end the rebellion had achieved a great victory. Alun Morgan said that "the Hampton bandsmen made more recordings in Europe than any previous touring group . . . the recordings revealed a literally astonishing amount of jazz talent and helped to set a number of hitherto unrecognized musicians in correct perspective."[17]

In Clifford Brown's case, the rebellion was responsible for launching his international reputation in jazz, which continued to grow from that point on. In addition it gave him the confidence to move his career ahead dramatically. The decision to leave college two years earlier had paid off in large dividends. Jimmy Cleveland assessed Brown's career at this time: "He was one of the most innovative trumpet players at that time alive, outside of Dizzy Gillespie. He knew he was good. He didn't know how good. He knew how the people reacted in Europe. He knew something was happening. He knew he had something. You can always tell it, because people that are informed about jazz *will* let you know. They will definitely come up and just tell you straight out how great you sound. Whether you believe it or not—it's one of those kinds of things. It matters to a person what a guy says and how people are playing your work and all that sort of thing and how popular you are. It is very important, but it does not deter you from continuing on your course because you want to get even better."[18]

This is an accurate picture of Clifford Brown's own assessment as he packed his bags and said good-bye to the Hampton tour. On December 1, 1953, the band flew back to the United States. Lionel Hampton sailed back on the liner *Liberté*, arriving in New York on December 10. Upon his return he immediately fired the rebellious band members, including Clifford Brown.

When I spoke to Lionel Hampton as I was researching this period, he revealed none of the animosity he must have felt at the time. He looked wistful and smiled as he remembered the feats that Clifford Brown had accomplished on that tour. Perhaps he put it best when he said to me, "Brownie set Europe on fire."[19]

Eight
New York
and Home

Once Clifford Brown had begun his recording career, there would never be a time in his life when musicians didn't press to perform with him. The plane had hardly touched the tarmac upon his return from Europe when the phone started ringing. This was mainly a response to the Blue Note recording he had done before the Hampton tour. By now, release dates were being announced, the publicists were at work, and disk jockeys were hearing more and more about the new trumpet sensation.

After freelancing around New York for a couple of weeks and checking out the scene, Brownie heard that Art Blakey called with news of a new group that he was forming. Together with the Blue Note producers, Blakey had convinced Lou Donaldson to join. Brown immediately accepted Blakey's offer to join him because he knew that the music would be to his liking and he had had a good experience with the Blue Note people. Blakey had also signed on veteran bassist Curly Russell and a budding piano talent who had scored well the year before with Stan Getz. His name was Horace Silver.

Early in the new year, the band began serious preparations for a recording date that the Blue Note producers had scheduled. They would record the group live at Birdland, where the band was making its debut. It was an exciting opportunity. Birdland was the most popular jazz club in New York, attracting top names who vied for choice dates. During these weeks Brownie had scarcely time to visit Wilmington and tell his family about Europe, see Ida Mae, and rush back for rehearsals.

Lou Donaldson had been acquainted with Horace Silver before the Blakey work had begun. As Silver recalled: "I used to play at a place called the Paradise Bar & Grill up on 110th Street and Eighth Avenue with Big Nick Nicholas, and we played just a tenor sax, piano, and drums, no bass. On the weekend we used to play for a floor show there, but during the week cats used to come in to jam. Lou was one of the guys who used to come in and jam. I think that is where Alfred Lion heard him and signed him to do a couple of recordings for him. He used to be on those records. That was my in to Blue Note records."[1]

This recollection illustrates that the origin of this quartet was more a creation of Alfred Lion and his staff than it was of the musicians. Art Blakey made the calls, but the group really had no leader. One day, Blakey would rise to the fore and stake his claim to leadership, as the group eventually evolved into the Jazz Messengers. But at this juncture things were pretty loose.

The record date was set for February 21. One afternoon as the group was rehearsing at Birdland prior to its opening, a stunning incident occurred. Horace Silver recalled it: "Miles came down there to listen to us rehearse, you know. This was afternoon down at Birdland. The place was closed up and we were rehearsing. In the middle of our rehearsal, Miles got up and started to leave. As he started to go out the door, he yelled back to Clifford jokingly, 'Clifford, I hope you break your chops!' And then Curly Russell said, 'Man, he ain't kiddin'. He means that!' "[2]

Whether Miles Davis was serious or not has been debated. But even if he was only joking, Brownie's playing must have been pretty awesome to warrant such a comment from a star like Davis.

According to Horace Silver, the live recording at Birdland was undertaken on two separate nights. This makes a lot of sense because the tunes average about seven minutes in length, and a couple of takes were made for "Wee Dot" and "Quicksilver." Rudy Van Gelder brought his portable recording equipment into Birdland, and the stage was set. February 21 was a Sunday night, but Silver recalled that the recording was made "Thursday and Friday" or "Friday and Saturday." One of the nostalgic bonuses of the recording for those who remember Birdland in those days was the voice of emcee Pee Wee Marquette. Marquette had a reputation for besieging the musicians who played the club and asking for "a taste" in return for special acknowledgment during his introductions. Indeed, on this recording Marquette saturates the audience with Art Blakey's name, lest there be any doubt who the leader was.

The album selections contained three originals by the young Horace Silver (twenty-five years old), who was already gaining a reputation for compositions that toyed with stereotypical bebop formulas. He later became known as a master of "hard bop"—a writer's term that started about this time to define the music of the post Parker/Gillespie boppers.[3] The first tune is Silver's "Split Kick," which, at 8:26, gives evidence that Alfred Lion was insistent on giving the composers and writers all the space they needed for their work. Blue Note records pioneered in encouraging these beboppers and hard boppers to do their thing, and let the three-minute record format be damned. As a result, all of the selections on "Live at Birdland" are unusually long. "Split Kick," a trademark Silver opus, opens with the melody stretching over different rhythm patterns. Initially, Lou Donaldson opens with a fluid triplet-figured solo that swings neatly. Brownie follows with some really inventive ideas; after his patented triplet run down the scale, he briefly refers to "Comin' Thro' the Rye," of all things, on his way to a stratospheric exploration.

On a new reissue of this recording, the liner notes marvel at his work: "On Silver's 'Split Kick,' Brown devotes one telling passage to an ascending scale; he plays it, then stops plays it again, stops. With each repetition, the tension builds. Finally he arrives at the top note he apparently was looking for all along, and then moves on, playfully baiting the listener with a new phrase that may or may not repeat. . . . These moments, and others, are not just the work of a clever button pusher. They're the product of a true thinker, an artist who was serious about communicating through his improvisations." After Silver works through his lines, constantly referring to "Joshua Fit de Battle of Jericho," the horns exchange, and then Blakey solos. They all return to the head and then go out.

Blakey next introduces Brown, "who has chosen for his musical vehicle, 'Once in a While.' " After a lush melody statement, Brownie plays a double-time chorus with a cascade of notes, and then follows with a $3/_4$-time passage that he would utilize a good deal from this time on. He clearly had worked this out in rehearsal.

After the ballad, Blakey tells the audience that the next tune is a Silver composition that has been named "Quicksilver" by the band members. The melody jumps out, containing a quote from "Oh, You Beautiful Doll," followed by another from "The Donkey Serenade." Donaldson solos first again; then Brownie launches into a clearly detailed triple-tongued chorus. His next chorus is a completely different solo with tricky fingering. Silver is up next, and then the melody is repeated by the horns. Blakey's tom-toms are cacophonous, and then the out chorus finishes things up.

What follows is an alternate cut of J. J. Johnson's "Wee Dot." Another bright-tempoed affair, the tune starts off with a fired-up Donaldson paving the way for an explosive Brownie, whose complex solo breaks new ground. After Silver solos, Curly Russell finally gets a brief chorus to solo, and a quick out chorus follows.

A blues, simply dubbed "Blues" with no composer credit, follows. Donaldson opens again, drawing upon some ideas from the southern R&B music that was so very important to him. Brown follows with a third chorus that the liner notes describe as "churchy, intervally interesting call and response between his low register and the extreme upper reaches of the horn."

Blakey then announces that he feels close to the next tune, "A Night in Tunisia," because he was "right there when Dizzy composed it in Texas on the back of a garbage can." Donaldson jumps in at a rhythm break, with a stupendous flourish of triplets. This suggests Charlie Parker's much more famous break solo at the famous Massey Hall concert in Toronto. A comparison of the two altoists in this context would be interesting.

During Clifford Brown's solo, Joshua mysteriously continues fighting at Jericho (why this quote abounds on this recording is anybody's guess), but what follows does not contain the inventiveness of the previous tunes. Silver follows, says hello to Joshua, and then gives way to Blakey's familiar tom-toms. The melody returns, and the tune ends with a brief cadenza from Brownie.

"Mayreh" is the third crisply composed piece by Silver of the session. Brown solos first this time, and his effort contains a lot of the "premeditated spontaneity" that characterizes his solos on the other Silver pieces. It becomes obvious that the Silver pieces were certainly the tunes that the band worked on the most during rehearsal.

"The title is kind of a tongue title," said Silver. "Lou Donaldson was from the South, and he talks with a southern accent [this is certainly not as true of Lou today as it may have been forty-odd years ago], so when Lou pronounces the name Mary, like Mary Smith, he says 'Mayreh.' That was a joke. So whenever I see Lou today, I call him 'Mayreh.' " In any event, at 6:02 it is the shortest cut of the night, except for Clifford's ballad. When it ends, the band segues into "Lullaby of Birdland"–further evidence that Gelder has decided to call it quits for the night.

Pee Wee Marquette hails "Art Blakey and his wonderful all-stars" in his introduction to the master of "Wee Dot." The tune begins with Blakey drum-rolling the band into the head followed by Donaldson whacking into his solo quoting "Swingin' on a Star." Some of Donaldson's ideas sound familiar, but he swings quite forcefully. Brownie, on the other hand, tries out some new ideas, finishing up with an ascending scale design that characterizes much of his work on this date. Silver's solo is, this time, free of quotes, containing some spicy chord melody work at the end.

Blakey tells the audience that "this is the first time [he] has ever enjoyed a record session" and introduces Lou Donaldson playing "If I Had You" in a sequence that replicates the music of the previous evening. Donaldson quotes Ferde Grofé's *Grand Canyon Suite* on his way to a fine performance.

Next comes the alternate of "Quicksilver," a much longer take than the original (8:26). Donaldson flies through some delicately phrased lines, followed by Brownie, who plays a startling phrase, repeats it and moves into "Donkey Serenade," a part of Silver's melody that stays pretty much in the middle and lower part of the horn. Silver's solo repeats some phrases we've heard before, and then comes Curly Russell, who is unforgivably shortchanged on this date. A Blakey chorus, and then out.

"The Way You Look Tonight" is a lengthy (9:55) treatment of the Dorothy Fields–Jerome Kern opus, but, like "A Night in Tunisia," it doesn't have the tight, well-rehearsed smoothness that the band revealed on the Silver compositions. Clifford's solos are filled with notes at rapid-fire pace. It is probably this tune and the following "Lou's Blues" that prompted Nat Hentoff to give a less than unqualified review of his performance. "He has one main trouble . . . he often plays too many notes. Clifford will be a great trumpet player not just a very good one, when he finds out the expressive value to economy."[4] After this comment, however, he proceeded to give the LP four stars.

Charlie Parker's "Now's the Time" is played in a medium swing tempo, and the solos are adequate but not up to the others, as the group seems to tire.

Blakey then announces his desire to "stay with the youngsters" (his sidemen), because "it keeps the mind active." If there was any doubt who the leader of this group was before the performance, it is certainly dispelled with Blakey's words here.

Parker's "Confirmation" is another long (9:56) exercise for the group. Here Brownie plays an opening long-lined solo that actually contains some strategic spacings. It is as if he himself feels that the session has already seen a bit too much multinoted blowing. Donaldson, however, rides merrily along with his roller coaster improvisation, not pausing for anybody. Silver's solo is an interesting two-handed battle, with more chord emphasis from his right hand than before. The horns trade briefly with Blakey, and then the band segues again into "Lullaby of Birdland," while Marquette urges the crowd to acknowledge "Art Blakey, Art Blakey, etc."

This album has become a jazz classic for many reasons: the

brilliant improvisations, the innovative Silver compositions, the quintessential hard bop musical statements, and the production standards rendered by Van Gelder and Blue Note. But perhaps most importantly for our story, upon its release, the jazz fans in America were now aware of the magic of Clifford Brown. From this point on he begins to receive the popular as well as critical praise that bring him to prominence.

Although the quintet had their two weeks in New York prior to the Birdland album and a week in Philadelphia before that, things came to an abrupt halt after the live recording. Although the jazz scene was not yet in the death grip of the rock 'n' roll era, things were tightening up generally, and Blakey did not respond to the structure very well. He was not at a point where he could network his way around the country's jazz clubs. As a result, the musicians very quickly became disenchanted and wondered what would happen. Despite the rumors of how well the live recording went, the phones were not ringing. Well, that's not entirely true. As before, there was one phone busy—Clifford Brown's. In March, a couple of weeks after the Birdland date, there was one call that was especially interesting—from drummer Max Roach.

By 1954, Roach had established himself as the world's seminal bebop percussionist. From the early 1940s he had been everywhere important bebop was being played and, with Kenny Clarke, had been responsible for revolutionary changes in percussive technique. He'd recorded the first great bebop records with Parker and Gillespie. He'd played with Thelonious Monk at Minton's and Monroe's (the twin New York homes of the bebop movement). He'd led the parade of "cool jazz" divertimentos with Miles Davis, and he had carried his melodic tom-toms into the world of hard bop in the 1950s.

In March 1954, Roach was in California working at the Lighthouse in Hermosa Beach. He had signed a six-month contract to be the house drummer and was basically vamping, waiting for something dramatic to happen, wondering when he would get moving again. California was certainly pleasant (despite the fact that he had a long drive from his house in L.A. down to Hermosa Beach); the social life was fun, and the music was OK. But still . . .

At the end of his contract at the Lighthouse, Roach was approached by Gene Norman, a record producer and music business veteran. Norman had a company—Crescendo Records—and he began urging Roach to start his own group, playing the kind of music that would once again revive his creative juices. Roach began to think seriously about Norman's suggestion and, according to his recollection, also began thinking about a record he had heard recently. It was a record by J. J. Johnson and . . . oh, yes . . . who was that trumpet player he "fell in love" with? . . . Clifford Brown. "So I called New York," said Roach, "and asked him how he felt about it. He said yes he'd like to come to California and . . . we got together."[5]

Max Roach had told Gene Norman that he would like to form a new group "if we had someplace to work." Norman provided further encouragement, and they went on to discuss recording contracts and tour possibilities. Roach flew to New York to meet Brown and talk further. "We talked about a lot of things," recalled Roach, and very soon he and Brownie flew back out to L.A. together.[6] Roach remembered vividly that they "played chess on the way back on the plane." He fancied himself a superior chess player. "I was all-city in New York," he said, "and I thought I was a killer at that time but he was murder with that chess board."

Max Roach was some six years older than Brownie and had come to Brooklyn when his family moved there from North Carolina during the Depression. A track and field performer ("I was pretty good") at Boys High School, Roach "moved to the City [Manhattan] as soon as I graduated." This was in 1942, a fortuitous time in jazz history. "I think I was just fortunate to be around New York at a certain time when most of the heavyweight players were all in the army . . . the government had slapped a 20 percent tax on entertainment" and "public dancing" and the big bands were suddenly in trouble. "Benny Goodman had the hottest band in the world," said Roach, "and was forced to work with his sextet. Basie had a septet . . . tap dancing went out, Sinatra couldn't sing . . . it was just a mess out here because an entrepreneur in New York City had to pay government tax, state tax, city tax, pay for his venue, buy booze and stuff . . . it was impossible to survive."[7]

"So," continued Roach, "the source of entertainment became the virtuoso players—the Coleman Hawkinses, the Art Tatums—and 52nd Street was of course in full swing." The "virtuosos" were the only ones "who could hold the attention of the audience in the little small joints" that sprang up all over to replace the large disappearing dance band venues. "I remember [Vladimir] Horowitz would come to the Three Deuces when Art Tatum was working," tell his stretch limo to wait, "and sit up in front all night. It was just a different kind of thing in New York . . . everybody came here and of course it was during that period when Charlie Parker showed up."

Roach's recollection of his bebop beginnings is worth quoting in its entirety: "I was working [in 1943] a joint on the west side downtown called George E J's 17th Street Tap Room when Bird wandered in. In those days we had bands, and the leaders of the bands were song and dance people. In our case the leader of this band was a man named Clark Monroe, and he had a club of his own which was after hours. The funny thing about that period was that they had two unions—a black union and a white union—and you worked seven nights a week for six weeks and had a week off." The "after hours" club that Clark Munroe had was, of course, Monroe's Uptown house, which opened at 4 A.M. "Charlie Parker came to New York City, and he used to come up to this joint. One night we had two gigs—we had a gig which we called in white town, and then we packed up and went uptown to Monroe's Uptown House, which was in black town. When we were young all we wanted to do was play, so this was a great opportunity."

At Monroe's "we heard Prez, Coleman Hawkins, Billie Holiday, it was just one of those places in Harlem, 132th Street between 7th Avenue and Lenox. The proprietor was Billie Holiday's brother-in-law, and he was a song and dance man. He had to have a guy who rehearsed the shows, and that was Victor Coolson. One night he said to the band, 'I'm gonna bring the greatest musician who ever lived in the club tomorrow night.' Next night here comes Charlie

Parker with sneakers on, and plays the show. The show had different acts, singers, dancers, etcetera, etcetera, and then we'd do a spot. Well, for the spot that night, Victor decided to feature Charlie Parker playing 'Cherokee.' He played and went past all of us! . . . That was the first time I met him. He went right past us all."

What happened after this 1943 meeting is, of course, jazz history. As Clifford Brown and Max Roach were meeting in Los Angeles in 1954, Brownie was, in his humility, hardly able to contain his excitement at being asked to join this legendary musician. Of course that didn't stop him from giving Max a rough time in the chess matches.

Nine
California
Surprise

"Bop" was a sudden eruption within jazz, a fast but logical complication of melody, harmony and rhythm. European and non-European components emerged according to what was increasingly a European pattern.

—Marshall Stearns, *The Story of Jazz*

As soon as they convened in California, Max Roach and Clifford Brown set up an apartment together. It was propitious for several reasons, the main one being their need to have long conversations about the kind of music they wanted to create together. The apartment doubled as a music library and rehearsal studio.

Max Roach's trademark as a percussionist had been the fixed pulse ride cymbal rhythm figure pioneered by Kenny Clarke. This approach freed up the other drums so they could supply counter rhythms, layered textures, and new spacings. Above all else, Roach sought to use a variety of tom-toms, each carefully tuned so he could explore the melodic and even harmonic possibilities of percussion. His technique was legendary, but what especially appealed to Brown was the peculiarly quiet sound of the ride cymbal. It allowed the melody instruments a much better opportunity for subtleties and gave bass players new confidence. For a change, the bass could actually be heard. What also appealed to Brownie was Roach's indefatigable chops. He could keep steady rhythm support at the meteoric tempos that Brownie loved and continually challenge his control.

When Roach came to the Lighthouse for his six-month residency, replacing the formidable Shelly Manne, he brought such stars as Miles Davis and Charlie Mingus along for some work. The Lighthouse owner, Howard Rumsey, said that Roach "set the whole town on fire" with his drumming, but even stars like Davis, Mingus, and others were not able to help him advance further musically.

When Clifford Brown arrived, Max Roach had an epiphany. At the apartment, a two-bedroom affair, "every morning we'd kind of wake up and dash for the piano," he said.[1] "He would always wake me up with it, in any case." Brown also played drums. "I had a practice set in the house and he kind of dabbled with everything."

After they had worked out concepts for the music they wanted to play, they needed to find musicians who could help them establish the new group. "Sonny Stitt was in California at that particular time," said Roach, "and we worked a place called the California Club." Stitt, a leading Parker disciple, although wonderfully creative, had a reputation for outmuscling musicians on the bandstand and not really being dedicated to cohesive band play. Thus, it was soon clear that Stitt would not fill the bill. But at this embryonic stage, they did acquire the bassist George Bledsoe, late of the Count Basie band, "who was a wonderful singer," according to Roach, who remembered Bledsoe more for his voice and less for his bass playing. On piano, they got luckier—Carl Perkins, "a fantastically gifted harmonic pianist," said Roach, "who did things differently than most people did with that instrument."

After Stitt quit (one account reports he stayed for about six weeks), Max Roach came across an old friend, Teddy Edwards. Although he had never worked with Roach, Edwards remembers that they had "played together in a big jam session in Tulsa, Oklahoma, in 1944." After "meeting together through the years," Edwards recalled a singular occurrence. "Max was the first guy that hipped me to Stravinsky," he said. "He had a little record player with him and he took me out to the hotel and he said, 'Man, I want you to hear somethin',' and he played the *Rite of Spring* and the *Firebird Suite*."[2]

Although Edwards remained with the group only a couple of weeks,[3] it was enough time to rehearse some music for a concert date that an anxious Gene Norman had set up for late April at the

Pasadena Civic Auditorium. When he had first spoken to Brown, Roach had made an unusual offer. He told Norman that he was willing to share billing with Brownie as co-leaders. And so in April 1954, the first appearances of the Clifford Brown–Max Roach Quintet took place.

During this frenetic creating and organizing period, Max Roach remembered that Clifford Brown was "constantly writing" and sorting out ideas for the new group. It appeared that he was in a singularly creative frame of mind, thinking of nothing but the music. But this was certainly not the only thing that preoccupied him in California.

After he had returned from Europe and the Hampton tour, Brownie didn't have much time to spend with friends and family down in Wilmington. Naturally, his relationship with Ida Mae had also become somewhat distant because of the European peregrinations and all of the work with Blakey that followed. Still, it is clear that he hadn't changed his feelings, so he was hurt and disappointed to discover when he returned that she had sought new companionship while he was away. Deanie Jenkins recalled that Clifford had been distraught to find out about the change and apparently spent a lot of time fretting over it.

When Brown joined Roach in California, his heart was still heavy, but that would change dramatically. The California scene was exactly the tonic that he needed—sunshine, exciting people, and great jazz.

One day, Max Roach introduced him to a diminutive young classical music student named LaRue Anderson. She was practically a native, hailing originally from Shreveport, Louisiana, and moving to Los Angeles when she was two years old. "From the time I was five years old, I played classical piano," recalled LaRue, "and I played with the Los Angeles Junior Philharmonic."[4] At the time she met Brownie, she was at the University of Southern California with an unusual major—"music psychology." She had been studying classically with Sam Browne, her teacher at Jefferson High School (who also taught Hampton Hawes and Don Cheny), and began "hanging out with the fellows" while at Jefferson. One of her fellow students was altoist Frank Morgan. "I used to do his music theory homework for him so he could stay in the jazz band," she said. In September 1953, LaRue Anderson was doing research on a strange topic—her thesis was essentially to disprove that jazz was an art form. Charlie Parker had come into the area that fall. "He was playing the L.A. area at the Tiffany, or a club like that. . . . When I met him it was at Hermosa Beach, at a place down from the Lighthouse."

This was the same time that Max Roach was doing his stint at the Lighthouse, so Anderson was now socializing with Parker, Roach, and other jazzers while studying classical music at U.S.C. She had begun at the Brooks Conservatory of Music and had continued her studies with Dr. Eurea and Elia Margorgsky, but "Sam Browne really was instrumental in continuing me along classical lines."

LaRue Anderson went up to the Lighthouse to meet Max Roach and approach him about an interview for her research. "He was very nice also," she said. "And he agreed to let me come over to his apartment and interview him, which I did. They found out that I could play chess, and we started to play chess. We got into all kinds of arguments about all kinds of things, and they adopted me as their little sister."

When Brownie arrived in L.A. Roach decided that LaRue should meet his young coleader and so introduced her to him. The musicians always hung out together, "and somehow I invited them back to my mom's house," said LaRue. "My mother fell in love with Clifford immediately, which meant that anybody Mom liked, of course I didn't like."

Very soon Brownie became a familiar face at the Anderson home. "He would go over to my house, and my mom and he would talk, and they would have dinner or lunch or breakfast or whatever together, and they really liked each other. He wasn't that bad—he was a nice young man, but I just wasn't interested in him." Also, LaRue was under the impression that Clifford was not available. "I don't know whether it was formally or informally, but he was engaged to someone else when I met him," she said.

During the first weeks that LaRue knew him, they had nothing but a friendship. "About a month must have been wasted before I even looked at him twice," she said.

Soon after Brownie began visiting the Anderson home, an incident occurred that caused LaRue to see the young musician in a different light. "One night I went over to play chess during intermission at the California Club," she said. The guys were on the bandstand, and bassist George Bledsoe "said something ungentlemanly to me from the bandstand out in the audience where I was." Bledsoe was quite tall, towering over Brownie's five foot nine, according to LaRue. Brownie became irate. "Cliff went up and very quietly told him never to talk to a lady like that, and if he ever did it again, he would be fired immediately, and that was it. So I had to look at Clifford again, and I really think that's when I started to like him."

One day, LaRue, trying to bolster her thesis that jazz wasn't an art form, took Clifford to Sam Browne's house, confident that he would back up the arguments about jazz that she had been having with Brownie. At the door her teacher practically knocked her over in order to shake Brownie's hand and usher him into the house, leaving LaRue outside. Naturally annoyed, she went in and said to Sam, "Are you telling me this man [Clifford] can play well?" "This man is a genius," said Sam and promptly began chattering away in idolatrous fashion with Brownie and ignoring a dispirited LaRue.

Clifford had by this time decided to pursue LaRue seriously. She was an educated, musically talented, young attractive woman, and he had, by now, developed a strong romantic attraction to her. While he was busy writing material for the new group, he decided to construct a ballad and name it "LaRue." Anxiously, he chose one night to take her out to the beach at Santa Monica. He brought along his trumpet and "with the beach and the ocean as the background for him playing," he performed the ballad for her. Then, he asked her "will you marry my music and me?" The night and the music were so special and personal to him that he never even considered recording the ballad. LaRue accepted, and then the couple was compelled to make wedding plans in the midst of all the problems associated with organizing the new group.

Sonny Stitt had by then left the group. (LaRue believed that one reason for his departure was "an ego problem with Sonny. . . . I don't think Sonny *could* be a side man. I think he had to be the star, and of course with Max and Sonny, I don't think that would have worked out very well at all.") Teddy Edwards had replaced him, and the band was rushing to get ready for the Gene Newman concert/live recording date in Pasadena. Despite the change in personnel and the time constraints, the April date worked out well. When the reviews of the recording came out, the musicians had to be pleased. "Despite poor recording quality and some heavy-handed editing of the tenor sax and piano solos,"[5] wrote one critic, "these sides give a clear indication of the excitement that the team of Brown and Roach could spark. 'All God's Chillun Got Rhythm' showcases Brownie's seemingly inexhaustible stream of ideas at a rapid tempo, and features one of Max Roach's fiery yet melodic drum solos. Unfortunately the solos of both Teddy Edwards and Carl Perkins have been edited to a chorus each. 'Tenderly' is Clifford's solo vehicle, and the mood is very similar to his already famous treatment of 'Once in a While' on the earlier Birdland album. 'Sunset Eyes' is an original composition of Teddy Edwards, and the tenor saxophone finally gets a chance to stretch out a little. The final cut from this concert is 'Clifford's Axe,' a medium-tempo swinger based on 'The Man I Love' changes. This one is Clifford all the way, sparked by Max's sympathetic yet forceful support. 'Clifford's Axe' gives notice of exciting things to come."

The next Gene Norman concert would not occur until August 30, but by then Brown and Roach had created great interest in their group.

The month of April also brought welcome publicity. Nationally known jazz writer Nat Hentoff had interviewed Clifford Brown for a feature in *Down Beat.* The piece came out in April and contained a careful biographical account of his activities up until that time. Hentoff was very generous with his praise, captioning the piece, "Clifford Brown—the New Dizzy." Brownie related the story of his father buying him a trumpet at thirteen, the teaching of Boysie Lowery, college, praise from Charlie Parker, the Lionel Hampton tour, and his recording career up till then.

He also made an interesting statement about a new "atmosphere" in jazz players. "A long time you weren't anywhere if you weren't hung on something, but now the younger guys frown on anyone who goofs. There's a different feeling now. You can notice how things are cleaning up." Here Brownie comments on this explosive issue in his usual quiet manner. For years he had seen the effect of drugs on his contemporaries. In Philadelphia with Charlie Parker, on the road with Chris Powell, and almost everywhere in the bop world, heroin use was pervasive. But Clifford Brown didn't view himself as a Messiah sent to cleanse the souls of his jazz colleagues. Indeed, he was aware that on occasion moderate indulgence could and did provide the framework for some inspired creativity—a complex process analyzed as far back as the early 1800s by English writers Samuel Coleridge and Thomas DeQuincey. For the beboppers, however, the drug life led to destruction—a lesson Brownie had most painfully experienced with the early death of Fats Navarro.

For these reasons Brown emphasized that great music and musicianship could best be achieved by hard work and vigorous personal discipline. Hence these observations in the Hentoff interview. He simply stated his views without fanfare. In the years ahead his modest, humble way of dealing with this problem would result in several prominent jazz players' quitting drugs because of his example and because they admired him so much—a sort of reversal of the Charlie Parker drug cult. In this regard, Quincy Jones declared: "Brownie had a very hard job. He constantly struggled to associate jazz, its shepherds and its sheep, with a cleaner element, and held no room in his heart for bitterness about the publicity-made popularity and success of some of his pseudo-jazz giant brothers, who were sometimes very misleading morally and musically. As a man and a musician, he stood for a perfect example and the rewards of self-discipline."[6]

Since the Hentoff interview had been conducted while Brown was still with Blakey, no notice was yet given of the new Brown-Roach group. Some reviews of Brownie's recordings were also included in the same issue of the magazine, and this resulted in even more publicity. Thus in the space of a few months, the media exposure in Europe and this new press attention in *Down Beat* had brought the name of Clifford Brown to the fore in jazz circles everywhere. He was regularly being asked for interviews, and he would soon be asked to fill out a questionnaire for Leonard Feather's *Encyclopedia of Jazz.*

LaRue recalls that the first gig at the California Club was billed as "The Max Roach Quintet featuring Clifford Brown," and that was not exactly the way coleadership billing normally read. In any case, in a few weeks, perhaps aided by the new publicity Brownie was getting, the name rapidly evolved into the "Clifford Brown–Max Roach Quintet."

Immediately after the concert at the Pasadena Civic Auditorium and the live recording, the group underwent more drastic changes. Teddy Edwards left (as he said in his interview, he was only there about two weeks), George Bledsoe left (his incident with LaRue didn't help matters), and so did Carl Perkins. But at this time something was happening in Los Angeles that could not have been more fortuitous for Brown and Roach.

Eric Dolphy, at the time a twenty-five-year-old reed player, was hosting a number of jam sessions at his home in Los Angeles. Dolphy, even then a brilliant eclectic, was experimenting with different sounds and instruments, and his jam sessions had become known far and wide as a must for black jazzers passing through the city. "Eric used to play from morning until night," said one visitor, noting that Dolphy's home had become a virtual laboratory for new ideas and players. What better place to search for talent when a new group was being formed?

Harold Land, a quiet twenty-five-year-old tenor player, was then jamming with Dolphy. Born in Texas and raised in San Diego, Land had come up to Los Angeles looking for work like everyone else and had run into Dolphy. They became very close friends, and Land became one of the steady players at the Dolphy home. Immediately after the departure of Edwards, while looking for a replacement, Brown and Roach visited Dolphy and came across Land. Harold

Land had a subtle tenor sound and a genteel personality—his meeting with Brownie was serendipitous. An intuitive, spiritual bonding developed immediately between them, and he was hired on the spot.

The marathon Dolphy sessions also included a soft-spoken bassist named George Morrow from Pasadena. Despite his considerable talent, it seems his tireless work ethic and understated personality had as much to do with his joining the band as did anything else. With the hiring of Land and Morrow, the ideas of Clifford Brown as a leader are evident. It was thought that Roach had actually seen Land first and then brought Brownie to Dolphy's house to conduct the full audition interview. It may seem strange that Roach, the much bigger star, would defer to Brown here. But in fact it says a great deal about the respect that the drummer had for his young partner. This sense of mutual respect and commitment to the group were to carry the organization and musical standards of the new aggregation a long way.

At about the same time that all of these meetings were taking place at Eric Dolphy's house, an old New York neighbor of Max Roach's arrived in town as the pianist with the short-lived Johnny Hodges band. Roach had been a sort of boyhood ideal of Richie Powell, the younger brother of bebop pioneer Bud Powell. A persistent youngster, Richie Powell would often drop by Roach's house for drum lessons, even before Max was awake, so the story goes. Perhaps because of his annoyance at the early-hour interruptions of his sleep, Roach suggested that young Richie take up the piano. Powell proceeded to do just that, and in the spring of 1954, when he was in Los Angeles with Hodges, and Roach was looking for a pianist to replace Perkins, Powell could hardly believe his good fortune. An opportunity to play with his hero was something out of a movie. Immediately, he accepted the invitation from Roach and Brown.

Thus the classic edition of the Clifford Brown–Max Roach Quintet was born and ready to begin work. With their new musicians in tow, the leaders scurried back to the Tiffany Club and began rehearsals. As this occurred, Brownie, now continually besieged by offers of all kinds, got an important call from producer Richard Bock over at Pacific Jazz. Bock had stood in line with producers from

Europe to California eager to get Brown to record for their respective labels. So, despite his upcoming wedding and all of the business of organizing, rehearsing, and writing for the new group, Brownie decided to make a commitment to Bock. In addition to the Pacific Jazz offer, the people at Mercury Records' EmArcy label were trying to bring the group into a studio as quickly as possible.

It was decided that Clifford and LaRue would marry on her birthday, June 26. Mrs. Anderson had some input into the wedding plans. LaRue was her only child, and she naturally had definite ideas about her daughter's wedding. Because LaRue was Catholic and was connected to a parish in Los Angeles, her parish priest made special arrangements because of the time constraint. An additional wedding would eventually take place in Boston, of all places. "I'm much married," said LaRue, recalling this happy time.

Clifford Brown's family at 1013 Poplar Street back in Wilmington was not exactly happy about these events. When Clifford telephoned his parents to tell them he was getting married, Estella became upset. Brownie had been with Ida Mae for a long time, and Estella heartily approved of her. From the very onset they were not receptive to this idea of their son's marriage to a "California girl" whom they had never even met. All sorts of suspicions arose as to who she was and what her motivations were. As LaRue recalled, "there was quite a little scene over the telephone when he called back home." It was also necessary to tell Ida Mae. This task would not be as difficult, because the couple had already become distant. Ida Mae was concerned enough to make a trip to California, however. When she arrived, she never even saw Brownie but "enjoyed meeting a lot of great people."

Despite the objection of his parents ("It didn't stop him," said LaRue), the wedding went off as planned. The "Mrs. Anderson" wedding occurred first, followed by a "champagne" wedding. The latter term is used to refer to the June 26 affair, which also doubled, predictably, as a jazz party. It was hosted by the musicians, and, according to LaRue, there were actually two bands. One featured "Red Norvo, Tal Farlow and Red Mitchell, and the other Roach, Morrow, Powell, Land and, of course, the bridegroom." The champagne wedding was held amid familiar musical surroundings at The Tiffany Club. There are some good photos of the event that reveal it as a happy time for the bride and groom.

As noted previously, when Brownie had asked LaRue to marry him, he said if she accepted she would also be marrying his music. Consequently, LaRue was not surprised to find herself smack dab in the middle of the music business before she finished eating her wedding cake.

One of the hallmarks of success in any art form is unequivocal determination. The British historian Thomas Carlyle once defined genius as "the infinite capacity to take pains." There are many other definitions, of course, but from the start Brown-Roach set a standard in this regard. They had a concept, had the energy and determination to actualize this concept, and had the necessary business savvy to market their music in the best way possible. And, of course, they had brilliant talent.

Once they had their musicians, the identity of the group had to be preserved at all costs. Acting almost as if they were lawyers at a mortgage closing, Brown and Roach obtained their record contracts and began diligently planning how to best execute the terms.

Brownie had to fulfill his commitment to Dick Bock at Pacific Coast Jazz Records. All during the spring of 1954, Clifford Brown had become intensely preoccupied with composing. Among the scattered pieces that he had written, he chose two for the initial record date with Pacific Coast Jazz: "Daahoud" (the Arab name for David) and "Joy Spring." The concept, or at least the title, for the former had perhaps taken form in Algeria the previous fall. As for the latter, it has always been de rigueur to suggest that Brownie's greatest source of joy in that spring was meeting LaRue. The Pacific Coast record date would contain two other Brownie tunes.

Bock had chosen Jack Montrose, a reputable West Coast arranger, to write material for the session. The group would consist of a front line of four horns—trumpet, trombone, tenor and baritone saxes—and rhythm. Montrose recalled the circumstances: "Art Pepper and I had a group that was playing opposite Brown and Roach at the Tiffany Club. For a couple of weeks there, I would go to his

[Brownie's] hotel room[7] during the day and go over his tunes, and then we'd play at night." Initially, Montrose constructed charts on four Brown tunes—"Daahoud," "Joy Spring," "Tiny Capers," and "Bones for Jones." At that point Montrose was prodded by Bock to write arrangements for "Blueberry Hill" and "Gone With the Wind." Montrose recalled that Brownie was not happy with these two insertions, "so I had to make something good out of them."[8] Montrose faced a further challenge. Brown's improvisational approach reflected the rapid-fire bebop style of America's East Coast players. By 1954, though, a well-defined West Coast style of jazz had also developed that emphasized a relaxed, subdued sound. Montrose thought there might be problems. "It [the West Coast sound] wasn't the kind of thing he'd been into—everything he'd played had more fire. But his tunes were terrific, and everybody was surprised by how warm he was. I think he was less hung up by the style than by the fact he'd never played with those musicians before. But he got over that. It was really a happy date."

LaRue also had apprehensions: "This was something so totally different from anything that he had ever done or would do again. I always thought it was strange that he could go into the studio during the daytime and play the kind of music that came out of Pacific Jazz and at night turn around and play something totally different with Max."

The musicians recruited for the date were indeed totally new to Brownie: Stu Williamson on trombone and vibes, Zoot Sims on tenor, Bob Gordon on baritone sax, Russ Freeman on piano, Joe Mondragon on bass (replaced on the second date in August by Carson Smith), and the quintessential West Coast drummer Shelly Manne.

"Daahoud" is the first tune of the session, and the emphasis from the outset is on crisp performances. The Montrose horns are neatly harmonized, punctually spaced and well rehearsed. Brown's opening chorus is carefully understated (with a small clam), and with trademark triple-tonguing as usual. Sims, Williamson, and Freeman follow. The fours are traded between the entire horn choir and Manne. Montrose's presence is felt throughout, and, if Brownie felt uncomfortable, it certainly doesn't show. A nicely arranged performance of one of his favorite compositions—always a rewarding experience for a young composer.

"Finders Keepers" is a Montrose composition done in a classic West Coast medium swing tempo. Manne's brushes keep the emotions carefully understated. Brownie's solo is once again an easy, swimming exercise—but hardly challenging. The West Coast formula is deeply etched here. Sims follows with a solo, and then we are immediately taken back to the horn choir and the Montrose sound. No drum solo.

"Joy Spring" has Clifford Brown playing the first half of the melody, with the horns sharing the release. His solo is initially more adventurous, with some initial doubling to start off with, but he then settles into the smooth West Coast style. Gordon gets his first licks in—a short chorus, and we go back to the head.

Jack Montrose had spent a great deal of time with Clifford Brown in the spring of 1954. "I had been playing with Art Pepper at the Tiffany Club on the same bill with Max and Clifford,"[9] recalled Montrose. "During the time we spent together it seemed like the horn was in his mouth all the time. He was always dedicated and committed and always so disciplined at a time when heroin was a badge of merit among musicians he never smoked or drank or did any drugs."

Montrose was amazed that Brown was utilizing "sophisticated chord changes that were not invented yet." As he constructed the chart on "Joy Spring," Montrose lowered the key to E♭ because he enjoyed Brownie's lower register improvisations. When Brown stepped up to play the arrangement, he was surprised at the key change. Seeing this, Montrose quickly suggested that they record the piece later on, but Brownie said, "No problem, let's do it in this key," and that's how the record was made. Montrose became a fan of Brown's compositional creativity, noting the half-tone change in the second eight-bar sequence of "Joy Spring." In "Daahoud," written in E♭ minor, Montrose noted the proliferation of minor sevenths that push the melody into new directions.

Montrose had spent a great amount of time with Chet Baker in

California. He compared him to Clifford Brown: "Chet would play a lot of wrong notes when he improvised but in Brownie's improvisations all the notes were correct—like they were written down by Beethoven."

Several things were accomplished in the West Coast session. Clifford Brown's compositional ideas were given exposure; a crackerjack arranger made them come alive; and Brown's ears got an interesting education. Lastly, his ability to be a complete player was given a big test.

Ten
Brown
and Roach, Inc.

The month of August 1954 brought about the flowering of the Clifford Brown–Max Roach Quintet. With the personnel completed and Brownie's new compositions in place, the time was ripe to record the new group and to develop plans for touring with it. With unbounded energy, the musicians launched into the recording studio. There would be seven sessions (including the second Pacific Jazz date) in less than two weeks.

On Monday, August 2, the band walked into Capitol Recording Studios at EmArcy Records and recorded three tunes. The first, "Delilah," is a Victor Young composition from the score of the movie "Samson and Delilah." In keeping with the Middle Eastern flavor of the tune, Roach uses mallets for the opening theme—a haunting minor-keyed melody played by a muted Brown with a Land countermelody. The intro is a vamp begun by Morrow. This vamp approach would quickly become a trademark of the new group. During the first bridge, Land's intonation truly captures the mood of the piece. While Brownie's solo utilizes the upper register in sharp contrast to the saxophone, Richie Powell's first recorded solo with the group is a minimalist single-lined affair in keeping with the theme. Brown and Land then do the trades with Roach. His tom-toms are well-tuned, and he plunges in medias res into his drum signature.

The mallets are used for a full chorus by Max, and then the haunting out chorus returns, ending on an oriental trill.

In choosing "Delilah" for their first session, the band is making an immediate statement. Their music would strive for innovative design. Careful thought would be given to composition, interpretation and execution. There would never be extended improvised choruses thrown into the date merely to fill up the time.

"Delilah" was an important milestone for the band. When people hear it, they immediately think of Brown-Roach. To the end of his days it remained Dizzy Gillespie's favorite Clifford Brown piece. Indeed, every time he watched the group perform, which was often, he asked for it.

If it isn't the definitive instrumental recording of the tune, then Harold Land's rendition of "Darn That Dream" is pretty close. Incorporating the smoky subtoned legacy pioneered by Ben Webster, Land presents this famous ballad with deep lyrical feeling. The sensuality of his lower register whispers is superbly delivered. This performance of a great jazz ballad has long stood as one of the best by any tenor man in the genre.

Richie Powell's legendary brother Bud had composed a brilliant piece called "Parisian Thoroughfare" a few years previously to commemorate his hiatus in France. With imaginative energy the band once again introduces the tune with a vamp, borrowed cleverly from Gershwin's *An American in Paris*. The rhythm captures the busy streets of Paris, and Clifford Brown's trumpet blares out the sounds of the traffic, with a reference to the *Marseillaise*. Acknowledging their new tenor man, the band starts off with a Land solo followed by Brownie, who doubles passages as he rolls merrily along. Powell provides a quote from "The Mexican Hat Dance" in the bridge, followed by a chorus from Roach. The coda returns to the Gershwin vamp, the band plays another chorus, returns again to the vamp, and fades.

The three tunes are all performed in one take, and it is certainly not an overstatement to say that the careful preparation resulted in a historic session. The pieces stress subtlety, economy of improvisation, and crafted understatement.

The next morning, the quintet was back again in the Capitol

studios. Their initial effort was the very first recording of Duke Jordan's "Jordu," which has since become a jazz standard. The melody is harmonized with Brown and Land. Brownie's solo utilizes bluesy doubling and strong scale work, with a typically warm tone. Land follows with some doubled figures, then relaxes into the medium swing tempo that had begun to characterize the quintet's preference. Powell's solo work is smoother than in the previous session as he quotes "Billy Boy." Again Brown and Land share the trades with Roach's tom-toms. One of Brownie's four-bar sequences is a rapid-fire lick that would be heard many times again; after Roach takes a chorus, the horns return to the head. Critic Dan Morgenstern has called this the definitive performance of "Jordu," which is remarkable considering all the outstanding groups who have since recorded this standard.

Max Roach's drum rolls the group into "Sweet Clifford," a Brown script based on "Sweet Georgia Brown" changes. A blazing tempo is set as first Land solos, followed by Brownie starting with some initially choppy runs that evolve into longer phrases. Powell begins by quoting "Popeye," and then Roach flies into high gear with a huge flourish. The trades follow and then an abrupt out. The next cut is a brief interlude with a Clifford Brown solo in what is an incomplete alternate take, once again exploring very different ideas.

After this, the session turns to Victor Young's standard "Ghost of a Chance." The ultimate take is abruptly halted with someone shouting, "That's the wrong tempo!" So the master commences at a slightly slower pace. Brownie's balladeering is splendid, especially the punctuation that takes place at the last four bars of the melody. A doubled chorus follows containing playful, yet natural lines. His feeling for the old standby reflects great maturity that has impressed critics ever since.

After a day off (from recording but certainly not from rehearsal), the group returned to Capitol on Thursday, August 5. It would be a day of standards, beginning with "Stompin' at the Savoy." The melody, halved between Brown and Land, starts things off in an easy swinging tempo. They play with exactly the same volume, and the sound is that of one horn rather than two. Brown's low register subtone quality makes his horn sound so much like a saxophone that this single sound effect is a predictable result. Land's solo is superbly creative, followed by Richie Powell in a quiet vein. Ira Gitler was impressed with Brownie's "sculpting long, unbroken beautiful lines that demonstrate a mastery of breathing with the horn"[1] in his solo. A walking bass by Morrow and out on the major seventh.

Before he left the group, Sonny Stitt had worked out an interesting approach to "I Get a Kick Out of You." Originally conceived by Thad Jones, the tempo alternates between $3/4$ and $4/4$ time with both rubato and rhythm figures. The $3/4$ idea is one that the group would explore again and eventually make a trademark. Brown's initial up tempo solo is a bit muddy at first, but he settles nicely into the changes later on. Land is confident at the tempo and wails through his solo effortlessly, while Powell halves the tempo initially, accomplishing little; he is followed by a melodic Max Roach, who plays almost as many notes as his pianist. The alternate take contains a more articulate Brownie solo of considerably greater length. Powell mentions "shave and a haircut" with some triteness, but Roach works out some more imaginative melodic figures as he zooms into mid-air once again.

Richie Powell has an opportunity to play without the horns in a trio cut of "I'll String Along with You." His playing is an unusual departure from his single note line approach and features heavily chorded patterns with intriguing flourishes.

The next day, August 6, the group began with "Joy Spring" and a solo by Clifford Brown (following Land) that has been critically acclaimed as one of his best. It is a lower register affair with that saxophone subtone quality. Richie Powell feels very comfortable here in this tempo, and the trades with Roach's brushes preserve the classy mood of the tune. Once again the unison sound of the horns on the head is the hook that will always identify this group. The alternate take sees Brownie take a very different direction—brighter, double-figured, and played at the top of the horn. It is a beautiful solo, but he obviously decided on the darker, softer feel of the first take. Indeed, this choice is a metaphor for his whole approach at this time. The search is for new vocabulary, always with emphasis on cohesiveness and design.

The next seven takes are all of "Mildama," a drum tour-de-force for Max Roach. The piece is divided into three parts. There is a free rhythm opening, then a pulsed pattern and a finale that climaxes big. Each segment has horn interludes that provide the same contrast to the percussion that the percussion would normally provide in a traditional tune. Roach wrote this piece, and it is perhaps his most important effort to explore the melodic-harmonic possibilities of his drums. The Max Roach music of the last twenty years or so has sought, at times, to embellish this idea by creating new percussion melody compositions.

The reissue edition of these seven takes of "Mildama" contains comments between Max Roach and the engineer that are often intriguing.

The standard "These Foolish Things" is for George Morrow. Bass melody performances were not favored by record producers, but democracy is certainly the rule of thumb with Brown-Roach, and the tune gives us a chance to hear Morrow uncluttered. His conservative low register approach reveals him to be a player happy with his singularly supportive role. A playful reference to "Holiday for Strings" reveals his sense of irony.

"Daahoud" is once again brought out, this time, of course, without the multihorned arrangement of the Pacific Jazz date. Clifford Brown's opening solo is beautifully, clearly spoken. Richie Powell's left hand is confident, and Harold Land is happy working through the changes. Again, solo time is limited for everybody. In the alternate take Brownie's solo is not quite as fluid, but the ideas are more adventurous. Once again, short and sweet. Delicious.

Predictably, after this session's playback, the producers began to drool. Like their colleagues at Crescendo and Pacific Jazz, the EmArcy brass were like kids in a toy store. As they jumped around with glee, somebody suggested a large jam session format, to include other Mercury jazz players. "Okay, let's do it," they all shouted, and so it went. Although not originally scheduled, the first jam session was slotted in a few days later on Wednesday, August 11. West Coasters rounded up included altoists Herb Geller and Joe Maini, together with tenorman Walter Benton alongside Brownie. The rhythm section had pianist Kenny Drew and bassist Curtis Counce alongside Max Roach. This studio jam was first issued as "Best Coast Jazz" and later as "Clifford Brown All-Stars," although he was never dubbed the leader.

The first effort finds the band rehearsing for the blues number "Coronado," with Max Roach in the middle of a solo. The exchanges between the horns sound like musical chairs after a while. They proceed from eights to fours to twos and then ones. One of the most unusual dialogues of its kind, the take ends abruptly with conversation. It is then followed by an alternate take of 17:56. The solos are as follows: Joe Maini—a rollicking but limited exploration in the middle of the alto with some triplet-playing; Clifford Brown—a leap into new blues territory with some swinging sequences on each twelve-bar chorus; Herb Geller—nicely spaced lines played within a medium range framework; Walter Benton—work in the upper register for this Texas stylist without the big sound. Kenny Drew's stride references are the look into the past. His blues consciousness is the most authentic of any of the musicians on the date. Curtis Counce plays a very melodic bass and works well with Drew. Roach's solo is quite interesting as he strays from his bebop style and reaches into the past. Snares play an important role. The trades follow again with the descending bar progression as the first fragment.

The master take is even longer—19:43. It is clear that the producers were wearing their "Jazz at the Philharmonic" faces hoping to reach that mass of jazz fans who scream for lots of notes, long solos, and rhythmic explosions. After all, Norman Granz had earned big payoffs for himself and his players.

Despite the artistry of Brown and Roach in this session, the sheer length of the pieces removes any feeling of drama or subtlety. The long jam session is directly opposed to the kind of music that Brown and Roach wanted to play, so they were very uncomfortable on the date. The session goes right for the gut without pausing at the brain. It is important, however, that we have these sessions because they act as a foil to the other EmArcy releases, which are so finely crafted.

After the blues that never ends, we go in the other direction. Kenny Drew begins "You Go to My Head" with an appealing theme and variations solo that leads to Joe Maini's alto solo. Maini is more inventive on the ballad than he was in the blues. Walter Benton follows with a nicely phrased example of his rarely heard ballad work. Herb Geller is next and enjoys Drew's comping—playing a variety of rhythm changes in his solo. Brownie's solo is particularly enjoyable. The softness of that horn just seduces. However, egged on by Roach, Brown is forced to double things. It is as if the producers are in the control room urging the players to s-t-r-e-t-c-h out the tune as long as they can. It goes on for 17:13!

The next marathon is "Caravan." It goes along endlessly for 15:10. By this time the album is beginning to sound like music by the yard. Once again, Joe Maini solos first (it was as impressive as anything he had done thus far), followed by Walter Benton. The tempo is way up there, but the tenor does well. Herb Geller enters in the (by now) familiar horn solo sequence. Clifford Brown's sequence is necessarily long-lined, but naturally he is up to the task. In the third chorus he clusters notes in short bursts and ties the clusters together with strategic spacing, aided by Max Roach. Drew's solo is adequate but repetitive. Roach's solo begins with an interesting tom-tom figure and develops from there, visiting some familiar melodic territory. He continues for awhile (the producers were probably in the control room urging for more). The trades are simple exchanges, and then the band returns to the head. Of all the marathon numbers, this "Caravan" master is by far the best.

The band did an alternate take, but all that remains is a Brownie solo that goes on for a time. The Clifford Brown phenomenon was so contagious, however, that producers actually issued this clipped solo on a Time LP and titled it "The Boss Man." It is a wonderful solo, and we are fortunate to have it.

The last entry on this day would be "Autumn in New York." Actually the tune celebrates all the seasons as it drones into winter, spring, and even summer for 21:35! Brownie's smoky attack is, how-ever, once again magnificent. Actually all the solos are well wrought, but the length . . . !

It is notable that the ballads offer more than the up tempo material in this jazz-for-money extravaganza. Here at least individual styles are more easily discernible and the cacophony departs. Herb Geller's tone is the closest to Paul Desmond's silky tone as that of any altoist of the time, but he surely must set some kind of longevity record for ballad solos.

Clifford Brown went back to Pacific Coast Jazz on the twelfth or thirteenth to finish up the album he had begun a few weeks before. This session would be important because Brownie would record two of his own compositions, "Bones for Jones" and "Tiny Capers," along with two standards.

Jack Montrose's chart on "Gone With the Wind," written as be-fore with his trademark horn choir harmony, begins the session. The personnel remain the same, with the exception of Carson Smith on bass. Brownie's solo is carefully fitted into the Montrose formula. An alternate take of this tune was discovered in 1997 but has yet to be reissued.

"Bones for Jones" is a lush medium swing tune, with Montrose's chart giving vitality to Brown's melody. The trumpet solo has ex-cellent turnback sequences at the end of the bridge and chorus. Zoot Sims plays simple lines on his short solo, as does Russ Freeman.

On "Blueberry Hill," Montrose makes use of some 3/4 phrases as he reconstructs the head rhythm. The ease of the Montrose-created sound is particularly echoed in Williamson's trombone solo and Bob Gordon's excellent baritone. Brown is the solo star, but the arrange-ment gets cobilling.

"Tiny Capers," Brown's next tune, uses a fugue treatment that proves a perfect instrumental response to his melodic ideas. Brownie gets the first solo, followed by Sims (an intriguing chorus), and then Russ Freeman, who brilliantly reconstructs the tune. Back to the head (really the most interesting of the Montrose treatments on Brown) and out. A shorter alternate take, with an excellent Brownie solo and some lovely lines by Sims, is also recorded.

The EmArcy producers had another jam session scheduled for Saturday, August 14. This time they would have a live audience present, and the session would feature blues queen Dinah Washington, whose career was then at a peak. She had significant clout with her producers and, according to Junior Mance, the pianist on the date, "wanted to do something different." Mance recalled an intensive catering effort with bar, buffet, and V.I.P. invitations given "to fifty people or so but to us it sounded like 50,000."[2] Clark Terry also remembered the setup: "At this point it [the jam session] had been advertised as one of the first of those audience kinds of dates. They sold tickets. In fact they were sold out. The tickets were printed and the people who were performing the date were printed on the tickets, and my name wasn't on there because I wasn't expected."[3]

Clark Terry had met Clifford Brown before. "We were very fond of each other. As a matter of fact, he used to call me Big Brother. I don't know why." At the time of the jam session, Terry was with the Duke Ellington band, "and we pulled into the Adams Hotel, which is where the Watkins Hotel was . . . it's the hotel where all of the traveling musicians stay in Los Angeles. As the bus pulls in front of the hotel, the Queen [Dinah] is hanging out the window." As they exchanged happy hellos, Washington informed Terry that she was recording that night and asked Terry to join her. He agreed, and this spur-of-the-moment arrangement is why his name was not on the tickets or preconcert publicity. The producers had signed on the entire Brown-Roach quintet plus Maynard Ferguson, Herb Geller, Junior Mance, Keter Betts, and Dinah Washington. Clark Terry got his name in the liner notes, and that was certainly the most important citation of all. It was billed as the "All-Star Live Jam Session," and to the delight of the producers there was enough music to fill two LPs—*Jam Session* and *Dinah Jams*.

The atmosphere was friendly. "It was a small studio, but it was packed,"[4] said Clark. "And Brownie was there, and he said, 'Hey, Big Brother.' We decided to do whatever she was doing and we'd just play one, two, three right behind the other (the trumpets, that is). I said, 'Let me play first, so I can get the hell out of the way.'"

Clifford Brown's bride, LaRue, was in the audience and had these thoughts: "I remember when he did the jam session. . . . He was so happy because he was playing with these giants. He was playing with Clark Terry and Maynard Ferguson! He kept saying, 'I won't be able . . . ' and he was in awe of them. He asked Dinah, 'Do you really want me to do this?' and she said, 'You're going to save me!' He said, 'Well, you know, I've got to do this because I'm under contract and you're under contract. But do you *want* me to do this? She looked at him and said these famous words, which I'd better not say . . . listen to that record sometime. You'll see where Clifford was in awe of Maynard Ferguson and Clark Terry and you will hear how he came out on the album.'"[5] LaRue's comments are interesting because, despite Ferguson's work with Kenton, he was hardly a trumpet star in 1954. But Brownie's humble comments sound typical of him.

Producer Bob Shad introduced the musicians. "What Is This Thing Called Love?" kicks off with a short solo by Herb Geller, followed by the first crisp Clark Terry solo. Maynard comes next, followed by Land with a nice long-lined affair interrupted by trumpet sequences. Brownie starts in the upper range and plays a soft solo, followed by Geller, who takes many choruses. Next comes a Ferguson offering, and then Max Roach follows with a crowd-pleaser. Finally, Richie Powell enters with some curious opera quotes.

Dinah Washington next sings a rhumba-rhythmed "I've Got You Under My Skin." It evolves into a swing piece when Terry enters for the second chorus, followed by Maynard and then Brown. The trumpets then exchange four-bar phrases—a hot sequence that ends abruptly with Washington returning for a rubato chorus that eventually leads back to the rumba tempo, and then the group goes out.

Dinah Washington then sings "No More," a relatively obscure ballad, with Clifford Brown's muted trumpet in the background.

"Move" starts its head out with the trumpets playing in unison. Then Clark Terry plays his little rolling lines. The tempo creeps up as Harold Land roars in with a multinoted extravaganza all over the horn. Maynard Ferguson follows, and by now his high register showmanship is standard operating procedure. A bass solo that sounds like Morrow is next. Herb Geller keeps the pace hot—Maynard returns with upper register sizzles—Roach flies in with a spectacular snare display—Powell returns for more quotes, and then the three trumpets hit the head and go out. Bob Shad says, "Let's do it over," as the crowd applauds.

Harold Land's velvet tenor introduces "Darn That Dream," playing a double-time chorus and then leading the rhythm section back home. Washington sings a chorus next with the trumpets playing harmony underneath. It is a memorable performance.

Dinah Washington starts out with rubato on "You Go to My Head." The next chorus sees the rumba rhythm returning with Dinah and the rhythm section. The soloists begin in a swing four—first Geller, then Mance with a piano solo. Terry's trumpet follows with a bare bones sequence that is refreshing, then Land enters the fray with some of his poetry. Brownie slides in with a triple-phrased array that is followed by Keter Betts, who stops in mid-phrase so that Dinah can come to the bridge, which she does rubato. Then the final section in rumba tempo and out. Applause.

Junior Mance then begins a ballad medley with "My Funny Valentine." The tune segues into "Don't Worry 'Bout Me," with Clark Terry at the helm. It ends in a playful quote of "Symphony Sid," getting a laugh from the audience. Herb Geller enters with "Bess, You Is My Woman Now." There is an applause segue, and then Clifford Brown takes center stage with "It Might As Well Be Spring." It is performed splendidly, and many of critics place it at the top of the list in his live ballad performances. The ballad medley proved to be a good idea. The EmArcy producers had a sense of performance and taste here.

Dinah Washington returns with the rhythm section and a swinging tempo in "Lover, Come Back to Me." At the beginning of the second chorus the horns enter—Clark Terry in his usual first solo spot. Harold Land, who takes second place to no one in these sessions, comes next, followed by Clifford Brown. After the bass solo, Geller takes the spotlight in one of his better efforts of this session. Maynard typically soars into the ionosphere, followed by Roach and Powell. Dinah returns for a couple of choruses, and everybody roars at the end.

Next the ballad medley format returns, introduced by Land with "Alone Together." His bottom notes are once again delivered so delicately one could hear the proverbial pin drop in the studio. Mance segues and vamps until Maynard's clarion sound enters with "Summertime." After the first chorus, he follows with notes that reach the ceiling and beyond. The audience gasps and then roundly applauds the king of the high C's. Dinah enters with "Come Rain or Come Shine," does a chorus, and the medley is over. Or is it? A brief pause and she floats into "Crazy He Calls Me." Her phrasing is flawless, and the mood she creates in these ballads is magical. Geller follows her, and the reverb is cranked up a bit. It is one of the many instances of uneven programming throughout the day. Dinah returns with Junior Mance and ends the tune flirting with the band. She then says, "I know a good one—'No Greater Love'--come on, Junior Mance," then does a short version of the standard.

With a mambo rhythm intro, Washington jumps into "I'll Remember April." Clifford Brown then takes a chorus, working a long-lined solo through the changes. The solo is a harbinger of a definitive performance of the tune that he would play at a later date. Land follows, and then Maynard steps in, and the microphone levels are lowered a bit. Roach's solo is a relatively subdued one, followed by a nice bit of playing by Mance. Geller comes on the scene, and then the trumpets, a bit uncertainly, exchange throughout the next chorus. The ending is a bit of a train wreck, but the audience likes it. The producer asks "Shall we wrap it up?" and that's it.

For saxophonist Herb Geller, the recording sessions of this August week had fulfilled a dream. He had become a Brown enthusiast back in 1952 and later attended many of the Atlantic City jam sessions, where he actually taped Brownie's solos "with a Webcor wire recorder."[6] He remembered saying to Russ Freeman (who had been working with Chet Baker), "I want you to listen to this incredible trumpet player," and then, even having to listen to the chopped-up sound of the primitive recorder, they sat awestruck at Clifford Brown's technique. In 1953, when Geller was working with Billy May's band at the Steel Pier, he frequently strolled over to the late night jams to hear Brownie. "That's when we became friends," said

Geller. "He would phone up and ask about chord structures on certain tunes, and I remember how polite and focused he was. I also became impressed with his clean living habits—no smoking, no drinking." But above all, said Geller, he admired Brownie's playing. "His playing was so consistent. I *never* heard anything bad, ever."

Ten months later, by the time Clifford Brown came to California to team up with Max Roach, Geller had a firm arrangement with Mercury records and was doing the studio work. "Miles Davis had hitched a ride out to L.A. with Max," said Geller, "and soon Max was playing frequently at Howard Rumsey's Lighthouse. When Brownie arrived, I kept running into him, and we continued the phone calling that we did back east. I remember a party at Max's house one day where a lot of people were hanging out smoking, drinking, and gossiping. Brownie was very shy at those gatherings, but a funny thing happened. Max had a set of vibes that he was trying to learn, and Brownie went over to them and picked up two mallets and started to play. I had seen him pick up many different instruments on occasion, but I was amazed when, after a while, he began playing the vibes with four mallets! Actually, Max got angry because he had tried to play the vibes, and here was Brownie playing so well at the party." Geller vaguely remembered a big band date with Hal Mooney's orchestra that Brownie played in, but the only jazz recording date that he and Brownie did together were the August sessions.

The pace slackened a bit for Brown and Roach after the Dinah Washington jazz jam. The group returned to their rehearsals, and the leaders made touring plans, once their records were pressed and on their way to the record stores.

During the short breaks between recording dates and jam sessions, Clifford finally had time to share with LaRue. She remembered: "We had puzzles where we would do the mathematical equations and do the musical equations, and they would come out the same, you know? This was wonderful because of my being a classical musician and not thinking that he knew how to play this music anyway; this was wonderful! And then we came across a Bach invention, and he sat down and he wrote out the parts based on a mathematical equation, and would you believe the darn thing came out the same way? He loved math, and he loved music, and he found the common denominator."[7]

On Friday, August 20, the band played for a Norman Granz Jazz à la Carte concert at the L.A. Shriner Auditorium with its 10,700 seats. The group would rarely play at such huge concert halls, and indeed, the size of such halls would always work against the intimacy needed for the small sound of many jazz groups.

As the month drew to a close, the Browns could break out and celebrate again. On August 25, *Down Beat* came out with the results of its famous critics' poll. The vote placed Clifford Brown fourth in the trumpet standings, behind Dizzy Gillespie, Louis Armstrong, and Roy Eldridge. In addition, the critics voted him the new star of the year in the trumpet category. Thus, in the space of one year, he had gone from virtual oblivion to a seat on the high altar of jazz. It was certainly a time to relax and enjoy the laurels. But as we have seen time and again, Brownie was never comfortable basking in the sunlight. There would always be work to do, and this time it was for Gene Norman.

The group still had a recording commitment for their original producer, so, on August 30, they hiked up to Crescendo Records for the very last recording session of the summer. By now they had developed a book, and for this session they simply picked four tunes that had become part of the repertoire. On "Jordu," Brown and Land solo energetically, and the group unity is stronger than ever. On "Parisian Thoroughfare," Land really outdoes himself with one of his more successful efforts. The group has certainly worked all the kinks out of "I Get a Kick Out of You" and glides over the music. "I Can't Get Started" has a good Brownie solo, but he doesn't seem to have as good a feel for the tune as he had for other ballads. Maybe because of its myriad associations with trumpeters through the years, the song had lost some of its appeal for him.

The band felt tested and ready. Now, at the end of August, it prepared to return east.

Eleven
Back
to the East

For the new group, planning a jazz tour represented a significant challenge. It was decided early on that the tour had to be based in the Northeast. There were many more clubs and concert halls, the press was centered there, and the coleaders had their most loyal followers there. This decision was going to be difficult for Harold Land and George Morrow, who were California residents and would be away from home for long periods.

The Clifford Brown–Max Roach Quintet was booked into the Blackhawk in San Francisco for two weeks beginning September 13. The club was one of the great homes of bebop during the period, and the positive reactions of the audiences gave the group new confidence. After this gig they flew east. Clifford and LaRue would set up housekeeping in Philadelphia, and from there it would be easier to reach the eastern and midwestern jazz meccas. The circuit they wound up following included New York, Boston, Pittsburgh, Philadelphia, Baltimore, Washington, D.C., St. Louis, Cleveland, Detroit, Chicago, Toronto, and scattered other locations.

When Clifford and LaRue arrived in Wilmington in the early fall, they had to take care of family matters. LaRue was now a part of a great extended family, so time had to be spent acclimating the Browns to their new daughter-in-law. Brownie's friends and neighbors were all eager to spend time with him—he had become quite a celebrity in the past year and the entire east side community was naturally proud of their favorite son. But, in the matter of pride, no one could outdo Joe Brown. The great dream of his life and more had been fulfilled, and his heart was full. Even with all of this recent excitement, the family continued to interact in the same way. Brownie still addressed his dad as he did when he was a toddler and behaved as if he had never left Delaware. Despite his sudden marriage, there was really no change at 1013 Poplar.

Initially, when they arrived back east, they lived with his sister Rella and her family. Soon, they would buy a duplex[1] on Samson Street and move there, and as soon as all of the normal adjustments to life as a married couple had been made, Brownie returned to his practice routine.

"His usual day was get up, practice his horn, then get on the piano and do something there," recalled LaRue. "I'm not sure what that was, but as a pianist, I had my ideas . . . I insisted he practice other things than whatever that mess was he was playing before. Then we would clean house, and we would do all the things that married people do. We would have friends over, and he loved to play Scrabble, so we would play Scrabble. The guys would go downstairs, where we had this basement fixed up with a bandstand, pool table, and shuffle boards and all this kind of stuff. We would play games, and they would jam, and we would eat, and that was his day. And then he would go back and practice some more and get ready to go to work, and that was that."[2]

In addition to these domestic activities, the Brown-Roach Quintet had to get ready for an important date—their home opener, so to speak—at the Blue Note in Philadelphia on October 29. Of course the club was packed with friends and well-wishers from all over the area, Max Roach's people from the New York area, as well as Richie Powell's family and friends.

Pianist Sam Dockery, one of the Philly jazzers, with whom Brownie had often jammed at Music City, remembered what things were like when Brown-Roach returned east in triumph. "Max became like the 'matinee idol' of the jazz world," said Dockery, "and

Clifford was the big giant. They were like pied pipers! They would come to town, and people would follow them wherever they went. Being a world-renowned trumpet player never seemed to faze Clifford one bit. It was always like that. And when he would play, people would just stand transfixed. The thing that made his playing so good was his sense of dynamics. He could build to a frenzied pitch! You would have to hear him in person to appreciate the true scope of his performing."[3]

After the gig at the Blue Note, the group picked up other important jazz club dates. Once again, the formula of record product, publicity, and live performance aided the band's success. The trick was to get the first two in generous helpings, and the third would follow. Brown-Roach's extensive recording that summer was stirring enough great interest in the eastern cities. On Tuesday, November 30, the quintet began a two-week engagement at the Crystal Lounge in Detroit. Detroit was a strong jazz town that had launched the careers of many talented local jazz players. It welcomed the band very enthusiastically, and local media was very cooperative.

Meanwhile, EmArcy records was eager to record their star trumpeter in as many settings as they could. The first in an eastern studio was set for New York on Thursday, December 16, right after Brown-Roach finished up in Detroit. This time Brownie would record with an old admirer—Sarah Vaughan—who had sought his services during the Chris Powell days.

Few success stories in American music could equal that of Sarah Vaughan in those days. The "Divine One" had scored heavily as a recording star. She waxed successful pop music (some of it bluntly commercial) for Mercury Records, but, because she would never neglect her jazz roots, she also had a deal with Mercury to record on their jazz subsidiary—EmArcy. She wanted Clifford Brown badly, and she got him. Because she was such a knowledgeable musician, Vaughan always found the best people. The arranger/conductor for the date was the redoubtable Ernie Wilkins. Along with Brown, Vaughan hired Herbie Mann on flute and Paul Quinchette on tenor. Her rhythm section at the time had Jimmy Jones on piano, Joe Benjamin on bass, and Roy Haynes on drums.

The LP starts out with a silky chart on "September Song." After Vaughan's opening chorus, a muted Brown enters playing doubled rhythm in a subdued long-lined stroll. Herbie Mann gets a brief solo, but back comes Brownie to finish up the instrumental part.

A slow-paced "Lullaby of Birdland" begins with Vaughan harmonizing the intro with the horns. After that, the rhythm section takes over, with short solos by Jones, Benjamin, and Haynes on brushes. Sarah then scats exchanges with Mann, Quinchette, and Brownie and then takes the out chorus to a harmonized end. Vaughan begins "I'm Glad There Is You" with a rubato verse that sets the rhythm at the beginning of the melody. As she sings, all we hear, in addition to the rhythm section, are soft lines from Mann, Quinchette, and a muted Brown. "You're Not the Kind" starts out with Brownie on an upbeat sequence that sets things soaring. Quinchette follows her vocal, then Mann and Brown bring up the rear with classic bop lines. Vaughan takes it out with the horns.

Two days later, December 18, the group is back to finish the LP. Initially, "Jim," a Chris Connor signature tune, gets the lounge-tempo-at-3-A.M. treatment. The horns fill up the long spaces with quiet lines. After Sarah's vocal, the lights turn up for Brownie, who livens things up with a bright-sounding chorus in double time. Vaughan comes back and takes us home, accompanied by Herbie and the rhythm. "He's My Guy" has Sarah Vaughan opening things up with rhythm, followed by an essential Paul Quinchette floater. Clifford Brown is next, with his triplets urging out big bop sounds. A short Jones solo, followed by Mann in double time, and we go back to Vaughan, the head, and out. The Yip Harburg–Vernon Duke standard "April in Paris" has Vaughan, with a rubato in her low range, opening things up. Her bottom range is not as rich as it will be twenty years later, but it is still remarkable. A slow rhythm sets in, with Jones soloing quietly. Quinchette follows at a bridge opening, and a muted Brown follows, taking the last eight. Vaughan begins another chorus, with the horns filling in to the end. Roy Haynes recalled that this tune, with its exchanges between Vaughan and Brown, still moved him after all these years. "It's Crazy" is a cutesy Dorothy Fields–Richard Rodgers tune that gets a swing treatment from Sarah Vaughan's opening chorus. Brownie follows with a chorus that pushes the feeling further. Jones solos, followed by Herbie who also swings. Quinchette brings up the rear, and the band gets looser. Vaughan returns, supported by the horns, to a dazzling seventh chord conclusion. The session ends with "Embraceable You," as Vaughan remelodizes the head with the rhythm section. The horns are quiet for this closer, which puts Sarah squarely in the spotlight where she certainly belongs.

This record date was an epiphany for Herbie Mann. Mann had first heard about Clifford in Trieste, Italy, as far back as 1949. An Army buddy, Gil Socolow, was a big jazz fan of his and said to Mann, "Wait till you hear Brownie, he sounds like nobody else."[4] Socolow hailed from Philadelphia, where Mann had played many gigs, including the Music City Jam sessions. On one of these sessions Mann recalled playing with Lee Morgan, "who was sixteen and in Bermuda shorts." When in New York Mann remembered hearing Brownie at The Bandbox with Lionel Hampton. "I didn't really hear much," said Herbie, "because he naturally didn't get much solo time in those arrangements." While in Gotham Mann had become a first call flutist for jazz record dates. "It was me and Sam Most," said Herbie. "No one else was playing jazz flute quite like us." By 1954, Quincy Jones had become a major figure on the New York recording scene and had helped Mann with several record date gigs. According to Mann, Quincy got him the Sarah Vaughan date and, at last, Mann was able to share a bandstand with Brownie. Mann recalled that the session date was very "loose," with Sarah Vaughan sitting down with her ideas and then abruptly saying to the horn players, "Paul, here's your note, Herbie, here's your note, Brownie, here's your note." The gig was a defining moment for Herbie. He said that, playing alongside Brownie was "like being on a basketball court with Michael Jordan."

What appealed to him most was Clifford Brown's great melodic sense. "I began to develop my melodic style from the trumpeters'," said Mann, "and Brownie became the conduit for this style later adapted by Lee Morgan and Freddie Hubbard." Mann adored Brown's melodic and countermelodic approach to improvisation. After Herbie began to emulate this style Steve Allen acknowledged the importance of it by telling him, "you're not just playing a chord. The reason why I love what you're doing is because you're playing melodies." In addition to this melodic innovation Mann admired his sense of spacing. "Brownie knew how to use silence," said Mann, and heaped more praise on him as he reveled in the special moments of the Vaughan record date. Later, Mann was able to catch Brown-Roach at the New York clubs, and what he saw and heard amazed him. "They were trying to figure out a way to get closer to the people," was his recollection of the group.

Only four days after Clifford Brown had recorded with Sarah Vaughan, EmArcy brought him back into the studio once more. Brownie was glad to see his old friend Quincy Jones, who had been very busy himself during the past year. For this date, Jones was conducting/arranging for a lovely blonde singer, Helen Merrill. Merrill had come to jazz via the big band route and possessed a unique dark voice–soft, smoky, and lush. The LP would feature Danny Bank on flute and baritone, Barry Galbraith on guitar, Milt Hinton on bass, Osie Johnson on drums, and once again Jimmy Jones on piano. Brownie's trumpet would be the chief solo instrument. On Wednesday, December 22, the troops assembled at the EmArcy studios in New York to cut four sides.

Milt Hinton remembered this record date as symbolic of new opportunities for black musicians. Although blacks had, of course, been widely heard on recordings for decades, the exposure had been limited to specific jazz styles and narrow repertoires that they alone could render authentic. However, in the period from 1930 to 1950 the recording industry had exploded into one of the leviathans of show business. Tens of thousands of record sessions were the order of the day in a market propelled by radio and record players. On a given day in a studio, dozens of producers would schedule time to record singles, albums, and a slew of commercials to feed the appetite of radio advertisers. A vital cog in this enormous engine was someone who became known as a "studio musician." These players were, of course, virtuosi but beyond their instrumental skills they needed one outstanding talent–sight-reading. Given this gift, musicians no longer had to live a bohemian life style; work in the studios was very steady and lucrative.

Born in 1910, Milt Hinton, despite his outstanding reading skills, had to sit on the sidelines for decades while white musicians filled the need for studio jobs. Eventually, after World War II, Hinton's great reading skills and affable personality enabled him to be "one of the first colored guys to get a chance in the studios."[5] Thus, he had done studio work at Mercury records (the parent company of EmArcy) and was a natural choice for the Helen Merrill LP. Fortunately, Hinton had met Quincy Jones years before in Seattle, and by this time Jones's writing skills had also opened studio doors for him. The Helen Merrill LP session, with Hinton, pianist Jimmy Jones, and Clifford Brown together, proves something of a milestone in the struggle to bring black musicians into steady studio jobs.

Billie Holiday's seminal ballad "Don't Explain" is the first selection on the Merrill LP. A synthesis of the lead instruments works behind her in Quincy's splendid arrangement. A muted Brownie is heard briefly in the distance. Then he removes the mute and plays a silky interlude. Merrill returns at the bridge and finishes the chorus. A soft coda and out. Barry Galbraith's guitar introduces "Born to be Blue." The tune was destined to be associated with Merrill. She steps lightly from phrase to phrase with subtle delicacy. Brown's solo follows, with some double-time work, and if he has been petal-like in his tone before, Merrill's voice encourages him even more. She comes back in at the bridge as before and takes us to a rubato final four, with a muted trumpet punctuating the ending. Cole Porter's "You'd Be So Nice to Come Home To" gets a light swing treatment from Quincy Jones. Hinton works well with Johnson's brushes (how many great dates like this would Milt do in the next forty years!), and Jones plays with the rhythm section. Brown's solo floats lightly along, continuing the mood. Danny Bank's baritone leads the horns back in to introduce Helen Merrill's last chorus. The last tune of the day is a bright-tempoed " 'S Wonderful," but Quincy Jones preserves the flavor of the date by having Johnson continue on brushes. Jones plays his feather touch solo, followed by Galbraith. Brownie's solo is multinoted and long-lined, but he plays softly as he seeks to keep things in the same vein.

In 1994, Helen Merrill did a fortieth anniversary version of this date to commemorate her association with Clifford Brown. She recalled in an interview how dreamy the first session had been despite the flurry of Christmas week activities. As a matter of fact, the final three sides of the LP were recorded on Christmas Eve, two days after the first session.

Brown leads the four-bar intro for Merrill's entrance in "Yesterdays," which starts the second record session. She sings magnificently, supported by Galbraith, Jones, and the rhythm. Her voice sustains the whole note passages with marvelous consistency—a quality so necessary in slow ballad work. Jones follows with a sparse solo, then Brownie enters, alternating doubled phrases and triplets in his solo. Oscar Pettiford has replaced Milt Hinton on this day, but there is no noticeable difference in the band sound. Merrill comes in at the bridge again—Quincy Jones certainly knew what he wanted in length. A muted Clifford Brown tags the ending. The Rodgers and Hart standard "Falling in Love with Love" is up next. As Helen Merrill launches the melody, the horns are heard in support, with the tempo up a bit. Pettiford solos once again, Brown solos, and Merrill returns, swinging beautifully slightly behind the pulse. "What's New?" would become another Merrill signature song. She phrases cleverly, injecting brief spoken passages that deliver some dramatic flair to the torchy tune. Brownie's solo doubles the time, but then he switches and plays whole notes over the doubled rhythm. Merrill's out chorus is done at practically a whisper. Jones ends the session with a celebration tonic chord.

This LP is a classical effort of collaborative art. Merrill is the perfect choice to vocalize the gently textured ballads, Brownie's subtoned innovations are given a new garden in which to grow, and Jones . . . well, Jones is simply Jones, a master arranger with all the talent in the world.

This album is also important because it set the stage for what would become Clifford Brown's best-selling LP.

The year 1955 started off in busy fashion, with the quintet's returning by popular demand to the Blue Note in Philadelphia. Once
again the group raised the rafters and kept the audiences clamoring
for more. To succeed this much in the heartland of bebop gave new
measures of confidence to the musicians who, by this time, had become like a working family.

The hype about the band had the jazz world spinning, so from
Philadelphia the group motored to Toronto. They appeared at the
Colonial Tavern for a week beginning Monday, January 10, where
the band received another overwhelming reception. Some fans there
made private tape recordings, which are now being slowly released.

By 1955, recording outstanding jazz virtuosos with strings had
become a common event. Charlie Parker, Dizzy Gillespie, and Louis
Armstrong had pioneered the tradition, and others, notably Bobby
Hackett, would enjoy great success with this format. Although Clifford Brown was only twenty-four years old, the EmArcy producers
decided to feature him this format. Brownie had now a worldwide
reputation, and his fat sound had already set new trumpet standards
for ballad playing. As they had done for the Helen Merrill LP, the
producers began wisely by obtaining a talented arranger. Neal Hefti,
a young trumpeter who had already enjoyed arranging success with
Woody Herman, among others, was the choice—and the project
could not have made a better one. Hefti would later become principal
arranger for Count Basie and Harry James and would become a
major figure in show business. He collected nine strings for the date—
six violins, two violas, and a cello—to support Brown and the Brown-
Roach rhythm section. In addition, guitarist Barry Galbraith, who
had worked out so well on the Merrill date, was called in.

After the Toronto date, the musicians scurried quickly back to
New York, where Hefti, Galbraith, and the strings had been rehearsing. On Tuesday, January 18, the group went into the EmArcy studios to begin recording the string album.

First up was "Portrait of Jenny," which proved to be a big winner.
Brownie begins with a bit more vibrato than usual, but this helps
sustain the whole notes more firmly. The rhythm is a slow four, and
the strings play the long lines of support; the mix is perfect as the

horn is strategically set off against the strings. They take over the bridge melody, and then Brown returns for a ritardando ending and brief cadenza. That's it. Short and sweet. But it would become a collector's item.

"What's New?" brings up the strings in the second four bars (a Hefti formula), with Brownie opening rhythmically. After his chorus, the strings begin the second chorus, but he returned on the second eight, and once again, a retard and out. "Yesterdays" is then resurrected. The strings use a pizzicato intro for the tune that the team had recorded on the Merrill date, and the dramatic entry of the horn on the last bar of the first eight is a delicious touch. On the second chorus the strings lay out until the last bar—a good contrast. In the last chorus, Brownie comes in with some tripping double figures, the pizzicato returns, and then it ends. "Where or When?" has the strings quoting a phrase from "Portrait of Jenny" to introduce Brown's horn. Once again his whole notes are rich, surpassing even his earlier success. The ending is another "Portrait of Jenny" reference.

In "Can't Help Lovin' Dat Man" the richness continues. Here Clifford Brown makes short crescendo changes on some whole notes. The tune is very rangy, but even in the upper register phrases he preserves the softness at all cost. In a bridge section by the strings, he plays scales over them with that same sense of balance and understatement. The length is only 3:44.

"Smoke Gets in Your Eyes" has a piano intro sans strings, which are introduced in the second eight measures. Clifford Brown all but abandons his triplets in an effort to keep things simple. Resisting all variations and embellishments, he allows the timbre of the instrument, as he plays it, to sell the tune. "Laura" begins a capella, with the horn wafting in pure sound. The subtone attack becomes so concentrated you can really hear the air coming out of Brownie's mouth. How much more air did he need to produce the dulcet sound? The trumpet theorists will have to figure it out. The sound is as fat as one can imagine. Then he plays over strong trills to an end that might be a bit unsteady.

"Memories of You" reveals that delicious column of air still accompanying the tone. There are no clipped endings at the ends of the whole notes; there is always enough breath to finish off the note properly, but is there a clam in the cadenza at the end? Jimmy Jones introduces "Embraceable You." Brown then enters, and the strings come in at the second four. Throughout, Hefti's strategic spacing and variation keeps the pace sharp—an essential ingredient in an LP of ballads. The ending gathers strings, piano, and trumpet.

An alternate melody phrase by the strings introduces "Blue Moon," and then Brownie enters with the faint echo of the piano behind him. The strings fill out the whole note measures in the third chorus, where subtle Hefti variations have just the right touch. Brown ends right in the middle of the note. "Willow Weep for Me" is begun with short violin tweaks, after which Brownie plays over the violas and cello. One or two phase attacks are slightly stronger, but the diminuendo quickly sets in lest the mood be jarred. A fade closes the tune. As he finishes the session with the difficult "Star Dust," two clams occur. They are two of three in the entire session, according to Hefti. They are more than atoned for in the sumptuous bridge that he plays over like a ballerina performing delicate entrechats.

And that's it.

The outing has become the standard trumpet-string ballad session. It is certainly the standard session by which all trumpet ballad albums should be compared. Actually, predictably, the album received a smattering of negative reviews by those critics who saw Clifford Brown as "selling out" by recording with strings. Earlier there were fatuous causes celebres raised about similar efforts by Louis Armstrong and Charlie Parker in their albums with strings, and they will certainly be made again by shortsighted purists. The fact is that in the forty-odd years since *Clifford Brown with Strings* appeared, its standard has remained sacrosanct. This album was an inspiration to many musicians; Wynton Marsalis, for one, has indicated that the LP was the reason he decided, at age twelve, to take up the trumpet.

With the completion of *Clifford Brown with Strings*, the quintet once again hit the road for the jazz club scene. There is some indication that they appeared with the Modern Jazz Quartet at Storyville in

Boston beginning on the first of February. What is certain is that they were at the club as headliners on February 11 for a gig, during which time a radio broadcast was made of their performance. Air checks of this performance have been circulated and indicate that the reception given to the group was more than generous.

It is on this trip to Boston that Clifford and LaRue were wed for the third time in a ceremony arranged by LaRue's local parish priest.

After the Boston gig the quintet motored back to New York to prepare for another recording session. All during this time (and whenever possible) Brownie, Richie Powell, and Harold Land were constantly exploring new musical ideas that could be incorporated into the Brown-Roach book. The next recording would reflect the fruit of their efforts.

As the musicians collected their manuscripts and prepared to record for EmArcy, it was decided to title the new release *A Study in Brown.*

On a cold Wednesday, February 23, the quintet convened at the EmArcy Records Capitol studios in New York.

The first selection was an ambitious construction of Clifford Brown's that was eventually dubbed "Gerkin for Perkin." Max Roach said, "This is a blues . . . the kind of thing I did a few years ago with Charlie Parker on 'Sippin' at Bells.' " The rhythm changes in the head are quite intricate, reflecting ideas that Brownie had been thinking about for a while. The composition is only 2:55 in length, which reflects a growing concern from the group for even more economy in solos.

The Land solo that starts things off in "Gerkin for Perkin" is a concentrated improvisational gem. Brown follows in fine form with a chorus of innovative ideas, and then come Powell and Roach. The head then has Brownie muted under Land for their unison melody statement. This performance is notable because of a new fluidity within the group (they had now been together for six months) and also because of Clifford Brown's compelling writing.

"Take the 'A' Train" begins with a clever introduction that has Powell and Roach simulating the sound of a subway train in Manhattan. The rhythm accelerates and leads into the head, taken at top speed. This intro is reminiscent of the kind of novelty thinking that went into the vamp of "Parisian Thoroughfare." The head is played crisply with spectacular triple-tongued articulation from Brownie. Once again, Land solos first and is marvelous. Occasionally, his work on this date eclipses that of his front-line mate. Brown's solo continues the staccato spraying of notes that will make it an object of wonder at the time of the album's release. Powell sounds stronger than ever on his solo, and then Roach exchanges with the horns, playing a unison pattern followed by a decelerando of the opening train simulation until the tune ends with his brushes coming to a stop—at 125th Street, of course.

"Land's End" is a beautiful bluesy composition that again reflects new ideas. The rhythm breaks in the opening eight bars are quite unusual. The head is shared by the horns, and then Land launches into his easy swinging solo. Brown follows with a solo of flowing doubled phrases. Powell's solo is a very comfortable affair, with his left hand lines dragging the rhythm nicely. There is no drum solo. The charming melody is repeated. An alternate take of the tune was made with another approach taken for an introduction. Land's and Brown's solos are even shorter here (this take is only 3:05 compared to the master, which is 4:54). "Land's End" is a thoughtful little piece of chamber jazz that goes a way toward achieving the group goal of a more cerebral sound. "Swingin'" is Brown's quick dash based on the changes of "I Never Knew." The fast head is a unison jump from the horns followed by a piano release. Brownie solos first, and it is vintage C.B., with a short tight explosion of notes. Another shorty from Land and then some elbow room for Powell. The horns return to exchange briskly with Roach, who jab-steps his way through his skins, the head, and then out. Few recordings in hard bop wind up "swingin'" as much as this.

The next day, the first cut is "George's Dilemma," a Clifford Brown triumph that has international flavor. Originally described by Max Roach as "a romance between Afro-Cuban and jazz rhythms," the tune resembles "A Night in Tunisia" in its structure and harmony. It begins with the percussion, followed by the bass in a fugue pattern, leading the horns in their harmonized melody statement. The melody has the haunting flavor of "Daahoud" and suggests the influence of the Hampton trip and Brownie's thoughts while there. His solo is played over the Afro-Cuban rhythm figures alternating with the straight four, and Land also does his solo work with these rhythms alternating. The piece exemplifies the new compositional and improvisitory level that immediately became a hard bop standard. Richie Powell's piano solo is also memorable.

On the standard "If I Love Again," Brown begins with a powerful break. He moves around the horn with as much dexterity as on any of the LP's solos. Land has the same success. A short solo by Powell and a chorus by Roach conclude the number. The economy of the pieces, together with the brilliant improvisations, makes a classic jazz performance.

"The Blues Walk" has a curious history. Sonny Stitt had written a blues titled "Loose Walk" that had been recorded in 1952. The idea of giving Clifford Brown credit for the title and song was evidently that of the producers. The horns provide memorable improvisation. Harold Land has never played better, and Clifford Brown goes beyond himself. Richie Powell is in absolute top form, utilizing some Horace Silver phrases with real confidence. After Max Roach takes an extended solo, during which he develops his rhythm motifs utilizing playful backbeat high-hat figures, something extraordinary occurs. Brown and Land begin a five-chorus dialogue that critic Thomas Owens says "has never been surpassed on record."[6] The first two choruses have the horns exchanging traditional four-bar sequences. Brownie works down the scale, moving from D to G. Then Land answers with his own descent, working F into a small motif and then stirringly moving down seven notes to another G. Brownie responds with his own G but at an octave higher and moving cleverly to F. This witty musical conversation continues into a third chorus, where the horns reduce their dialogue to two-measure phrases. Land responds to Brown's descents with subtle variations that lead to real drama—the fourth chorus reduces the conversation further into one-measure shouts:[7]

By the fifth chorus the trades are reduced to two-beat blips:

Because "Blues Walk" is fast paced (♩ = 260), any further dialogue would be a reductio ad absurdum, so the horns return to the head with two traditional choruses. In an alternative take of "Blues Walk" the Brown-Land dialogue continues for seven choruses, but the last three exchanges are somewhat tenuous.

On "What Am I Here For?," Land breaks his lines up a bit with some uncertainty, but Richie Powell seems to retain the confidence of "The Blues Walk." This tune was the first one recorded on February 25, the last day of the session.

"Cherokee" has received the most praise of any of the tunes played in the session, and deservedly so. No one has ever recorded this tune at this tempo with such success. In his solo, Clifford Brown achieves more than seems humanly possible at this torrid speed. The notes are naturally clipped more, but the articulation is right there. Land also rises to the task with aplomb. Powell's hands move well. Max Roach provides one of classic tom-tom displays. The Indian powwow motif in the introduction itself is a piece of jazz history.

Richie Powell's "Jacqui" swings mightily. The melody unites the horns in a parallel-third harmonic pattern that works splendidly. Brownie's solo is a wonderfully imaginative exercise in subdued articulation—a fluid gem. Land explores some curious new areas, and Powell loves his melody so much he plays a little theme and variations on his solo. Roach is superb. At the close the horns play alongside some bowed lines delivered by Morrow. Neat, classic hard bop.

"Sandu" is yet another Brownie composition whose title suggests foreign inspiration. It is a fine blues line played in a seductive medium swing. Roach and Morrow play in a sweet and quiet unison, with Max's high hat lightly stroked. It is the kind of percussive support that lead players dream of. The horn solos are tranquil, followed by Morrow's solo, which remains squarely in the bottom register. The unison horn delivery of the head is mellow and sumptuous. Another memorable performance.

"A Study in Brown" provided the group with further ammunition for its continuing tour. As the LPs of 1954 kept being released, more and more record buyers showed up at the clubs and concerts. The money was starting to come in for the musicians, but the hassle of motoring around the tour was grueling. Max Roach recalled: "There were times when we'd close in Chicago at 4 A.M., pack all our gear after working all night, and make a matinee in Philadelphia at 4 P.M.

that afternoon. We'd play from 4 until 7, have a two-hour break, and come back and play from 9 to 2 the rest of the week and do a matinee Friday and Saturday."[8]

Under such conditions it is always important for musicians traveling together to be very flexible with and tolerant of one another. This is often a difficult thing to achieve in a group of creative personalities. With Brown-Roach harmony prevailed. Harold Land recalled: "There was a camaraderie among the five of us, like a family out there together on the road. Different people said that they could really feel that when we played together, that everything was so tight. This doesn't usually happen with every group. I think it was because of that closeness and mutual respect that we had a close-knit family."[9]

For Clifford Brown this "family" existence was an extension of his own life experience. But Land also had had this kind of experience—very close family ties—so he was able to assist Brownie in conveying this spirit to the group. No one should interpret these comments to mean that there were five cloistered monks in the band, however. Land remembered with a smile, "Richie was a little busy with the ladies. He had harems in almost every city." Morrow, however, was also a family man, and perhaps the most subdued one in the group. Roach has already been characterized as a "matinee idol," but this never distracted him from his duties and responsibilities as coleader of the group. In this area, however, he got great inspiration and cooperation from his much younger, coleader. "To be so young and to be so wise," Max said were characteristics about Brownie that continually amazed him and strengthened his resolve to work harder and harder. Worrying about performing well and doing one's best for each audience is one thing, but being totally committed to the business details of payroll, equipment, booking, and travel arrangements is something else. Jazz history is littered with tales of great geniuses who fell tragically because they could not take care of business.

Max Roach continued to marvel at his young colleague's organization, determination, and sense of responsibility. "We were working a club in Buffalo," Max recalled, "and each week we'd take turns in who collects the money and who takes care of the books on the band. There was a rough guy in Buffalo who said that week was a bad week. It snowed, and he just couldn't give us all his money. Buffalo is known to be one of the enclaves for Mafia-type characters, I put that in quotes. But this guy was really that type . . . cigar, vest, stayed in the back room all the time. It was Clifford's week to collect, and I knew he was going to have a tough time because it *was* a rough week. I remember, when we left the club that night, he stayed in the man's office maybe about an hour and a half . . . later [the proprietor] walks up to me and said, 'You know that kid is really tough?' . . . We got our money." Roach never found out what Brown did to secure the paychecks, but he was to become more and more relaxed because when Brownie was in charge, "we never had any problem."

Roach was also amazed at Brownie's structured domestic life. "I found out that he had his house that he had bought [on Samson Street in Philadelphia], insured to be paid for in case anything happened to him . . . [it's] unusual for a young person that age to have that kind of insurance . . . these are maybe small things to some people, but for musicians it's almost like you don't think about things like that." Max had spent the better part of his career in a world where most musicians lived a predictably bohemian existence, for example, Charlie Parker, who often disappeared for weeks, sleeping in different locations with nobody knowing where he was. In addition it is certainly true that the Parker-inspired drug use by many beboppers resulted in disorganized life styles. Most musicians, of course, had some sense of responsibility, but Clifford Brown went far beyond that. He became a role model for so many of his peers, just as they had previously idolized Charlie Parker. Because of Parker, many players used drugs in a foolish attempt to match his genius. Conversely, those influenced by Brown were as eager to emulate his very different lifestyle. Although he was never judgmental, Clifford Brown had very definite views about how jazz players should live. As we have seen, discipline, responsibility, dedication, and proper social behavior were things he had learned from his family. Wherever he worked, these characteristics made deep impressions upon musicians with whom he came in contact.

It is, of course, important to note, as we have previously, that Clifford Brown never intended to be, nor should he be remembered as, some kind of saint. Brownie was Brownie. He shot pool, had an occasional drink, smoked a cigarette now and then, socialized with women, and enjoyed going to the racetrack. "I found out after we had been together maybe a year or two," said Max Roach, "that he played the horses." The quintet personnel were constantly with each other on stage at night and together when they traveled. During daytime hours, however, "you pretty much stay to yourselves," said Roach. It turned out that Brownie enjoyed horse racing and went often to racetracks around the circuit. In typical fashion, however, he simply didn't carry on too much about his social life.

During March 1955, the tour kept rolling along, gathering pace. On Friday, the eleventh, the group was in Detroit, appearing at the Madison Ballroom. Detroit was rapidly becoming a prime location for the group because of the success of their earlier appearance and the increasing sales of their records in the Midwest. In typical routing fashion, the next step from Detroit was Toronto. On Monday, March 14, the group returned to the Colonial Tavern there for a week and from there made their way back to Philadelphia for a Parker benefit at the Blue Note on Monday, March 28. This was followed by a regular stint at the beginning of April at the club, with the usual guest appearance for Ellis Tollen at a jam session in Music City on the eleventh.

When Clifford Brown was in the Philadelphia, he saw his family, visited relatives and friends in neighboring Wilmington, practiced, dealt with his house and financial needs, and then went back and practiced some more. LaRue had this recollection: "I'll put it like this: We would have breakfast, and Clifford would practice. We would go out, and then Clifford would practice. We would have lunch, and Clifford would practice. Clifford practiced anytime he possibly could, and even if we were in a place where he couldn't blow his horn, even with the mute, he would do lip exercises and tongue exercises or he would just simply play his mouthpiece. He played constantly."

He also devoted more time to the piano. "He would practice scales," said LaRue. "He would play for his own enjoyment. He would go through various chord changes and sometimes he would just want to see what he wanted to do with a particular piece. So he would go to the piano and work it out." As for writing, "he would write anywhere, anytime. He might wake up in the middle of the night and write something down or write it on a napkin or a piece of paper or anything. He was forever writing."

On occasion Brownie launched into song. LaRue recalled that "he would do something from *Figaro* or he would sing something from Muddy Waters." He also enjoyed singing Broadway show tunes and pop standards. When she was asked how well he could sing, LaRue replied bluntly, "Unfortunately, he couldn't." So much for that. Unlike his sister Geneva, who became a serious opera singer, Brownie did not have it in the vocal chords.

When LaRue and Clifford married, she had made it clear to him that she wanted to wait quite a while before having children. But soon after the nuptials, he began to try to change her mind. She had no inclination. In his inimitable persistent fashion he kept broaching the subject, however, and his determination being what it was, she finally consented. So in the early spring of 1955, LaRue became pregnant, and the couple began to prepare their residence for the new arrival. Such preparations had to be organized around the schedule, but organization was Brownie's middle name, so things proceeded in an orderly manner in anticipation of the December arrival of their child.

At the end of April, the quintet came into New York to perform at Basin Street, a posh new place in sharp contrast to the old 52nd Street dives. Clubs like Basin Street were venues where everyone wanted to perform. As they had so many times, on opening night the group stunned the New York audience used to the best in jazz. Gotham jazz fans were still reeling from the tragic death of Charlie Parker the month before. Also, the demise of 52nd Street had left the scene in an uncertain state. Older clubs were becoming strip joints, rock 'n' roll music was taking the nation into very different territory, and the jazz scene was hurting. But when Brown and Roach played Basin Street, it was as if an explosion had occurred on Broadway. Crowds poured in, musicians dropped by, writers sought interviews, and disk jockeys brought tape recorders. The whole jazz scene got a lift from this exciting quintet.

On Friday, May 6, a benefit concert for the Lighthouse, in memory of Charlie Parker, was held at Carnegie Hall. Jazz stars from around the world gathered at the venerable concert hall. The list of performers included the very top names: Count Basie, Billie Holiday, Buddy Rich, and Lester Young. Brown-Roach was on the bill. With his usual humility, Brownie stepped up and performed brilliantly on this bill of legends.

A recording of the group's performance was made, and it is remarkable. They chose to open with "I Get a Kick Out of You" from their book. But the tempo was beyond belief. In the excitement of the evening, they perhaps had become rather ambitious. Somehow Brown and Land performed their solos with all the notes intact. Land actually received more applause for his work than the others, and Richie Powell was roaring. Max Roach's solo got strong applause. The tempo is outside the pale, and the crowd went wild.

Next was "The Blues Walk," and again the accelerated tempo went way beyond what the group had done in the studio. This time, however, Brownie's solo can be truly heard. Actually, he performs several sequences of high range pyrotechnics for the crowd, and they respond fervently. Again, Land follows playing brilliantly, somehow managing to stay pretty close to his thoughtfully worked-out lines. Brown-Roach students will easily recognize some licks from Richie Powell that will be heard on later recordings. He also returns to his old quote habits—this time it's a nursery rhyme. But his solo produces a great amount of applause. The performance is also notable because of the long solo space given to George Morrow. It might have even been longer, but Roach was eager to get in. And when he does, it is for a marathon solo. The trades of four, two, and one between Brown and Land follow. The end is a bit ragged, but it works, and the crowd responds wildly.

At this point, *Down Beat*, which had already been more than generous in covering Clifford Brown and the success of Brown-Roach, published a piece by Nat Hentoff titled "Roach & Brown, Inc., Dealers in Jazz." This proved to be a pivotal piece, because in it Brown articulates clearly the musical goals of the group and indicates the primacy of their aesthetic concerns over popular tastes. "Our own policy," Brownie stated, "is to aim for the musical extremes of both excitement and subtle softness whenever each is necessary, but with a lot of feeling in everything. The majority of our book consists of originals with some standards. And we have a definitely organized sound because organization is the trend in all modern jazz groups today. We're trying more and more to have our solos built into each arrangement so that it all forms a whole and creates emotional and intellectual tension."[10]

In order to achieve the goals of the group, however, many pragmatic hurdles had to be avoided. "We realize," said Brownie, "that one thing that has hurt small jazz units is the fact that bookers often haven't been sure they'd get the same personnel the next time they hired a unit. A club owner would hire a name musician one week, and the next time the name came around, he'd have different men with him and a different sound. In a small band, if you can stay together at all, you have a responsibility to maintain your identity. But club owners themselves sometimes don't realize this fact. Some of them look for a shortcut. For example, they want to lure stars, but try to save money by putting in a local rhythm section. If these new men are weak, musically, they hurt the stars' reputation too, in the long run. Max and I have had offers while in New York to headline as singles at a couple of places. But unless they hire the unit as it is, we won't do it. We've been determined to play New York first with our group as a whole. That's the only way we're going to keep together. We've got to work together all the time."

Unfortunately, few musicians have heeded Clifford Brown's advice. It is all too common to hear a new jazz album, look at the list of personnel playing with the leader, and then go immediately to a club performance supporting this effort, only to find out that the leader is appearing with different sidemen. The tunes are the same, the arrangements are identical, but, because the personnel are different the performances are almost always sub par precisely because the cohesiveness gained from constant playing with identical partners is absent. Of course, as Brownie mentioned, there are pragmatic reasons for these changes, almost always due to economics. But if musicians ignore this vital factor, their music is sure to fall short of their aesthetic vision. All anybody has to do is listen to the Clifford Brown–Max Roach quartet and discover the remarkable sense of unity–all due to Brownie's theory of identity–to appreciate the value of his ideas.

In the entire Hentoff piece, Clifford Brown speaks for the group virtually all of the time. Max Roach offered only one small addendum to his comments, suggesting that he felt that his coleader, despite being only twenty-four, had the philosophic and intellectual vision of the music, and, what's more, he could articulate it with thoughtful precision.

Twelve
Into 1956

At the end of May, the group was booked for their fourth appearance in seven months at the Blue Note in Philadelphia—some sort of record. The gig began on Monday the thirtieth, and on the following night Brownie, Billy Root (who was playing in the Blue Note house band), and others were asked to play for a jam session at Music City, as they had done many times before. We have frequently referred to the hour-long jam sessions intended for younger audiences held at Music City, usually from 7:30 to 8:30 on Tuesdays.

This particular session is historic for two reasons: first, Clifford Brown's solo on "Donna Lee," one of three tunes recorded privately that night, has been the subject of much scholarly analysis—that he had created a new improvisational standard is the consensus opinion. Second, for reasons that are quite complex, many musicians, writers, producers, and critics have assigned the wrong date for this jam session; as a result, it has been assumed that the session took place on June 25, 1956.

Let us first describe the circumstances of the event. As usual, on May 31, 1955, the proprietor of Music City, Ellis Tollin, was leading the rhythm section on drums with Ace Tisone on bass and Sam Dockery on piano. That evening Brownie was to play trumpet, with

159

Billy Root on tenor sax, together with local legend Ziggy Vines. Root recalled: "Clifford and I were working at the Blue Note, where I was in the house band. So, Ellis Tollin had us come over, and we played that night. A man named Fred Miles recorded that session."

The first tune is "Walkin'," and, after the head, Brownie solos quite energetically. The tape, first released in 1973, is certainly not studio quality, of course; we hear more crowd noise and Tollin cymbals than anything else. After Brown, the two tenors get long solos, and after a break in the tape we hear Sam Dockery's piano. Then the exchanges begin, with Brownie leading the way. They are long—suitable jam-session length—and after this the horns unite for the out chorus.

Next "A Night in Tunisia" has Clifford Brown playing the top melodic line and the saxes playing the vamp. After the usual break, Brownie begins a series of choruses that toss out new ideas in a virtual improvisational seminar. In a particularly intricate doubled sequence, he sets out what one writer has called "a definitive statement of this anthem and one of the great recorded solos." After tenor and piano solos, Brownie returns with a rare upper register scream, and then the final chorus arrives, ending with his struggling to reach a Z and finally doing it at the end.

"Donna Lee" begins unsteadily for Brown, but he soon launches himself into an improvisational orbit that has had listeners gasping ever since. The triple-tonguing sequences are simply nonpareil. New York disc jockey Bob Porter has remarked, "When I heard 'Donna Lee' I knew that Brownie was the best." Another writer referred to the solo as "meteoric, mind-boggling." After a series of solos by the rest of the group, Brownie returns in ever more brilliant form. His last chorus has been termed a defining moment in trumpet history. After the applause, he says, "Thank you very much . . . you make me feel so wonderful." One wonders if his humility allowed him to comprehend what he had just accomplished.

As for the disputed date, a weekly newsletter published by Music City to advertise the concerts records quite clearly in an article accompanied by photos that this show took place on May 31, 1955, as Billy Root has correctly remembered. Why so many people chose to date the session in June 1956 can only be understood in the light of later events.[1]

In May 1955, George Wein, producer of the Newport Jazz Festival, was gearing up for his second season. After an enormous success the previous summer, Wein, who would go on to become the world's most important jazz festival producer, had his pick of the top names in jazz. Newport had dramatically rescued the music from the onslaught of rock 'n' roll, and the attendant publicity received by the artists who performed there had jump-started many struggling careers. On May 18, Wein announced the performers for the festival slated for July 15–17, among them Duke Ellington, Count Basie, Woody Herman, Dinah Washington, Gerry Mulligan and Chet Baker, Stan Getz, Erroll Garner, Thelonious Monk, the Modern Jazz Quartet, Charlie Mingus, Lester Young, Kai Winding and J. J. Johnson, Jimmy Rushing, Lee Konitz, and Art Farmer. Even the usually recalcitrant Miles Davis quickly accepted an invitation. Because the astute organizers had carefully followed the meteoric progress of Brown-Roach, they vigorously pursued them for the festival.

Following the group's successful first week at the Blue Note in Philadelphia, Max Roach was involved in an automobile accident. Suffering minor injuries, he took a few days to recuperate. Such accidents were not uncommon among road musicians. The extraordinary amount of time musicians spent driving from one gig to another created a serious problem. They were constantly tired from the long hours they had to play, and many times they had to drive long hours at night over roads that were often in need of repair. With Roach out, the group did not have to look far for a replacement; Art Blakey sat in for Roach for five days.

When Roach returned, the band drove to Chicago for a two-week triumphant return to the Bee Hive. Because the group had done such outstanding business on a previous engagement, the club owners had discussed a longer stay, but the band was already committed to Newport.

Once again the traveling took a heavy toll. The group completed their Bee Hive gig on July 15, which was the day the Newport Festival began. One can only imagine the stress and fatigue incurred in driving from Chicago to Rhode Island and then having to be ready to play at the festival on Saturday, the sixteenth.

Newport had opened on a bad note. *Down Beat* reporter Jack Tracey wrote in a review dated August 24, that "the sound system advertised previously and hailed in the press as 'high fidelity outside' was nothing short of miserable." True to their word Woody Herman, Erroll Garner, and Louis Armstrong played for the Friday night opening before a reported gate of 7,100 people. (Tracey estimated that about 20,000 total attended the three-day festival—a huge number for 1955.) The weather, however, was not cooperating, as rain constantly threatened.

On Saturday, Tracey wrote, the "concert opened to murky skies and threats of rain, but any mental gloom on the part of the audience was dispelled immediately . . . Max Roach and Clifford Brown ignited a fire right away . . . they swung hard and rousingly with Max's driving drumming the highlight. Clifford was to come into his own later in the evening."

When Teddi King and Dave Brubeck finished their turns, Gerry Mulligan, Chet Baker, and Brown and Roach came on to "jam the evening to a close." Brown and Roach "were swinging something fierce on 'Tea for Two,' " when Wein walked out on the stage to close up the show, fearful, no doubt, of the curfew that had been imposed on the festival by the town fathers. The crowd went wild after Brownie's solo and ignored Wein's pleas. So did Clifford, who "dug his neck into his shoulders and screamed another chorus." After he quit, rain began to fall heavily.

Newport brought the band rave notices. In its festival debut, it had more than held its own against an array of important jazz players. During the next few weeks, the band visited Canada, opening up new territory in the eastern part of the country; on July 28 they did a performance in Quebec, where some private recording was done. Involved in the performance were some Canadian locals, one of whom was Rob McConnell.

After the trip to Canada, the group made its way back to Philadelphia. This time they played at the Showboat. Now Clifford could spend as much time as possible with LaRue as they continued to prepare for the baby. Just a couple of years before, Brownie had been one of many talented locals who had jammed at the Showboat with Charlie Parker, Ernie Henry, and J.J. Johnson. Now he was returning as a star. There to greet him was the usual contingent of family from Wilmington and some friends from Poplar Street. Kelly Swaggerty, his old friend from the days with Todd Dameron, took his cab up to the club on Lombard Street and dropped by. Even though Brownie was swarmed over by adoring fans, he spotted Kelly. "Hey, man, let's go have a Coke," he muttered to his old pal, and Kelly remembered they hung out for a while as in the old days. "I didn't idolize him as Clifford Brown," said Swaggerty. "He was just Brownie."

LaRue had gone along on many of the road trips. She and her husband enjoyed visiting museums. "We would browse the museums in all of the cities," she said. On one of their early jaunts, LaRue discovered that Brownie had a passion for doughnuts. "I don't mean *like*," she said, "I mean *love* of doughnuts. Whenever we would pass a doughnut shop, this man would have to stop and buy dozens of doughnuts. Now he knew he was never going to eat them, he just had to have them. I never did understand that one. They'd get stale, and we would have to throw them out. But he wanted doughnuts around him all the time."

Following the gig at the Showboat, the quintet began a two-week stay at Basin Street, beginning on Friday, August 26. The producers at the club were on a roll. They had decided to follow up their previous success with a dramatic bill featuring Brown-Roach, the Dave Brubeck Quartet, and an opening act dubbed the Australian Jazz Quartet. After opening night the word got out that the show was a big winner, and the crowds poured in. Gary Kramer in *Billboard* magazine reported the news: "Basin Street in New York has one of the most potent draws in its history. On weekends, customers have been queuing up a block long to get inside, and even during the week it's been packed to capacity. The house has not seen this kind of business since Louis Armstrong's appearance there a years ago." This was big news at a time when Elvis Presley dominated the headlines.

The *Billboard* writer continued with a review of the show: "In contrast to the Brubeck group, the effect produced on their listeners by the Brown-Roach quintet is immediate and electric. Both Brown and Roach, now at the high points of their respective careers, effortlessly perform with such supreme virtuosity on their instruments that aficionados at the nitery are simply staggered. The fanciful flights of Brown on trumpet never serve a cheap effect, however. The fireworks are brilliantly patterned and thoroughly thought out. In a drummer, the modesty and complete lack of exhibitionistic tricks of Max Roach are almost as impressive as the variety of sounds that he coaxes from his drums in his tasty solos. These two artists are currently combining their rich talents in one of the most stimulating modern jazz combos extant."[2]

After the record-breaking run at Basin Street, the musicians headed for the Midwest. In Chicago, at the Bee Hive, they really outdid themselves. They opened on Friday, September 30, for their usual two-week engagement, and the audiences swarmed the club. Business had never been so good, and an extension was absolutely necessary to accommodate the demand. The owners were so excited that an unprecedented deal was struck; the band was held over for another month.

It certainly was a heady time for the group. Their successes in the summer at Newport and their colossal run at Basin Street enabled them to raise the ante in Midwest clubs.

In the flush of this great success, Brownie celebrated his twenty-fifth birthday. His life was in great shape, his family was growing, and his art was finally paying off. He had every reason to feel confident—crowds mobbed him and critics raved. But he never had a swelled head. Just as he had striven for higher standards at Howard High, with Boysie Lowery, and at every step in his career, he kept gritting his teeth and moving on.

One night at the Bee Hive, Brown stole a few moments to walk outside. Barbara Gardner reported the event in *Down Beat:* "After a particularly burning session in Chicago's Bee Hive, Clifford quietly walked out of the club and stood sucking in the cool night air. He confided in a friend: 'I feel as though I have just had acid thrown in my face. My lips are on fire. Sometimes I wonder if I can keep up with Max when he really gets that cymbal going.' "[3] Keep up with him he did—with greater communication than any other player with whom Max had ever appeared on a bandstand.

While in Chicago, Harold Land got news that his grandmother was very sick back in San Diego. Land had been away from home for over a year and, except for a couple of visits with his wife when the quintet was in the Midwest, was unable to be with his family. He often brooded about his young son and had shared his worries with Brownie, who had the same family concerns. Word soon came that his grandmother was in the hospital, and "they didn't think she was going to make it." As it turned out, she did die. Agonized, Land soon decided that with his mother, wife, and son needing him in California, he would have to leave the quintet permanently. It was a difficult decision for him. Not only was he sharing in the great artistic success, but he felt deep affection for Brownie and the whole band.

Before Land left, the quintet had been tape-recorded by fans lucky enough to catch the action at the Bee Hive. One of the private recordings of the group—probably made in October—still has Harold Land playing, but on November 7, a Monday night, there is a new voice playing tenor with the group. Brown and Roach spent countless hours wondering who they could get to replace Land; finally, fate lent a hand. Living in Chicago at that time was one of the formidable tenor saxists in jazz—Sonny Rollins. Rollins was already enjoying a good measure of fame in his own right. After establishing himself in the late 1940s as a master improviser and gifted composer, Rollins had been having a tough time with drugs, but still he had just had completed a successful run with a rejuvenated Miles Davis quintet. Playing alongside Philly Joe Jones, Paul Chambers, and Miles, Rollins had attracted considerable attention. At this time he was alternating with John Coltrane in the Davis group. But Davis considered Rollins his "favorite tenor at that time."[4]

The tape made of Rollins playing with Brown and Roach on that Monday in November included a rhythm section of Billy Wallace sitting in on piano, Leo Blevens on guitar, and Nick Hill on bass.

They play "Walkin'," "Cherokee," and "Hot House." It is an exciting session, quite long. Although it was poorly recorded, it is still a significant tape, for it has often been described as Sonny Rollins's "audition" for the group.

Recognizing the challenge of playing alongside Brown and Roach, and immediately captivated by Brown's grace and magnanimity, Rollins leaped at the chance to join the group. What was happening with Brown-Roach was infinitely more interesting to Sonny than his work with Miles Davis. He had fended off the best improvisers in jazz with ease, but he sensed that he would be in a different arena with his new cohorts, and he was right. His own recording career would soon reach a peak,[5] and his drug problems would quickly disappear. Indeed Brown would have a similar effect on the lifestyle of many jazz musicians.

When the group finished its historic run at the Bee Hive on Armistice Day, they headed east, with Sonny Rollins firmly in tow. The quintet made their first stop back at the Showboat in Philadelphia for a two-week run.

Less than two months older than Brownie, Walter Theodore[6] Rollins had experienced as dramatic a rise as his new colleague. After making a debut recording with Babs Gonzales at age nineteen, Rollins performed with J.J. Johnson and by the end of 1949 had recorded with Bud Powell and Fats Navarro on Blue Note. Later he'd worked alongside Charlie Parker, Jackie McLean, Thelonious Monk, and Milt Jackson before joining Miles Davis in the months before the fateful Bee Hive jam session. Sought by nearly every leader in jazz, Sonny was as monstrous an improviser as you could want on a bandstand.

As the two horns dueled each other during the Showboat gig, observers began to sense that Brown-Roach had definitely taken a new turn on their journey. Like Brownie, Rollins had that keen desire to find new lines in each chorus he played, and he had the ability to play whatever his mind conjured up.

When he began to dig into the Brown-Roach repertoire, Rollins underwent an epiphany of sorts, both in his playing and in his personal life. During his time with Miles Davis, he had languished, feeling unchallenged by Miles. But after playing alongside Clifford Brown, he was both intensely challenged and inspired to change his ways. Brownie had paved the straight road, and Sonny was eager to ride along. In recent times, Sonny has spoken frequently about the transformation that took place when he joined Brown-Roach. As a young player in Harlem, he felt he had to get high in order to play well. Also, his efforts to secure heroin had led him to crime. But when he encountered Brownie, he quickly saw the light and went straight. At once, inspired by Brownie's abstemious regimen, he intensified his practice efforts and his dedication. The results were immediate. Rollins later said: "Clifford was a profound influence on my life. He showed me that it was possible to lead a good, clean life and still be a good jazz musician."

After the Showboat, the band opened at the Patio in Washington, D.C., on Monday, November 28, following with a week in Baltimore at the Las Vegas Club. Audiences responded with great enthusiasm. Fans and critics poured into the clubs to see if what they had been hearing was really true.

EmArcy producers came as well. What they heard was so stunning that plans were quickly formulated to record the quintet anew. When the group arrived back at Basin Street in New York on Tuesday, December 20, a plan was set to record them live from the club.

During this month I had been making the rounds of the New York jazz clubs with my saxophone, hoping to join whatever jam sessions would permit a young high-schooler to sit in. At one club in lower Manhattan, I had finally managed to crash a session and was feeling pretty good about things when a buzz came into the room that Clifford Brown was going to come on stage and play. I knew very little about the jazz scene in those days and nothing about Brownie. But when he came up and started to play, I couldn't believe what I was seeing and hearing. Later, going home on the subway, I couldn't decide whether I had participated in fantasy or reality.

The following week, several fellow musicians and I attended a dance at my high school in Brooklyn. Following the dance, I persuaded the group to go to Basin Street, where our dates had to sit ignored while we all went wild over Brown-Roach. George Shearing's quintet shared the billing, but when Brown-Roach began their fireworks, we all but abandoned our dates as we listened to the incredible music. The girls never spoke to us again.

During this Basin Street run, LaRue had given birth to a son—Clifford Jr.—on Wednesday, December 28. The engagement was over on Sunday, New Year's Day, and Brownie, who had been commuting between Philadelphia and New York by train during this gig, went home to spend some time with his new son. When he returned to New York, he quickly began to prepare for the group's first recording in nearly a year.

On Wednesday, January 4, the Clifford Brown–Max Roach Quintet, including their new saxophonist, marched into Capitol studios in New York to begin work. It was a joyful time for Brownie, who was elated over the birth of his son and excited at having a new opportunity to record. After grueling months on the road, the musicians were eager to create some new music and move forward.

During his Chicago wanderings, Richie Powell had met an artist named Gertrude Abercrombie, among whose many attributes that Powell admired was her walk. Richie sought to emulate this in the first cut of the day, which he jocularly dubbed "Gertrude's Bounce." The intro has a holiday flavor about it, before the ensemble jumps into a seductively swinging tempo. Brown presents a long, brilliantly articulated solo with his classic imprimatur all over it—triple-tonguing, exploratory chord work, and fat, fat sound. Rollins's short solo smacks of warm-up, and Powell's is also short. Roach's tom-toms rat-tat-tat briefly, and then we are back to the lively ensemble passages of the head, a repeat of the intro, and a fade. "Gertrude's Bounce" has intriguing originality, cohesive unison sound, and a great Brownie solo, but above all that gemlike economy that the group had long labored to achieve.

Benny Golson, long a friend of Clifford Brown's, had written a tune called "Step Lightly," which got renamed "Junior's Arrival" during these happy days following the birth of Clifford Jr. Written in a minor key, it doesn't exactly sound like a song for a newborn. Brownie's solo is a doubled blast from the outset, and Rollins follows the doubled rhythm with a nice rangy swinging chorus. Powell's short interlude leads to a brief four-bar sequence from Roach, then a quick return to the head, which is itself abbreviated. This cut never made it to the collection on the new LP.

"Powell's Prances" is the burner of all burners. After a two-bar drum intro, Brown and Rollins come together on one of the great up-tempo ensemble performances of the era. After the head, Roach's snare rolls Brownie into a masterpiece solo. Rollins next provides a nicely spaced response that counters Brown's lines thoughtfully. Roach's solo utilizes all of the percussion imaginable, but the length is tantalizingly brief. Back to the head with a colossal closer. "Powell's Prances" is a modal composition, with Brown and Rollins improvising on the scale rather than on the usual chord changes. Modal jazz would become a favorite jazz style in the 1960s. Miles Davis was credited with creating a modal revolution three years later, yet this 1956 performance by Brown-Roach in the modal style contains improvisations far superior to some best-selling modal recordings done much later. You have to search far and wide to find anyone else in jazz who will touch this tune. This tune is owned for all time by Brown-Roach.

Although they had recorded only three tunes for the new LP, Brown-Roach had to get back on the road again to fulfill club engagements. It was tough for Clifford, who naturally wanted to be home with his new son. But this was not to be. After the record date, the group found themselves on a wild spree of dates, zigzagging back and forth. They started with an opener on January 10 at the Las Vegas Club in Baltimore, and following this, in a bit of unfortunate routing, they had some dates at Storyville in Boston, then a last-minute replacement gig at Basin Street for three nights before they scooted to Detroit, opening on Monday, January 30, at the Loop Lounge. It was another venue for them in the growing Detroit jazz market. During the first two months of 1956, Brownie would barely have two weeks to help LaRue with the baby, but his brief presence was deeply meaningful.[7]

LaRue remembered Clifford as a new father: "He was a fantastic father. He would take the baby, put him on his lap, talk to him, have a whole conversation with him about philosophy, art, or music.

Current events . . . just anything—talk, talk, talk, talk. When he would practice, he would lay him across his lap and play something, and he'd say, 'Now, that was so and so and so.' I swear to you, our son to this day says he remembers, he remembers some of the things his father said to him. I personally think it's impossible, but who's to say? He was absolutely wonderful with his son."

After the week in Detroit and some time home with the family, Brownie rejoined the quintet back in New York to finish up the Basin Street LP. It was Thursday, January 16, 1956, when the group got back to Capitol Studios. First came "I'll Remember April." The tune was recorded twice (each take is over nine minutes long), plus one short false start fragment. The musicians decided on a Latin fugue introduction, which has become quite famous. Brown attacks the head with one of his fatter-sounding passages, and Rollins follows with the bridge. At the break, Brownie launches into orbit—a multi-noted fanfare celebration. Rollins follows with a pared-down contrast that soon heats up, aided by Powell's excellent comping. Powell's solo follows with clearly articulated single-note lines played with great confidence. Max Roach's solo simply soars, combining all of the tonal elements he had been working on for so many years. The horns exchange eights, then fours in a dialogue that is breathtaking. A last chorus follows, but then the trades return briefly before the Latin rhythm takes the tune out. Most critics would agree that this is the finest jazz performance of this oft-recorded standard.

After the fragment, the engineer spouts, "Take three," and the group is off again. They stay with the Latin intro far longer on the alternate. Although Brownie's solo is again a multinoted roller coaster, the lines do not have the flow of the master. Rollins's power and imagination operate nicely again. Powell's solo refers briefly to some oriental phrases, and Roach's solo sparkles. The trades are nowhere near as vibrant—it sounds as if the players realize that they've left their best work in the master. The Latin rhythm returns at the conclusion.

Richie Powell's ballad "Time" is next. He said that the title refers "to the time a man spends just sitting in jail, wondering when he's going to get out." The trumpet and saxophone have a dual melody line that is quite poignant, accompanied by Powell on celeste. For his solo he switches to piano and delivers a mournful line, punctuated by Roach's cymbals. The head returns with a lovely combined ending.

"The Scene Is Clean" signals the return of Tadd Dameron into Brownie's life. Dameron composed and arranged all the rest of the material on the *Basin Street* LP and would record this tune with his band a few weeks later. Opening with a bass and drum dialogue, the tune settles into a light swing melody that is pure Dameron. Powell's "shave and a haircut" quote leading into Max's delicate tom-toms is a real treat. The horn solos are understated and finely wrought. In the ensemble playing, Brown and Rollins play in unison brilliantly.

"Flossie Lou" is another Dameron piece that took four takes to do and then never made it to the finished LP. The tune is based on the changes to "Jeepers Creepers" and is a medium romp with an airy feel, containing a couple of lazy Max Roach solos and good Brown/Rollins work. The multiple takes are probably the most valuable collection in the group's canon because there are new ideas constantly developing and novel changes attempted. One of the bonuses on the CD reissue of the EmArcy material is a brief conversation that Brownie has with producer Bob Shad on an alternate take of "Flossie Lou." The feeling of being in the studio with the group, as the record spins, is intoxicating.

Dameron's arrangement of Cole Porter's "What Is This Thing Called Love?" is up next in two takes. Once again a vamp gets things going. The alternate take has a longer version of this vamp, and the solos are solid, with Rollins's effort a bit more interesting. But the exchanges are powerful on the alternate, and some banter in the studio suggests everybody is pretty happy. The shorter vamp on the master is more in keeping with the Brown-Roach sense of economy. After the head is introduced by Brownie, Rollins delivers the bridge splendidly. Brown's solo is excellently played and becomes memorable despite a couple of false starts. Rollins's is brief but sensational, as is Richie Powell's. A welcome interlude from George Morrow leads into an ensemble insert of Dameron's. Roach enters, playing head melody figures followed by innovative trades with both Brown and Rollins excelling. Roach rolls them into the vamp again, and the tune fades. This Dameron arrangement and the solo variations created a great jazz collaboration.

"Love Is a Many-Splendored Thing," a Richie Powell arrangement, returns to the $3/4$–$4/4$ ideas that the group had had when they started out in California. On the alternate take, after a false start, the tempo accelerates unevenly after the head, but the horns are playing some splendid figures. Things fall apart in the out chorus, so we go to the master. Once again there is a slight tempo change during Brownie's superb solo. Rollins follows with an intricate line embracing several different ideas. Powell is very articulate once again, and Roach's solo leads logically into the $3/4$ tempo of the head. The Brown-Roach economic formula makes this a historic selection. Thus we have *Clifford Brown and Max Roach at Basin Street*, one of the great recordings in jazz history.

The group returned to the Rouge in Detroit for an engagement beginning Monday, February 20. While making the rounds of the local publicity stops, Brown and Roach were the guests of one of the most ardent jazz fans among comics—Soupy Sales. It was a typical zany Soupy Sales television show. The star appeared with a mock bald head, parodying the then-current popularity of Yul Brynner in *The King and I*. Directly, he introduced a "new jazz star, Cliff Brown." After a brief interview, during which Brownie responded to Soupy's inquiry about the recent birth of his son—that he was "six pounds, four ounces"—and told him that his latest LP was *A Study in Brown*, Brownie played two numbers. There were good close-ups of his playing, and the viewer can clearly see Brownie's embouchure and facial expressions.

For years, the kinescope of this show lay buried in Soupy Sales's archives. He periodically reminded himself to search for it every time he ran into Max Roach. Finally, forty years later, he got it to him, and I happened to be at Max's apartment soon after it arrived. We sat there marveling at the quality of this bit of early television and the sight of Brownie conversing with Soupy was enough to make us teary-eyed. There were also rumors that Brownie had been a guest on one of the early Steve Allen TV shows. I spoke to Allen's archi-

vists, who informed me that NBC unfortunately destroyed the kin-
escopes from his 1955 and 1956 programs, and, if indeed Brownie
did perform for Allen, the evidence is lost. Outside of these instances
there is no present evidence that Clifford Brown made any other TV
appearances.

During the same period, Brownie began suffering from an aching
wisdom tooth. In terrible pain, he finished a night's work, exclaiming,
"I couldn't play." Despite this, according to LaRue, he received "one
of the best reviews that night that he had ever had in his whole life."
Following dental work, he returned the following night, complaining
again that he couldn't play properly. This time Soupy Sales was in
the audience and rushed up to Brownie, praising his great performance, adding jokingly, "Man, why didn't you sound like that when
you did my show last week?"

The group then drove back to Boston for an appearance at Storyville beginning Monday, February 27. After Storyville, the musicians moved back "home" to the Blue Note in Philadelphia. It appears that on his way from Boston to Philadelphia Max Roach had
stopped off for a day or two at his home in New York. Suddenly,
disaster struck. "I got a call from Brownie," said Roach. "He told
me that Sonny Rollins and Richard Powell were in an awful accident,
and the car was totaled. So I jumped into my car and went down to
Philadelphia, and in those days it was almost like Bessie Smith: they
would not take Sonny Rollins and Richard Powell in the hospital.
[Max is evidently referring to some latent racism in the city of broth-
erly love.] They were in Richard Powell's mother's house in Philadelphia at that time in shock, Sonny's teeth hanging out of his head.
I wondered why they did not take them to the hospital."[8]

Actually, Sonny Rollins had avoided serious permanent damage.
But the incident did not augur well for Roach. He had worried about
the driving schedules of his musicians ever since he had witnessed
another incident a few months before. On one of the quintet's visits
to Detroit, he recalled: "We all had a little money so Clifford and I
traded in our cars and bought two new cars,[9] and Richard Powell
of course bought himself a car, too. And I remember at that same
week we were at a party, and it was about 7 or 8 o'clock in the

morning, and it was in one of those streets that was a dead end street, and you have to make a U-turn. I saw Richard's young wife negotiating this turn in the dead end street, so I walked over the car and said, 'Richard, what are you doing? She's having a difficult time with the car.' So he chastised me and said, 'You guys, you older guys are always telling us younger guys what to do.' " Max "let it go," but when Rollins and Powell totaled their car, Roach was beside himself.

The musicians didn't have much choice in those days. Commuter flights between the cities were rare, and in any case the costs would have been prohibitive. Also, they could always have a day or two at home between gigs and catch up with the group at the next job. With the big bands who played one-nighters, a bus was mandatory, and the musicians were forced to stay in hotels. But the jazz club circuit consisted of one- or two-week bookings or longer, so the cost of a bus wasn't possible. Automobiles were the answer. But each month Max worried more and more.

The group drove long hours to Pittsburgh for a brief stint and then headed to Toronto for a gig at the Colonial Tavern. Here an interesting incident took place, as veteran rhythm 'n' blues tenor saxist Jimmy Cavallo related: "The Colonial had two performance rooms—upstairs and downstairs. I was working with a group in the smaller room, and when I heard that Brownie and Max were going to headline I got very excited. When the gig started, I couldn't wait to go to the big room to listen to them during the breaks in my sets. They were really cooking up there. When I approached Clifford one night, he asked where I was playing, and I modestly told him about the blues honking that I was doing at the other room of the Colonial. He was very supportive and told me to stop putting my gig down because that music was just as important as his bebop thing. He was very adamant about it, and I was surprised. What we were doing was nothing compared to his stuff, and yet he showed me great respect. I've never forgotten his demeanor and seriousness. He seemed to be so mature and knowledgeable. As for as his playing, he was simply phenomenal."[10] After a great reception in Toronto, the group began the long trek back to New York.

Sonny Rollins had caused such a stir in his young career that many record companies had attempted to sign him. Finally he did make a deal with Prestige. After recording some LPs as a leader while part of Brown-Roach, he faced a dilemma. He did not want to leave the quintet, so he asked if they would record an album with his name listed as the leader. Brown and Roach readily agreed. The group operated as a team, and Rollins was impressed with their lack of ego.

On Thursday, March 22, the musicians convened at Rudy Van Gelder's Hackensack, New Jersey, studio, where Clifford Brown was reunited with his old friend from the Blue Note days. The album was titled *Sonny Rollins + 4*, and for the date Sonny rolled out of his archives two compositions that he had been working on for just such an opportunity: "Valse Hot" and "Pent-up House."

"Valse Hot" is a jazz waltz that derives inspiration from Thelonious Monk's "Carolina Moon" (which had Max Roach as the drummer). After a four-bar intro, the horns played the head. There seems to be a little uncertainty in the reading, but after the head Rollins takes the first solo in 3/4 and doubles many of the phrases. The 3/4 pulse by the rhythm section is very steady—no rhythm adventures here. The head statement is repeated before Brownie's solo, which also doubles the rhythm in many phrases. The 3/4 doesn't hamper him, but, like Rollins, he does not venture outside the framework at all. Richie Powell follows with a straightforward single-note line effort, playing with the rhythm only for a couple of bars. Again the head for four bars with Max Roach, who organizes his lines to fit the 3/4; next came the out chorus, and again a couple of missed notes and an abrupt ending. "Valse Hot" has remained one of Sonny Rollins's most durable compositions.

"Kiss and Run," a work of Sam Caslow's, is an up-tempo swinger with a stop-time head. The musicians seem very comfortable with the familiar 4/4, although there are some sound problems at the start. Rollins begins with a lengthy and quite imaginative solo. Brownie follows with his usual triplet figures, but each chorus is totally different, the last one very new in its structure. Richie Powell has a very long solo, which is followed by some brisk exchanges between Roach and the horns, and then Brownie and Rollins divide fours. In conclusion the stop time head statement is repeated.

A vamp starts off "I Feel a Song Comin' On," with Brown playing the melody over Rollins and the rhythm. Rollins's bridge sounds sweet staccato before he launches into his first short solo; then Brown toots brilliantly through the changes, followed by Powell's quick solo. The melody returns as the basis for trades with Roach, then Brownie and Rollins do some trades themselves and reach the ending with some uncertainty. It finally ends with a Roach solo.

Sonny Rollins starts "Count Your Blessings Instead of Sheep" right on the tonic note of the melody. His ballad-playing is marvelous—we haven't heard this yet in the Brown-Roach connection. He is very adventurous, and his tone is very rich.

"Pent-up House" has become a true jazz standard, for which Stephanie Nakasian has recently written lyrics. Sonny Rollins begins the melody on a pick-up, and things just start flying from there. Brown repeats the pick-up in the second eight, and they keep alternating. Brownie's solo is performed above Morrow's walking bass and then above Roach's high hat. Richie Powell stays out. Brownie explores new regions with some shorter lines than usual. After an almost noiseless interlude, Rollins begins a half-noted tranquil solo that develops its own character. Comping under most of this, Powell seems to start a solo at one point, but Rollins continues. When Powell begins his solo a few bars later, it is a familiar-sounding affair. The horns return to trade with Roach, then Roach solos nicely before the magical head returns. That's it—only five tunes in the album.

Although this LP is not as explosive an outing as is the recording of the previous month, it reveals a new sense of searching on the part of Rollins, Brown, and even Roach. The leaders are now fully confident that their musical concept can develop freely with Rollins on board, and they feel certain that the group sound that audiences recognized will continue. As soon as this happens they are free to roam, and this is what characterizes much of *Sonny Rollins + 4*.

In early April Clifford Brown was glad to have a few days at home. LaRue remembered that Brownie and Max Roach and a few other friends talked about religion, philosophy, and sociology. She recalled that some of their friends were interested in the teachings of Malcolm X, and expostulations of his ideas were a main topic of conversation. Brownie was also examining Buddhism in a general spirit of "searching around." Naturally, the chess games continued, intermixed with baby feedings and practice sessions. The Brown home in Philadelphia had become both a haven for artists and musicians and a secure place to raise Clifford Jr.

One of the perks of jazz stardom during this time was "The Blindfold Test" that Leonard Feather ran in *Down Beat*. As most jazz fans know, the column featured selections played for the artist profiled, who was then asked to identify the piece and the musicians, and to give the mystery recording a rating. On February 22, *Down Beat* ran the Clifford Brown blindfold test. Some of Brownie's comments reflected important musical ideas that he embraced. While analyzing Harry James's performance on a tune called "James Session," Brown said: "One thing I did like: he played the full range of his instrument, utilizing the lowest and highest notes effectively . . . the low notes didn't have the same body and fullness and purity of tone as the high notes." As we have seen, low-register playing was a Brown specialty. Later, in discussing a Kenny Dorham piece dubbed "Minor's Holiday," which he liked, he said, "I think it's possible for a rhythm section to support a soloist so that he can play long flowing lines, instead of getting in the way."[11] This latter comment reflects one of the basic ideas that went into the Brown-Roach formula.

On April 26, the quintet went back to New York's Basin Street. This time there would be a new wrinkle—live broadcasts. The first show was aired on Saturday, April 28, and for this performance the group pulled out two of the charts they had recorded on the Sonny Rollins LP of March 22—"Valse Hot" and "I Feel a Song Comin' On."

The commentator for the broadcast announces "Valse Hot." After the melody, Rollins solos and feels freer to explore in the $3/4$ than he did on the recording. The same is true of Brownie, who produces some new ideas and doubles several $3/4$ phrases. Powell follows with some familiar licks that develop into new high-register lines. The entrances and exits between solos are sloppy, but when Roach solos, this is soon forgotten. He breaks the $3/4$ more often than he did in the recording, obviously feeling freer. Although this performance is interesting, it never quite comes off.

"I Feel a Song Comin' On" starts with the same vamp, but the tempo is much quicker than the recording. Clifford Brown tongues at this machine gun tempo far more than he did at the same tempo the year before. Rollins follows with a brief Coltrane-like modal reference. After Powell's solo, the group uses the vamp to introduce the trades as on the record.

On Sunday, May 6, the national radio crew was back at the club for more broadcasting. This time, however, Max Roach was ill and could not make the show, so Willy Jones subbed for him. Included in this broadcast were "What's New?," "Daahoud," and "Sweet Clifford," which the MC announces as "Sweet Georgia Brown." These broadcasts together with the May 6, 1955, All-Star Carnegie Hall concert, have been produced on CD by the Fresh Sounds label in Switzerland.

"What's New?" begins with a pick-up cadenza by Brownie. His ideas are naturally very different from his earlier recording of the tune. He does a great amount of melodizing, trilling, and high-register work. It is a very unusual solo.

"Daahoud" is also taken at a quicker tempo than on earlier recordings. Brownie's solo after the head is again unique, as the changes from upper to lower register are broken and the lines don't flow—but this is intentional. Rollins follows with his clever half-note legato answer to Brownie's barrage, repeating his ideas from the Basin Street recording. Powell follows with a few new quotes. There is no drum solo.

"Sweet Clifford" is counted off by Clifford Brown as the announcer voices over the music. Rollins's solo swings, and Brown follows with some more heavy artillery. Morrow seems to be working harder in the absence of Roach, and Powell's solo is right on target—and singular. Morrow trades with the horns. The trades are high voltage, and then the band is out.

A few days after these national broadcasts, Don Manning, a jazz musician/fan from Portland, Oregon, conducted a phone interview with Brown. The interview alludes to the ailing Max Roach and his temporary replacement, Willy Jones. During the conversation, Manning asks Brown what the travel plans for the group might be, since they hadn't been seen on the West Coast in a long time. Brownie inquires whether Manning might actually help book the group on the coast and is very glad to accept Manning's praise for his playing. The interview indicated the importance of recording and broadcasting in musicians' careers. Even though Brown-Roach hadn't been on the coast for over a year and a half, there was great interest in them among core fans, and Brown was certainly aware of this fact.

On Tuesday, May 22, Brown-Roach was on the road again, beginning a schedule that had them at the Patio Club in Washington, D.C. After the week there, with well-planned routing, they motored to Cleveland for a week at the Cotton Club. The audiences in these smaller clubs were definitely building, and the group was gratified that the outpouring of records, reviews, broadcasts, and media publicity was translating into more financial freedom—a rarity for small bebop combos.

Beginning Tuesday, June 5, the group worked at the Rouge in River Rouge, Michigan, for a few dates, had a few days off, and then was scheduled for a club in Milwaukee dubbed Tutz. Between gigs and during daytime rest periods, Brownie and Max spent long hours on the phones talking to promoters, club owners, and the like, constantly trying to take care of business and keep things moving.

While they were in the Midwest, Brown and Roach made contact for a new booking in Norfolk, Virginia, at the Continental Restaurant. As he prepared for the date, Brownie was communicating with LaRue about a planned trip to the West Coast for her and Clifford Jr. LaRue's mother was anxiously awaiting a visit from her daughter and first grandchild, so on Monday, June 18, as the group was opening at the Continental, LaRue and Clifford Jr. were flying to Los Angeles.

Of the many private recordings and tapings made of Brown-Roach during their existence, the one made at the Continental is surely the most significant. The announcer, Bob Story from WNOR in Norfolk, notes the small crowd, but assures them of the excellent music ahead. You can hear someone shout "Just One of Those Things" as Max Roach launches the set. The tempo is astounding, and Clifford Brown plays his solo after the melody at a pace that would have short-circuited a metronome. In addition, it is long lined and characterized by some upper-range thunder not heard before. Chorus after chorus comes flying out so fast it defies description. Sonny Rollins follows the pace, not starting with his accustomed half-note lines but simply whooshing along at light speed. The crowd doesn't really know what they're hearing as Richie Powell solos. What you can hear is George Morrow playing his bass and wondering if his hands will start to bleed. Max Roach is not playing the ride cymbal; the sound would muddy things up at this tempo. Meanwhile Powell spirals along in a lengthy solo that certainly challenges him. Morrow then solos with spectacular intonation, and there follows an exchange between the horns and Roach. Some of these four-bar lines are uncanny. Max's chorus is right out of his melody bin; some cymbal and bass drum work is new as he goes on and on in his longest solo to date. When Brownie returns, it is not to the head but to more trades with Rollins, as he recognizes a defining moment when he sees one. Finally, the melody returns and decelerates to the end. It is as if the musicians had made bets to see how fast their music could be played.

Next up, as Clifford Brown eases into "You Go to My Head," the listeners get comfortable for a brief moment, only to be jarred again by his octave leaps—a rare occurrence. Sonny Rollins then plays some figures that really push the remaking of the melody to an extreme, and Brownie is impressed, yelling out "Yeah!" Morrow follows without surprises. But Powell's effort stuns. Gone is the left-handed single note line. In its place are lush chorded sequences, with arpeggio endings. Brownie doubles the pace, finally returning to tempo with high note wailing over Rollins's whole notes. The ending sees Brown, with Maynard Ferguson–like screams, in a wild fanfare ending.

Some banter is barely heard over Richie Powell's changes that lead into an introduction for "Good Bait." Brown's bridge continues his high-note playing. After the melody, there is uncertainty, with the horns finally blowing in unison. Then a Brownie solo up top with never-heard-before broken clusters. "Anything You Can Do" from *Annie Get Your Gun* is a final statement. It is a metaphoric reference to the theme of this jet-propelled session. Rollins knee-jerks around his solo, playing variations on a three-note motif and then briefly modulating à la Coltrane. He cannot resist answering Brownie's *Annie Get Your Gun* quote, but he uses another Berlin tune, "Doin' What Comes Natur'ly." The crowd barely applauds, totally unaware of the drama taking place on the bandstand. Richie Powell comes on with George Shearing–like chords over Morrow's low-register. He quotes "I'm Beginning To See the Light" as Max Roach is subdued for a Powell-Morrow low-key interlude. Powell next hurls out some barrelhouse figures that take us way back. "I'm Gonna Wash That Man Right Outa My Hair" gets a citation, followed by an Irish jig quote. Morrow is next with a nice melody line quoting "Let's Fall in Love" before the tape runs out. There's no telling where this tune wound up.

The lounge set continues with Richie Powell playing the melody of "One for My Baby (And One More for the Road)." One wonders if there might have been dancers that night! The trio continues until he dutifully winds things up, accompanied by Max Roach's brushes.

Clifford Brown announces Sonny's interpretation of "Someone To Watch Over Me," which Rollins begins by playing the melody of "In a Sentimental Mood." He does some octave jumps in his last chorus before a cadenza that gets solid applause. A segue, and Brownie continues the slow dance tempo with "What's New?" Gentle ringlets of sixteenth notes adorn his playful upper register, hidden a bit by the conversation of the patrons. He emulates Rollins's cadenza ending and also gets a good reaction.

Clifford Brown tells the audience that "Georgie Morrow will now give his unique conception of 'These Foolish Things.' " Morrow is alone in this only-time-ever-heard feature that eventually gets support from Powell.

The group's oft-heard "I Get a Kick Out of You" begins normally, but at the bridge the tempo once again races into space à la "Just One of Those Things." Brownie is first to solo, then he and Max Roach get into a call-response that sees the speed of Brownie's notes evolve into a blur. Sonny Rollins follows with another sackful of notes and continues the duel with Roach. Most of this contrasts with some bluesy half-note catch-your-breath sequences. Things quiet down rhythmically for Powell, who is accompanied again by Roach's brushes. The left-hand single notes are back but in clusters that are so fast they even bury a quote from "Yankee Doodle." Powell yields to George Morrow. The horns then have lightening-speed exchanges with Roach, who is indefatigable in this never-ending set. The trades go on . . . the crowd roars . . . the crowd applauds . . . the crowd laughs . . . Brownie quotes "This Old Man" . . . the trades end . . . Roach continues alone . . . the crowd urges him on . . . will he ever stop? Finally he rim-shots his way into the 3/4 and the melody returns, but the ending is delayed! More tom-toms from Roach, and then— at last—it is over. Much applause. Segue to Max Roach's closing remarks acknowledging the musicians and referring to himself as Zutty Singleton. The announcer acknowledges "Dotty the Manager and Ben." And the tape runs out.

What is going on here? There can be no doubt that this performance pushes jazz tempos to their outer limits, but there are other things happening too—new ideas for improvisations, new ideas for exchanges, etc. Has the Brown-Roach formula with Rollins as the catalyst outrun its course? Plans are being made to issue this remarkable tape on CD. It will certainly evoke much discussion.

With the wildness of Norfolk behind them, the group separated: Max Roach and Sonny Rollins for Rudy Van Gelder's Hackensack recording studio (Rollins was set to record "Saxophone Colossus," one of his most important LPs) and Brownie for a relatively quiet weekend at home (LaRue and the baby were still in Los Angeles). He would need some rest because on Wednesday, June 27, the group would convene in Chicago for their first-ever appearance at the Blue Note. The club had specialized in major orchestra bookings such as Ellington, Goodman, and Basie, so performing there would achieve a new high for Brown-Roach. There would be new financial and publicity benefits, so anticipation was in the air.

When Clifford Brown and Richie Powell arrived home in Philadelphia, the word came to them that Julian "Cannonball" Adderley was appearing that week at the Blue Note. Junior Mance was Adderley's keyboard player and recalled that "halfway through the gig (which probably meant Thursday or Friday night) Richie and

Brownie sat in." Mance had spent some time sharing ideas with Powell, who often complained that his famous brother "would never show me anything." Jack Field, the owner of the Blue Note and also a jazz trumpeter, was delighted to see Brownie on the bandstand of his club, and, according to Mance, the evening turned into an improvisational extravaganza.

Having some free time for the weekend would enable Brownie to drive down to Wilmington to see his family and friends. In addition, during the mini-vacation he would be able to stop off at the local racetrack to indulge himself and have some fun.

His friends were naturally excited to see him, and Bop Wilson mentioned casually that he was playing with a group over at The Transit Bar in Chester, Pennsylvania. Maybe Brownie would like to join him. Although considerably fatigued, Brownie traveled to Chester to oblige his friend. "I was working with Charlie Robertson and the Jazz Men," said Bop. "Brownie showed up on Sunday at 7 P.M. and played with us all day."[12]

On Monday, Brownie and some chums decided to go fishing. Joe Brown had for years taken his sons down to the local rivers and streams, where the boys had often been successful. This day would be no exception. Brownie was back at his ol' fishing hole and having a good time reliving some of his childhood memories. The fishing was good, and it was very relaxing to have some fun on a warm summer day in the way he had years ago.

When they returned to 1013 Poplar, Clifford Brown was pleased to see his sister Geneva visiting the family. She had been married years before, and Brownie had not had much chance to see her recently. Proud of his catch of fish, he said to Geneva: "Somebody told me you think you're such a good cook. Well, I want you to cook something for me, and I'll see whether you can cook or not."[13] Geneva accepted the challenge. "I cooked him soul food," she said. "I fried the fish, and we had black-eyed peas and cornbread. I believe I cooked greens. But it was a typical soul food dinner. And he piled up his plate."

It was a wonderful day for Clifford, enjoying Geneva's meal and sitting back relaxing with his family. However it was a bit of a tease, since he had so little time to be with them. Geneva remembered him sitting at the table in the dining room, saying, " 'Boy, I sure wish I didn't have to go. I'm not in the mood to go. I just wish I didn't have to.' He kept saying that over and over," said Geneva, who remembered that Joe tried to console him. "Well, Cliff, once you get on the road and everything, it'll be okay," said his father. But Brownie answered, "Oh no, I just wish I didn't have to go." Just before he departed, Geneva remembered, "My daddy hit him on his rear end and said, 'Well, take it easy. When you get to Philly, let Richie drive.' He told him to let Richie drive because Clifford would sit at the wheel and go to sleep at the wheel," said Geneva.

Finally, Brownie bid farewell to his family, took his luggage into his Buick, and drove to Philadelphia. The plan had been to meet Max Roach there. He was on his way from New York, and they could drive together to Chicago in time for the Blue Note gig. But on Tuesday Brownie decided that on the way to Chicago, he wanted to stop for a while in Elkhart, Indiana, to try out some new horns. As musicians know, Elkhart was home to several important brass instrument manufacturers, and it was just south of Chicago. From Philadelphia, Clifford Brown called Max Roach in New York that morning to tell him about the change in plans, and Max said, "Fine, I'll see you in Chicago." Roach recalled that it would be the first time that Brownie had not traveled with him in his car.

That Tuesday, June 26, was indeed a special day—it was LaRue's birthday and their second wedding anniversary, so there was plenty of last-minute family business to attend to before the trip.[14] Perhaps as he was making his preparations, Brownie was reminded that, since it was Tuesday, it was jam session night at Music City. There is a bit of confusion on this because in the context of events recalled years later, many seemed to think that this Tuesday, June 26, 1956, was the night of the famous "Donna Lee" jam session. But as we have seen, that session occurred the previous year.[15]

In any event, there was jam-session activity going on in town that night, for when Clifford Brown left Philadelphia for Chicago with Richie and Nancy Powell, it was late evening. Roach believes that Brownie started out driving but then turned over the keys to Powell and retreated to the back seat to take a nap. After a while, Powell decided, contrary to Roach's edict, to turn over the wheel to Nancy. It was raining heavily that night, and the Pennsylvania Turnpike was badly rain-slicked. After stopping for gas outside of Bedford, Pennsylvania, shortly after midnight, Nancy resumed driving. A short distance down the road, after gaining considerable speed, she failed to negotiate a curve and struck the guardrail. The car then careened across the road, hit a bridge abutment overlooking Route 220, jumped the barrier, and rolled down a seventy-five-foot embankment. Clifford Brown and Richie and Nancy Powell were instantly killed. A piece in the *Bedford Gazette* on June 28 indicates that the accident was one of several occurring on the turnpike "in this area in the past few weeks," raising the death toll to eight people.

The news of the accident quickly spread to Brownie's family in Wilmington, where Joe and Estella were devastated to hear of the death of their youngest child. In Los Angeles, a twenty-three-year-old LaRue Brown was suddenly widowed with a six-month-old son. When Max Roach arrived in Chicago, his agent told him the news, and Max said: "I locked myself in the hotel room and finished two bottles of cognac." He would mourn his friend for a long time to come. When news of the tragedy reached the media that Clifford Brown's life had ended so suddenly and violently, the jazz world went into deep mourning. One of the major jazz voices had been stilled at an inordinately young age.

Epilogue

"I don't know if we'll ever hear the trumpet played like that again."

–Nicholas Payton, 1997

As the Wilmington east siders mourned the loss of their favorite son, tributes poured in to the Brown family. Despite his brief life, Clifford Brown had inspired the jazz world with his unique talent and improvising genius. Speculation began on the "what-if-he-had-lived," as is so often the case when great artists die young. But it was also realized that in just a few years of recording Clifford Brown had set a new standard for trumpet players. Although he died young, he had achieved greatness. Benny Golson said it all simply: "Clifford Brown was a genius."

Clifford Brown was buried quietly in Wilmington, in a segregated cemetery. The ignominy of his resting place echoed the altered circumstances of bebop itself in the years that immediately followed Brownie's death. Hordes of boppers left America as they could not sustain themselves in a music business that no longer had much room for them. Art Farmer would live in Austria for decades; Bud Powell, Dexter Gordon, and others would seek refuge in Paris; Johnny Griffin, Ed Thigpen, and others would scatter throughout Europe as the bebop legacy ebbed steadily.

Those jazz figures who remained–such as Miles Davis, Thelonious Monk, and John Coltrane–found themselves living in a different

186

jazz world, one with more limited audiences and more difficult challenges.

After experiencing severe shock and depression, Max Roach got himself together and tried to move on. He hired Kenny Dorham, a stalwart trumpeter with whom he had worked before, to play alongside Sonny Rollins in the band. The players all pulled together, but after a while it was just no good. Brown and Rollins had broken new ground in the time before that fateful June night, and Dorham could not fill the void. Sonny Rollins became distracted and began to focus more on his own recordings. The brilliant art that Brown-Roach had achieved had ended, and for Sonny Rollins that was tantamount to another kind of death—a lack of creativity.

Brown's untimely death at age twenty-five indeed coincided with a violent change in the music business. By 1956, the rock 'n' roll revolution was in full stride. The age of jazz and its ascendance in music like swing and bebop had ended. By this time, big bands had all but disappeared, and pop vocalists was struggling to keep their record contracts because all the attention had turned to the rockers. But of all music, jazz suffered the most. Clubs closed everywhere, jazz concerts were no longer as successful, and, as we have noted, many beboppers fled to Europe.

The rock roller coaster roared on, and despite the stabs made by jazzers at fusion, rock jazz, modal, avant-garde, and free form expressions, the music became buried in the vaults of labels whose names became extinct in the world of mergers and acquisitions.

Shortly before his death in the early 1980s, the great bebop trombonist Kai Winding made a sagacious comment one night as we were discussing the loss of bebop and the sad state of music in America during that time. Winding said simply, "The valid things remain." The statement was, of course, a truism, but its articulation at that time had prescience, because shortly after Winding's death a stirring began to occur in music colleges, concert halls, and clubs. By the end of the 1980s, young players from the music schools began playing the bop tunes of their grandfathers, and the sounds of the 1940s and 1950s returned to the jazz world. The advent of the compact disc made record companies realize that they could make money reissuing the music of the bebop years, and soon the records of the beboppers could be found in record stores across the country. Magnificent boxed sets of the CDs containing "complete" collections of these artists, with fresh liner notes for the new listeners, filled the stores. One of the best of these collections bore the name of Clifford Brown.

In the 1990s, an integrated city government in Wilmington, Delaware, organized a Clifford Brown Festival. Each June, the old east siders and their children throng to Rodney Square to pay tribute to their old friend.

One evening in 1995, while visiting the city during festival time, I wandered into a small community hall—the Christina Arts Center—that had a room named after Clifford Brown. It was a jam-session night, and the grandchildren of Brown's high school friends were gathered around a weathered upright piano playing some well-worn brass, reed, and percussion instruments, probably borrowed from the studio trunks of nearby Howard High. These youngsters had grown up in the tradition of rap, hip-hop, and other post-jazz sounds. Indeed, they were clad in the apparel of the 1990s, with their earrings and body-piercing metal. But as they began putting horns to lips and sticks to hands, a strange sound emanated from the group. The tune was "Joy Spring," and after an inexperienced trading of fours, the group segued into "Daahoud" and other Clifford Brown compositions. The youngsters were finger-popping and foot-stomping in the manner of their grandparents. As the sound of Clifford Brown's music filled the room, I found that I could not fight back the tears.

Notes

Chapter One

1. All Leon Brown quotes in this chapter are from an interview with Alan Hood, June 17, 1992.
2. Carol E. Hoffecker, "The Politics of Exclusion: Blacks in Late Nineteenth-Century Wilmington, Delaware," in *Delaware History* (Wilmington: Delaware Historical Society, 1974–75), 16: 60.
3. Harold B. Hancock, "The Status of the Negro in Delaware After the Civil War, 1865–1876," *Delaware History* (Wilmington: Delaware Historical Society, 1968–69), 13: 57.
4. Hancock, "The Status of the Negro," 59.
5. Hancock, "The Status of the Negro," 54.
6. *New York Times*, November 8, 1870.
7. Telegraph from Higgins to Grant, November 8, 1870, Attorney General's Papers, Letters Received, Delaware, 1812–1870, National Archives.
8. *Delaware Gazette*, November 11, 1870.
9. John A. Munroe, "The Negro in Delaware," *South Atlantic Quarterly* 56 (Autumn 1957): 438.
10. Hoffecker, "The Politics of Exclusion," 70.
11. J. Sanders Redding, *No Day of Triumph* (New York: Harper & Row, 1942), 3.
12. Redding, *No Day of Triumph*, 3.
13. Ralph Morris interviewed by Alan Hood, March 11, 1992.

14. Kay Lacy interviewed by Alan Hood, June 15, 1992.

15. Dick Russell, *Black Genius* (New York: Carroll and Graf, 1998), 24.

16. Kay Lacy interviewed by Alan Hood, June 15, 1992.

17. All Geneva Griffin quotes in this chapter are from an interview with Alan Hood, June 15, 1992.

18. Interview with Cynthia Oates, June 1, 1996.

19. Nat Hentoff, "Clifford Brown–The New Dizzy," *Down Beat*, April 7, 1954, 15–16.

20. Hentoff, "Clifford Brown," 16.

21. Interview with James Moody, June 7, 1989.

Chapter Two

1. Interview with Boysie Lowery, June 1, 1995.

2. Hollie West, "Clifford Brown–Trumpeter's Training," *Down Beat*, July 1980.

3. Phil Schaap, radio interview with Robert "Boysie" Lowery, WKCR-FM, Columbia University, New York, N.Y., October 31, 1990.

4. *The Complete Encyclopedia of Popular Music and Jazz*, ed. Roger D. Kinkle, 1065–1066.

5. Interview with Ernie Watts, June 10, 1998.

6. S. B. Arban, *Arban's Complete Conservatory Method for Trumpet*, ed. Edwin Frank Goldman and Walter M. Smith and annotated by Claude Gordon (New York: Carl Fischer, Inc., 1982). The Arban Method is still considered a bible by trumpeters. This edition updates the work of the famous cornetist S. B. Arban. He originally published his theory in *Arban's Complete Celebrated Method for the Cornet* in 1894.

7. This nonpressure system of playing a brass instrument that Andrews speaks about is based on identifying and then strengthening the facial muscles that hold the lips in an idealized embouchure formation, which trumpeter Roy Roman calls "the ultimate position." See Roy Roman, *The Ultimate Position*, Vols. One and Two (Cleveland, Tenn.: Mighty Horn Records, 1988), instructional videocassette. Instead of pressing the mouthpiece against the lips to move into the high register or to achieve other effects, a brass instrument player merely alters the aperture between the lips that is formed by this idealized embouchure formation. Coupled with breath control and articulation effects achieved both by tonguing and valve manipulation, this technique allows for increased range, power, and stamina without sacrificing expressivity.

8. West, "Clifford Brown."

9. Alan J. Hood, "Clifford's Contemporaries Speak: Interview Excerpts About Clifford Brown's Life and Music," in *Jazz Research Proceedings Yearbook* (Chicago: International Association of Jazz Educators, 1997).

10. Marcus Belgrave, liner notes to *Clifford Brown: The Complete Blue Note and Pacific Coast Jazz Recordings*, Blue Note CDP 7243 8 34195 2 4, 11.

11. Kenyon Camper interviewed by Alan Hood, June 2, 1996.

Chapter Three

1. Deanie Jenkins interviewed by Nick Catalano and Alan Hood, June 1, 1996.

2. Ralph Morris interviewed by Alan Hood, March 11, 1992.

3. Bop Wilson interviewed by Nick Catalano and Alan Hood, June 1, 1996.

4. Annette Woolard, "Parker v. The University of Delaware: The Desegregation of Higher Education in Delaware," *Delaware History*, Vol. 22 (1986–87), 113.

5. Gary Giddins, "Adventures of the Red Arrow," *Riding on a Blue Note* (New York: Oxford University Press, 1981), 235.

6. Mark Gardner, liner notes to *The Clifford Brown Quartet in Paris*, Prestige Records PR7761, 1970.

7. Whitney Balliett, "Fat Girl," *The New Yorker*, June 12, 1978, 116–17.

8. Thomas Owens, "Fats Navarro," *The New Grove Dictionary of Jazz*, ed. Barry Kernfeld (New York: Macmillan, 1988), 163. A helpful discography of Fats Navarro's most important recordings is included in the Owens entry.

9. Golson interviewed on *Shades of Brown*, radio program on National Public Radio, narrated by Bob Wisdom, 1982.

10. Leonard Feather, *Jazz Encyclopedia* Questionnaire, 1954.

11. *New Grove Dictionary*, 510–11.

12. Johnny Coles interviewed by Alan Hood, May 28, 1996.

13. Billy Root interviewed by Alan Hood, March 15, 1994.

14. Billy Root, "Interview," *Cadence Magazine*, November 1990, 8–9.

Chapter Four

1. All Leon Brown quotes in this chapter are from an interview with Alan Hood, June 17, 1992.

2. Johnny Coles interviewed by Alan Hood, May 28, 1996.

3. Dave Clark interviewed by Alan Hood, March 22, 1992.

4. Dan Morgenstern, "Clifford Brown," liner notes to *Brownie: The Complete Emarcy Recordings of Clifford Brown*, EmArcy/Polygram Records, 838 306-2, 1989, 17.

5. Interview with Tommy Walker, February 25, 1997.
6. Ralph Morris interviewed by Alan Hood, March 11, 1992.
7. Deanie Jenkins interviewed by Alan Hood, April 22, 1992.
8. According to Ken Vail, *Bird's Diary: The Life of Charlie Parker, 1945–55* (Chessington, Surrey, England: Castle Communication, 1996).
9. Tom Darnall interviewed by Alan Hood, June 3, 1996.
10. Nat Hentoff, "Clifford Brown–The New Dizzy," *Down Beat*, April 7, 1954, 17.
11. Interview with Roy Haynes, July 21, 1998.
12. Morgenstern, "Clifford Brown," 17.
13. Jimmy Heath interviewed by Alan Hood, June 3, 1996.
14. Hentoff, "Clifford Brown," 15.

Chapter Five

1. Unless otherwise indicated, all Vance Wilson quotes in this chapter are from an interview with Alan Hood and Don Glanden, May 28, 1996.
2. Brian Madden, "Clifford Before Max," *S&F*, February 1966.
3. Billy Taylor quotes in this chapter are from an interview with Alan Hood, Austin, Texas, October 13, 1992.
4. All Ida Mae Bey quotes in this chapter are from an interview with Alan Hood, June 3, 1996.
5. Ralph Morris interviewed by Alan Hood, March 11, 1992.
6. Vance Wilson interviewed by Alan Hood, March 15, 1994. Also quote on p. 63.

Chapter Six

1. Leonard Feather, liner notes to *Clifford Brown Memorial Album*, Blue Note B–81526, 1969.
2. Mark Gardner, liner notes to *The Clifford Brown Quartet in Paris*, Prestige Records PR 7761, 1970.
3. Ira Gitler, liner notes to *Clifford Brown Memorial*, Prestige Records PRLP 7055, 1956.
4. Tadd Dameron, quoted in Ira Gitler, *Jazz Masters of the Forties* (New York: Macmillan, 1966), 272.
5. Interview with John Lewis, July 21, 1998.
6. Jimmy Heath interviewed by Alan Hood, March 23, 1992.
7. Johnny Coles interviewed by Alan Hood, May 28, 1996.
8. Interview with Kelly Swaggerty, October 16, 1995.
9. Leonard Feather, liner notes to *Clifford Brown Memorial Album*, Blue Note BLP1526, 1956.

10. Raymond Horricks, *Quincy Jones* (New York: Hippocrene Books, 1985), 18–23.

11. Peter Landsdowne, *Joy Spring: The Life and Music of Clifford Brown* (Upton, Mass.: Peter Landsdowne, 1992), 35–36.

Chapter Seven

1. Interview with Annie Ross, November 4, 1996.

2. Interview with Art Farmer, February 15, 1996.

3. Raymond Horricks, *Quincy Jones* (New York: Hippocrene Books, 1985).

4. Leonard Feather, *The New Edition of the Encyclopedia of Jazz* (New York: Bonanza Books, 1962), 76–77.

5. Kenny Matheson, "The Dude Is Back," *Wire*, New Year 1991, 50.

6. Art Farmer interview.

7. Barbara Gardner, "The Legacy of Clifford Brown," *Down Beat*, October 12, 1961, 17–21.

8. Art Farmer interview.

9. Phil Schapp, "Brownie Birthday Broadcast," WKCR Radio, October 30, 1994.

10. Horricks, *Quincy Jones*.

11. Mark Gardner, liner notes to *The Clifford Brown Quartet in Paris*, Prestige Records PR 7761, 1970.

12. Mark Gardner, liner notes.

13. Mark Gardner, liner notes.

14. Jimmy Cleveland interviewed by Alan Hood, March 18, 1993.

15. Xanadu Records: Xanadu 122, Xanadu JX6603/506603, and Xanadu JC7023.

16. Louis-Victor Mialy interviewed by Alan Hood, July 18, 1996.

17. Alun Morgan, "Jazz Under Cover: A Report of the Recordings made by the Lionel Hampton Band Personnel in Europe during 1953," *Jazz Monthly*, April 1955, 1–8.

18. Robert D. Rusch, "Jimmy Cleveland Interview–Part One," *Cadence Magazine*, January 1991, 18–19.

19. Interview with Lionel Hampton, September 12, 1975.

Chapter Eight

1. Interview with Horace Silver, August 2, 1996.

2. Horace Silver interviewed by Alan Hood, April 21, 1992.

3. The term "hard bop" is a controversial one, which has never been given a meaningful definition. It was invented to attempt to describe the musical growth that the second-generation beboppers brought to the music in the

early 1950s, when they incorporated blues, funk, and folk ideas into bebop. An excellent book that deals with the subject is David H. Rosenthal, *Hard Bop* (New York: Oxford University Press, 1992).

4. Nat Hentoff, liner notes to *Clifford Brown: The Complete Blue Note and Pacific Coast Jazz Recordings*, CDP 7243 8 34195 24, 29–30.

5. Max Roach, transcript of "Tribute to Clifford Brown," Highlights in Jazz concert, June 26, 1978.

6. LaRue Brown-Watson distinctly recalls going to L.A. airport *with* Max Roach to meet Clifford Brown flying in from the East alone.

7. Interview with Max Roach, May 22, 1995.

Chapter Nine

1. Max Roach, transcript of "Tribute to Clifford Brown," Highlights in Jazz Concert, October 6, 1977.

2. Interview with Teddy Edwards, April 8, 1996.

3. According to one account, Edwards didn't remain with the group because his wife was expecting a baby and he didn't want to go on the road.

4. Interview with LaRue Brown-Watson, January 22, 1999.

5. Robert Gordon, *Jazz West Coast: The Los Angeles Scene of the 1950s* (London: Quartet Books, 1986), 108.

6. Quincy Jones, "A Tribute to Brownie," *Down Beat*, August 1956, 10.

7. According to LaRue Brown-Watson, Clifford never spent "one day in a hotel or motel" in Los Angeles. She mentioned that Clifford lived with Max until he got married.

8. Jack Montrose, liner notes to *Clifford Brown: The Complete Blue Note and Pacific Coast Jazz Recordings*, Blue Note CDP 7243 8 34195 24, 10.

9. Interview with Jack Montrose, August 11, 1998.

Chapter Ten

1. Dan Morgenstern, "Clifford Brown" liner notes to *Brownie: The Complete Emarcy Recordings of Clifford Brown*, Emarcy/Polygram Records 838 306-2, 1989, p. 31.

2. Interview with Junior Mance, July 14, 1998.

3. Interview with Clark Terry, April 2, 1996.

4. Clark Terry interviewed by Alan Hood, December 19, 1992.

5. LaRue Brown-Watson interviewed by Alan Hood, February 3, 1992.

6. Interview with Herb Geller, July 31, 1998.

7. LaRue Brown-Watson interview (see note 5, above).

Chapter Eleven

1. According to LaRue Brown-Watson, "each apartment had three bedrooms, two baths, living room, separate dining room and kitchen. Our apartment also had a full finished basement that was used as a recreation or family room with a half bath."
2. LaRue Brown-Watson interviewed by Alan Hood, February 3, 1992.
3. Sam Dockery interviewed by Alan Hood, April 7, 1992.
4. Interview with Herbie Mann, July 29, 1998.
5. Milt Hinton interviewed by Alan Hood, July 15, 1998.
6. Thomas Owens, *Bebop: The Music and Its Players* (New York: Oxford University Press, 1995), 216.
7. Owens, *Bebop*, 217.
8. Max Roach, "Tribute to Clifford Brown."
9. Interview with Harold Land, October 13, 1995.
10. Nat Hentoff, "Roach & Brown, Inc.–Dealers in Jazz," *Down Beat*, May 4, 1995.

Chapter Twelve

1. This problem is referred to again in n. 14, following.
2. Gary Kramer "Trio of Jazz Combos Rock NY's Basin Street," *Billboard*, September 10, 1955.
3. Barbara Gardner, "The Legacy of Clifford Brown," *Down Beat*, October 12, 1961.
4. Eric Nisenson, *Round About Midnight–A Portrait of Miles Davis* (New York: Da Capo Press, 1996), 105.
5. Because of Sonny Rollins's enormous reputation, developed over the last forty years, his role in the Brown-Roach groups has taken on an importance that tends to downplay the "classical" days of the group's existence with Harold Land. This history is shortsighted. As we have seen from recording sessions, tours, and longevity, the achievement of Brown-Roach with Harold Land alongside Brownie is the principal chronicle of the group's contribution. What happened when Rollins joined was, of course, highly significant, but not as defining as has been reported. It is important to note that Rollins was constantly recording on his own when he played with Brown-Roach. As a matter of fact, some of his greatest recording success as a leader took place during this period, for example, *Work Time* (12/2/55), his first date as a leader after joining Brown-Roach; *No Line* with Miles Davis (Prestige 7047, 3/16/56); and *Tenor Madness* (Prestige 7047, 5/24/56). In view of Sonny's prolific success as a recording leader during this time, it is doubtful that he would have remained a Brown-Roach sideman for very long. De-

spite the events of the summer of 1956, his own recording success continued right through 1959 when he undertook a long hiatus from jazz.

6. Rollins's name has always been recorded as "Theodore Walter," but recently he indicated this was incorrect.

7. All LaRue Brown-Watson quotes in this chapter are from an interview with Alan Hood, July 18, 1996. Actually, LaRue recalls that she and the baby were on the road with the band during part of this two-month period. She remembered leaving to go back to Philadelphia to have the baby checked and for her own six week check-up during this time.

8. Max Roach, transcript of "Tribute to Clifford Brown," Highlights in Jazz concert, June 26, 1978.

9. According to LaRue Brown-Watson, "Clifford only owned one car during his lifetime. It was a 1955 turquoise and creme Roadmaster Buick. Therefore, he did not have a car to trade."

10. Interview with Jimmy Cavallo, January 15, 1998.

11. Leonard Feather, "Brownie Digs Only Modern Sounds," *Down Beat*, February 22, 1956, 29.

12. Bop Wilson interviewed by Nick Catalano and Alan Hood, June 1, 1996.

13. All Geneva Griffin quotes in this chapter from an interview with Alan Hood, April 21, 1992.

14. LaRue Brown-Watson remembered that "Cliff sent flowers to me in L.A. and told me he was bringing a special gift with him when he joined us in L.A. after the Chicago job." This is a reference to a mink coat Brown had bought for his wife.

15. Because of the sheer number of writers who have incorrectly listed the "Donna Lee" jam session of 5/31/55 as taking place on 6/26/56, we quote the following from an interview with Billy Root, who was an eyewitness:

Q: You were on the last recording of Clifford Brown.

BILLY ROOT: See, that was a lie. . . . I was working with Clifford at the Blue Note in Philadelphia and there was a place called Music City where the kids used to come and play and hear the great players in town—they'd let them in because they couldn't get in the clubs. So I went over with Clifford and they took a tape and it was 8–9 months, maybe a year before he passed away. But they said he had just done it, which was not true, that had been done a year or so before he passed away.

Q: They said it was like the stop before the night he was killed.

BILLY ROOT: Not true, that's a falsehood.

Cadence Magazine, November, 1990, 9

Selected and Annotated Discography

As this biography goes to press, most of Clifford Brown's important recordings have become available on compact disk. Because of this fortunate circumstance, I have dispensed with the old format of individual recording lists and instead provided descriptions of the dates included in these CD reissues. Scholars interested in more detailed history should consult the excellent compilation of the English discographer Bob Weir.

Instruments are abbreviated as follows: (as) alto saxophone, (arr) arranger, (bs) baritone saxophone, (b) bass, (cl) clarinet, (cr) conductor, (d) drums, (fl) flute, (g) guitar, (p) piano, (ts) tenor saxophone, (tb) trombone, (tp) trumpet.

Clifford Brown Memorial Album (Blue Note CDP 7 81526 2)
Included herein is Clifford Brown's first jazz recording session, made on June 9, 1953. Alto saxophonist Lou Donaldson is the leader for the date, with Elmo Hope (p), Percy Heath (b), and Philly Joe Jones (d). Also included is Clifford Brown's first session as a leader, performing for Blue Note on August 28, 1953, and a session from the 1953 Lionel Hampton tour from September 15, 1953, originally advertised as "Clifford Brown and Art Farmer with the Swedish All-Stars." Quincy Jones wrote the charts.

197

Clifford Brown Memorial (Original Jazz Classics OJCCD-017-2)
This album, recorded on June 11, 1953, was originally performed on the Prestige label. Tadd Dameron is the leader of a nonet group that includes Clifford Brown (tp), Idrees Sulieman (tp), Herb Mullins (tb), Gigi Gryce (as), Benny Golson (ts), Oscar Estelle (bs), Percy Heath (b), Philly Joe Jones (d), and Tadd Dameron (p/arr)

The Clifford Brown Sextet in Paris (Original Jazz Classics OJCCD-358-2)
This is the first of the Paris sessions recorded on October 8, 1953, for Vogue Records, with Clifford Brown (tp), Gigi Gryce (as), Henri Renaud (p), Jimmy Gourley (g), Pierre Michelot (b), Jean-Louis Viale (d).

The Clifford Brown Big Band in Paris (Original Jazz Classics OJCCD-359-2)
This CD includes a big band date from October 9, 1953, with many of the French musicians from October 8 sextet recording. In addition, Walter Williams (tp), Jimmy Cleveland, Al Hayse, Benny Vasseur (tb), Anthony Ortega (as), and Clifford Solomon (ts) from the Lionel Hampton band join in the session originally billed as "Gigi Gryce and his Orchestra." Music recorded the following days (October 10 and 11) in a Vogue album originally issued under the title *The Gigi Gryce Octet* is also included here.

The Clifford Brown Quartet in Paris (Original Jazz Classics OJCCD-357-2)
This music was recorded on October 15, 1953, listing Clifford Brown as the leader with Henri Renaud (p), Pierre Michelot (b), Benny Bennett (d).

Art Blakey: A Night at Birdland, Vol. 1 (Blue Note CDP 7 46519 2)
One of the legendary albums in the hard bop tradition, this live recording took place on February 21, 1954, with Clifford Brown (tp), Lou Donaldson (as), Horace Silver (p), Curly Russell (b), and Art Blakey (d).

The Best of Max Roach and Clifford Brown in Concert (GNP Crescendo GNPD 18)
Recorded live in April 1954, this is an early incarnation of the Max Roach–Clifford Brown quintet with some of the first musicians hired when the co-leaders initially formed the group. Heard on the CD are: Clifford Brown (tp), Teddy Edwards (ts), Carl Perkins (p), George Bledsoe (b), and Max Roach (d).

Brownie: The Complete EmArcy Recordings of Clifford Brown (EmArcy/Polygram [USA] 838 306-2; 10-CD boxed set)
One of the first CD boxed sets of the contemporary reissue cavalcade, this 10-

CD set is easily the most valuable package for Clifford Brown devotees. It includes the classic Max Roach–Clifford Brown quintet recordings with Harold Land (ts), George Morrow (b), and Richie Powell (p). In addition, there is a jam session with Dinah Washington and a host of all-stars, vocal dates headlining Sarah Vaughan and Helen Merrill, and a notable date on January 19, 1955, that presented Clifford Brown with strings. It also includes the historic recording dubbed *Max Roach and Clifford Brown at Basin Street* that features Sonny Rollins (ts).

Brownie Lives! (Fresh Sound Records [Switzerland] FSCD-1012)
This CD produced in Switzerland includes live broadcasts from Basin Street in New York recorded April 28 and May 6, 1956. It also includes music from a benefit concert (following the death of Charlie Parker) featuring Brown-Roach at Carnegie Hall on May 6, 1955.

Sonny Rollins Plus Four (Original Jazz Classics OJCCD-243-2)
This is the last commercial recording of the Brown-Roach group. It was recorded under the leadership of Sonny Rollins for his own company, Prestige, on March 22, 1956.

The Beginning and the End (CBS [Japan] 32DP-663)
This CD includes the earliest Clifford Brown recordings, made when he was a member of the rhythm 'n' blues group the Blue Flames, led by Chris Powell. It also contains music from a controversial jam session recorded at Music City in Philadelphia.

Clifford Brown: The Complete Blue Note and Pacific Jazz Recordings (Blue Note CDP 7243 8 34195 24; 4-CD boxed set)
The most recent of the CD reissues includes the session with Lou Donaldson (June 9, 1953), Brown's first session as a leader (August 28, 1953), and a session with J. J. Johnson as leader recorded on June 22, 1953. These dates were all recorded for Blue Note records. Also included here is music recorded in July and August 1954, when Clifford Brown lived in California. These sessions (for Pacific Coast Jazz) featured arrangements of original Brown compositions (i.e., "Joy Spring" and "Daahoud") by Jack Montrose.

Index

200

LaVergne, TN USA
26 October 2010

202340LV00002B/36/P